SEVENTH EDITION

GRAMMAR IN CONTEXT 2A

SANDRA N. ELBAUM

NATIONAL GEOGRAPHIC LEARNING

Australia · Brazil · Mexico · Singapore · United Kingdom · United States

National Geographic Learning,
a Cengage Company

Grammar in Context 2A, **Seventh Edition**
Sandra N. Elbaum

Publisher: Sherrise Roehr

Executive Editor: Laura Le Dréan

Managing Editor: Jennifer Monaghan

Director of Global Marketing: Ian Martin

Heads of Regional Marketing:

Joy MacFarland (United States and Canada)

Charlotte Ellis (Europe, Middle East, and Africa)

Kiel Hamm (Asia)

Irina Pereyra (Latin America)

Product Marketing Manager: Tracy Bailie

Content Project Manager: Beth F. Houston

Media Researcher: Leila Hishmeh

Art Director: Brenda Carmichael

Senior Designer: Lisa Trager

Operations Support: Rebecca G. Barbush, Hayley
Chwazik-Gee

Manufacturing Planner: Mary Beth Hennebury

Composition: MPS North America LLC

For permission to use material from this text or product,
submit all requests online at **cengage.com/permissions**
Further permissions questions can be emailed to
permissionrequest@cengage.com

Grammar in Context 2A ISBN: 978-0-357-14028-4
Grammar in Context 2A + OLP ISBN: 978-0-357-14054-3

National Geographic Learning
200 Pier 4 Boulevard
Boston, MA 02210
USA

Locate your local office at **international.cengage.com/region**

Visit National Geographic Learning online at **ELTNGL.com**
Visit our corporate website at www.cengage.com

Printed in China
Print Number: 01 Print Year: 2019

CONTENTS

1 ANIMALS

2 ACROSS GENERATIONS

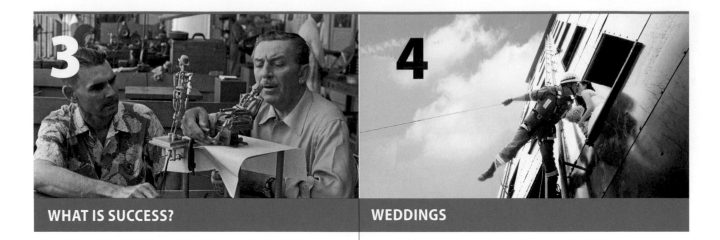

3

WHAT IS SUCCESS?

4

WEDDINGS

5

AMERICAN HERITAGE

6

A HEALTHY PLANET, A HEALTHY BODY

7

A NEW START

APPENDICES

ACKNOWLEDGMENTS

The Author and Publisher would like to acknowledge and thank the teachers who participated in the development of the seventh edition of *Grammar in Context*.

A special thanks to our Advisory Board for their valuable input during the development of this series.

ADVISORY BOARD

Andrea Gonzalez, BYU English Language Center, Provo, UT, USA

Ellen Rosen, Fullerton College, Fullerton, CA, USA

Erin Pak, Schoolcraft College, Livonia, MI, USA

Holly Gray, Prince George's Community College, Largo, MD, USA

John Halliwell, Moraine Valley Community College, Palos Hills, IL, USA

Katherine Sieradzki, FLS Boston, Boston, MA, USA

Maria Schirta, Hudson County Community College, Jersey City, NJ, USA

Oranit Limmaneeprasert, American River College, Sacramento, CA, USA

Susan Niemeyer, Los Angeles City College, Los Angeles, CA, USA

REVIEWERS

Adriana García, Institut Nord-America, Barcelona, Spain

Alena Widows, Institut Nord-America, Barcelona, Spain

Augustine Triantafyllides, So Easy, Athens, Greece

Bilal Aslam, GTCC, High Point, North Carolina, USA

Carmen Díez, CFA Les Corts, Barcelona, Spain

David Finfrock, QU, Doha, Qatar

Deanna Henderson, LCI, Denver, CO, USA

Ellen Barrett, Wayne State University, Detroit, MI, USA

Francis Bandin, UAB, Barcelona, Spain

Jonathan Lathers, Macomb Community College, Warren, MI, USA

Karen Vallejo, University of California, Irvine, CA, USA

Kathy Najafi, Houston Community College, Houston, TX, USA

Katie Windahl, Cuyahoga Community College, Cleveland, OH, USA

Laura Jacob, Mt. San Antonio College, Walnut, CA, USA

Leah Carmona, Bergen Community College, Paramus, NJ, USA

Luba Nesterova, Bilingual Education Institute, Houston, TX, USA

Marcos Valle, Edmonds Community College, Lynnwood, WA, USA

Marla Goldfine, San Diego Community College, San Diego, CA, USA

Milena Eneva, Chattahoochee Technical College, Marietta, GA, USA

Monica Farling, University of Delaware, Newark, DE, USA

Naima Sarfraz, Qatar University, Doha, Qatar

Natalia Schroeder, Long Beach City College, Long Beach, CA, USA

Paul Schmitt, Institut d'Estudis Nord-Americans, Barcelona, Spain

Paula Sanchez, Miami Dade College, Miami, FL, USA

Paulette Koubek-Yao, Pasadena City College, Arcadia, CA, USA

Robert Yáñez, Hillsborough Community College, Tampa, FL, USA

Samuel Lumbsden, Essex County College, Newark, NJ, USA

Sarah Mikulski, Harper College, Palatine, IL, USA

Steven Lund, Arizona Western College, Yuma, AZ, USA

Teresa Cheung, North Shore Community College, Lynn, MA, USA

Tim McDaniel, Green River College, Auburn, WA, USA

Tristinn Williams, Cascadia College, Seattle, WA, USA

Victoria Mullens, LCI, Denver, CO, USA

A WORD FROM THE AUTHOR

My parents immigrated to the United States from Poland and learned English as a second language as adults. My sisters and I were born in the United States. My parents spoke Yiddish to us; we answered in English. In that process, my parents' English improved immeasurably. Such is the case with many immigrant parents whose children are fluent in English. They usually learn English much faster than others; they hear the language in natural ways, in the context of daily life.

Learning a language in context, whether it be from the home, from work, or from a textbook, cannot be overestimated. The challenge for me has been to find a variety of high-interest topics to engage the adult language learner. I was thrilled to work on this new edition of *Grammar in Context* for National Geographic Learning. In so doing, I have been able to combine exciting new readings with captivating photos to exemplify the grammar.

I have given more than 100 workshops at ESL programs and professional conferences around the United States, where I have gotten feedback from users of previous editions of *Grammar in Context*. Some teachers have expressed concern about trying to cover long grammar lessons within a limited time. While ESL is not taught in a uniform number of hours per week, I have heeded my audiences and streamlined the series so that the grammar and practice covered is more manageable. And in response to the needs of most ESL programs, I have expanded and enriched the writing component.

Whether you are a new user of *Grammar in Context* or have used this series before, I welcome you to this new edition.

Sandra N. Elbaum

For my loves
Gentille, Chimene, Joseph, and Joy

WELCOME TO *GRAMMAR IN CONTEXT*, SEVENTH EDITION

Grammar in Context, the original contextualized grammar series, brings grammar to life through engaging topics that provide a framework for meaningful practice. Students learn more, remember more, and use language more effectively when they study grammar in context.

ENHANCED IN THE SEVENTH EDITION

National Geographic photographs introduce unit themes and pull students into the context.

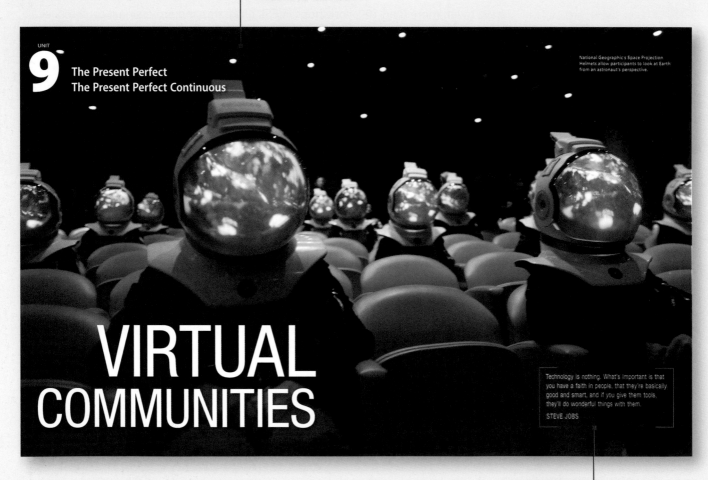

UNIT
9
The Present Perfect
The Present Perfect Continuous

National Geographic's Space Projection Helmets allow participants to look at Earth from an astronaut's perspective.

VIRTUAL COMMUNITIES

Technology is nothing. What's important is that you have a faith in people, that they're basically good and smart, and if you give them tools, they'll do wonderful things with them.
STEVE JOBS

Unit openers include an inspirational quote to help students connect to the theme.

New and updated readings introduce the target grammar in context and provide the springboard for explanations and practice.

New Think About It questions give students the opportunity to personalize and think critically about what they are reading.

CROWDFUNDING

Read the following article. Pay special attention to the words in bold. 🔊 9.3

■ **Have** you ever **had** an idea for a business but no way to fund it? **Have** you **asked** relatives and friends for money to help you? If you **have done** these things, you know it isn't easy to get people interested in investing in your dream. After getting money from relatives and friends, it's hard to find more people willing to invest. Lately, people **have found** a different way to raise cash: through crowdfunding. Crowdfunding is a method of "collecting small amounts of money from a lot of different people, usually by using the Internet." While the idea **has been** around for possibly hundreds of years, the word *crowdfunding* **has** only **existed** since 2006.

Crowdfunding websites, which started to appear on the Internet in 2010, **have helped** individuals raise billions of dollars worldwide. So how does it work? A person demonstrates his idea in a short video and states his financial goal and the time frame for raising money. Usually the first investors are family and friends. Little by little, strangers become interested and donate money.

Not all crowdfunding plans are for profit. Some people **have used** crowdfunding websites that are specifically for philanthropic[1] projects. These sites **have attracted** people who want to make the world a better place. The 97 Supermarket in Changchun, China, is one example of this. Jiang Naijun used crowdfunding to get the money to open a supermarket. She named her market 97 because that was her age when she did this. Since she became profitable, she **has given** at least half the money she earns to charity[2], to help children in need. "I wanted to do more for society," she said.

If you want more information, just google "crowdfunding" and you will find a number of different sites specializing in different types of projects.

[1] philanthropic: intended to help others
[2] charity: an organization that helps people in need

Crowdfunding has become one of the most popular ways for people to raise money for a cause, project, or event. In 2017, $34 billion was raised globally. This number is expected to grow to more than $300 billion by 2025.

98-year-old Jiang Naijun used crowdfunding to start her supermarket and donates the profits to charity.

COMPREHENSION Based on the reading, write T for *true* or F for *false*.

1. _____ Sometimes strangers help fund a crowdfunding project.
2. _____ The idea of crowdfunding is old, but it has become easier to do with the Internet.
3. _____ The "97 Supermarket" project didn't reach its financial goal.

THINK ABOUT IT Discuss the questions with a partner or in a small group.

1. What would you like to crowdfund for? Why?
2. What might be some challenges with crowdfunding? Explain.

9.4 The Present Perfect—Overview of Uses

EXAMPLES	EXPLANATION
People **have used** crowdfunding since 2010. Google **has been** in existence for over 20 years.	We use the present perfect to show that an action or state started in the past and continues to the present.
I **have used** my laptop in coffee shops many times. How many articles about crowdfunding **have** you **read**?	We use the present perfect to show that an action repeated during a period of time that started in the past and includes the present.
Have you ever **asked** relatives for money?	We use the present perfect to show that an action occurred at an indefinite time in the past.

EXERCISE 7 Tell if the sentences show continuation from past to present (C), repetition from past to present (R), or an indefinite time in the past (I).

1. Larry Page has been interested in computers since he was a child. _C_
2. How many emails have you received today? _____
3. I've had my laptop for one year. _____
4. The word *crowdfunding* has been in existence since 2006. _____
5. Internet security has become a big problem. _____
6. Has your computer ever had a virus? _____
7. My cousin has used crowdfunding two times. _____
8. Have you ever used your laptop in a coffee shop? _____

> **GRAMMAR IN USE**
> When an event happened in the recent past, and the effect is still felt, we often use the present perfect. This is especially common for speakers of British English. In American English, we use either the present perfect or the simple past.
>
> | | |
> |---|---|
> | *Someone has just donated $10,000!* | *Someone just donated $10,000.* |
> | *I have forgotten my password again.* | *I forgot my password again.* |
> | *Have you heard the news?* | *Did you hear the news?* |

New Grammar in Use notes highlight practical usage points to help students communicate more effectively.

New listening comprehension activities encourage students to listen for meaning through natural spoken English.

EXERCISE 17 Listen to the information about the U.S. Census. Write T for *true*, F for *false*, or NS for *not stated*. 🔊 9.6

1. _____ At first, children were not counted in the census.
2. _____ All census information is available to everyone.
3. _____ Most Americans complete the census questionnaire.

New Fun with Grammar allows the class to practice grammar in a lively game-like way.

Summary and Review sections help students revisit key points and assess their progress.

SUMMARY OF UNIT 9

The Present Perfect and the Simple Past

PRESENT PERFECT	SIMPLE PAST
The action of the sentence began in the past and includes the present.	The action of the sentence is completely past.
Sergey Brin **has been** in the U.S. since 1979.	Sergey Brin **came** to the U.S. in 1979.
Khan's videos **have been** available for many years.	Khan **created** his first math videos in 2004.
I've always **wanted** to learn more about my family's history.	When I was a child, I always **wanted** to spend time with my grandparents.
How long **have** you **been** interested in genealogy?	When **did** you **start** your family tree?

PRESENT PERFECT	SIMPLE PAST
Repetition from past to present	Repetition in a past time period
Khan Academy **has created** over 5,000 videos so far.	Khan **created** several videos for his niece in 2004.

PRESENT PERFECT	SIMPLE PAST
The action took place at an indefinite time between the past and the present.	The action took place at a definite time in the past.
Have you ever **used** Cyndi's list?	**Did** you **use** the 1940 census in 2012?
My brother **has raised** $5,000 on a crowdfunding site already.	He **put** his project on a crowdfunding site six months ago.
I'm interested in the DNA project. I've **received** my kit, but I **haven't sent** the sample back yet.	My friend **sent** her DNA sample to the Genographic Project last month.

The Present Perfect and the Present Perfect Continuous

PRESENT PERFECT	PRESENT PERFECT CONTINUOUS
A continuous action (nonaction verbs)	A continuous action (action verbs)
I **have been** interested in genealogy for five years.	I've **been working** on my family tree for five years.
A repeated action	A nonstop action
Cyndi Howell's website **has won** several awards.	The U.S. Census Bureau **has been keeping** records since the 1880s.
Question with *how many/how much*	Question with *how long*
How many times **has** Khan **been** on the cover of a magazine? How much time **has** he **spent** on Khan Academy?	How long **has** Khan **been living** in Boston?
An action that is at an indefinite time, completely in the past	An action that started in the past and is still happening
Many teachers **have started** to use Khan lectures in their classrooms.	Dr. Wells **has been collecting** DNA for several years.

254   Unit 9

REVIEW

Fill in the blanks with the simple present, the simple past, the present perfect, or the present perfect continuous form of the verbs given. Include any other words you see. In some cases, more than one answer is possible.

A: What do you do for a living?

B: I ___work___ as a programmer. I _ve been working_ as a
     1. work   2. work
programmer for five years. But my job is boring.

A: _____ about changing jobs?
     3. you/think/ever

B: Yes. Since I _____ a child, I _____ to be an actor.
                    4. be   5. always/want
When I was in college, I _____ in a few plays. But since I
                              6. be
_____ , I _____ time to act. What about you?
7. graduate   8. not/have

A: I _____ in computer security.
         9. work

B: How long _____ that?
              10. you/do

A: For about six years.

B: I _____ the field of computer security is very important.
         11. think

A: Yes, it is. But lately I _____ the computer for other things, too. My hobby is
                              12. use
genealogy. I _____ on my family tree for about a year. Last month, I
                 13. work
_____ information about my father's ancestors. My grandfather
14. find
_____ with us now, and he likes to tell us about his past. He
15. live
_____ born in Italy, but he _____ here when he
16. be   17. come
was very young, so he _____ here most of his life. He
                            18. live
_____ much about Italy. I _____ any information
19. not/remember   20. not/find
about my mother's ancestors yet.

The Present Perfect, The Present Perfect Continuous   255

From Grammar to Writing gives editing advice and practice to set students up to successfully apply the grammar to writing.

FROM GRAMMAR TO WRITING

PART 1 Editing Advice

1. Don't confuse the *-ing* form and the past participle.
                          taking
   I've been ~~taken~~ a course in genealogy.
                     given
   My parents have ~~giving~~ me family photos.

2. Use the present perfect, not the simple present or present continuous, to describe an action or state that started in the past and continues to the present.
      had   have you been
   He has his laptop for two years.   How long ~~are you~~ studying math?

3. Use *for*, not *since*, with the amount of time.
                                          for
   I've been interested in my family's history ~~since~~ three years.

4. Use the simple past, not the present perfect, with a specific past time.
      studied
   He ~~has studied~~ algebra when he was in high school.
      did   study
   When ~~have you studied~~ algebra?

5. Use the simple past, not the present perfect, in a *since* clause.
                                      put
   He has collected $5,000 since he ~~has put~~ his project on a crowdfunding site.

6. Use the correct word order with adverbs.
               never studied
   I have ~~studied never~~ my family history. Have you ~~heard ever~~ of Dr. Spencer Wells?
                                            ever heard

7. Use the correct word order in questions.
                 has your family
   How long ~~your family has~~ been in this country?

8. Use *yet* for negative statements; use *already* for affirmative statements.
                                          yet
   I haven't taken advanced algebra ~~already~~.

9. Don't forget the verb *have* in the present perfect (continuous).
      have
   I been studying my family history for two years.

10. Don't forget the *-ed* of the past participle.
         ed
   He's watch a math video several times.

PART 2 Editing Practice
Some of the shaded words and phrases have mistakes. Find the mistakes and correct them. If the shaded words are correct, write *C*.
                    have you
   How many changes you have made since you came to the U.S.? For our journal, our teacher
                  1.   2.   C
                                                                               3.
asked us to answer this question. I have come to the U.S. two and a half years ago. Things have
                                   4.
change a lot for me since I've come here. Here are some of the changes:
   5.   6.

256   Unit 9

First, since the past two years, I am studying to be a software engineer. I knew a little about
         7.   8.   9.
this subject before I came here, but my knowledge has improve a lot. I started to work part-time
                                                     10.   11.
in a computer company three months ago. Since I have started my job, I haven't have much time
                                              12.   13.
for fun.

Second, I have a driver's permit, and I'm learning how to drive. I haven't took the driver's test
                                                                    14.
yet because I'm not ready. I haven't practiced enough already.
                          15.   16.

Third, I've been eaten a lot of different foods like hamburgers and pizza. I never ate those in
         17.   18.
my country. Unfortunately, I been gaining weight.
                           19.

Fourth, I've gone to several museums in this city. But I've taken never a trip to another
         20.   21.
American city. I'd like to visit New York, but I haven't saved enough money yet.
                                              22.   23.

Fifth, I've been living in three apartments so far. In my country, I lived in the same house
         24.   25.
with my family all my life.

One thing that bothers me is this: I've answered the following questions about a thousand
                                   26.
times so far: "Where do you come from?" and "How long time you have been in the U.S.?" I'm
                                              27.   28.
getting tired of always answering the same question. But in general, I been happy since I came to
                                                                   29.   30.
the U.S.

WRITING TIP
When you write a paragraph or essay about a change in your life, start your paper with a sentence that states how the new situation (technology, for example) has changed your life.

Since I got a cell phone, my life has greatly improved.

Then use the simple past to talk about what you used to do and the simple present to talk about what you do habitually now.

Before I got a cell phone, I went to work in the morning and only talked to my family at night. Now, I call before I go home to ask if they need anything.

PART 3 Write
Read the prompts. Choose one and write a paragraph or two about it.
1. Write about the changes that you have made since you came to this country, city, or school.
2. Write about new technology that you've started using recently. How has that made your life different?

PART 4 Edit
Reread the Summary of Unit 9 and the editing advice. Edit your writing from Part 3.

The Present Perfect, The Present Perfect Continuous   257

New Writing Tips further connect the grammar to the unit writing task.

ADDITIONAL RESOURCES

FOR STUDENTS The **Online Practice** provides a variety of interactive grammar activities for homework or flexible independent study.

GO TO ELTNGL.COM/MYELT

FOR TEACHERS The **Classroom Presentation Tool** allows the teacher to project the student book pages, open interactive activities with answers, and play the audio program.

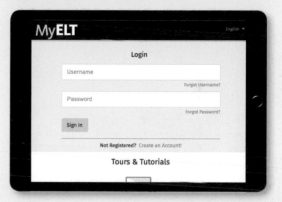

The Teacher's Website hosts the teacher's guide, audio, and ExamView® Test Center, so teachers have all the materials they need in one place.

ELTNGL.COM/GRAMMARINCONTEXTSERIES

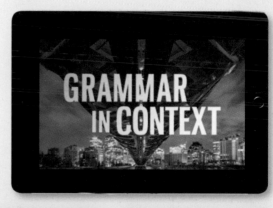

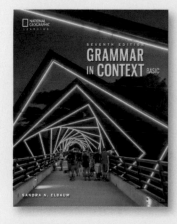

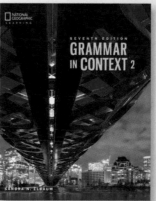

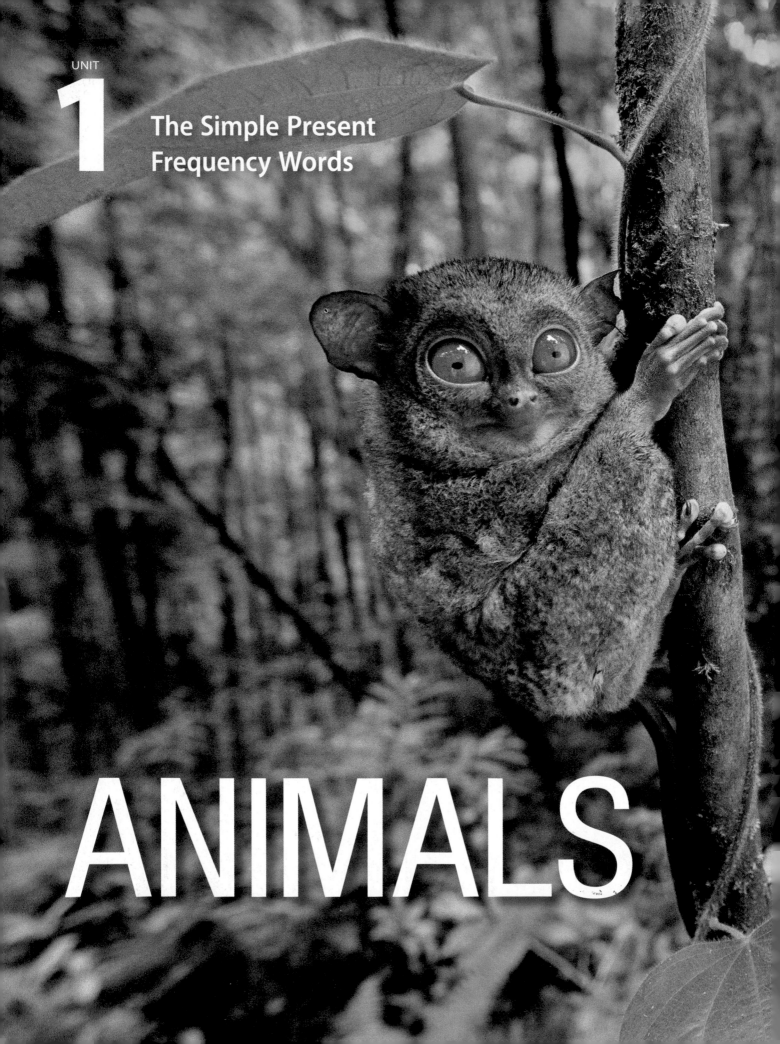

ANIMALS

The Western tarsier is nocturnal. Its big eyes and ears help it see and hear in the dark.

Some people talk to animals. Not many listen though. That's the problem.

A.A. MILNE

Special Friends

Read the following article. Pay special attention to the words in bold. 🎧 **1.1**

They **are** our friends. We play with them. We talk to them. We spend a lot of money on them. We love them. Who **are** they? Our pets, of course. About 68 percent of Americans live with one or more animals. There **are** about 94 million pet cats and 90 million pet dogs in the United States. There **are** more pets than children in the United States! The most popular pets **are** cats and dogs. Other popular pets **are** fish, birds, and rabbits.

Pet ownership **isn't** cheap. Americans spend more than $69 billion a year on their pets. There **are** schools, toys, hotels, clothes, and cemeteries for pets. The average dog owner spends over $257 a year on vet[1] bills.

For many Americans, pets **are** part of the family. Many owners sleep with their dogs or cats. Some people travel with their pets. (The average cost to fly with a pet **is** $125 each way.) Some hotels allow guests to bring their pets.

Pets **are** great for your health. Contact with an affectionate[2] dog or cat can lower a person's blood pressure. Also, pets **are** a comfort to lonely people.

Pets **are** fun, but **they're** also work. Animals need a lot of attention. Before you buy a pet, it **is** important to answer these questions:

- **Are** you patient?
- **Are** you home a lot?
- If you have children, **are** they responsible?
- **Is** this a good animal for children?
- **Are** pets allowed where you live?
- **Are** you or your family members allergic[3] to pets?

It's important to understand that a pet **is** a long-term responsibility—and a long-term friend.

---

[1] vet: short for *veterinarian*; an animal doctor
[2] affectionate: loving
[3] allergic: very sensitive to a particular animal or plant

A man and his dog check in for their flight.

COMPREHENSION Based on the reading, write T for *true* or F for *false*.

1. ___T___ The most popular pets in the U.S. are dogs and cats.

2. ___F___ About 94 percent of Americans have a pet.

3. ___F___ Pets are not allowed on airplanes.

THINK ABOUT IT Discuss the questions with a partner or in a small group.

1. Do you have a pet? If so, what kind? If not, what kind do you think you would like?

2. In addition to lowering a person's blood pressure, what other ways can a pet make a person's life better?

1.1 *Be* Simple Present—Form

EXAMPLES			EXPLANATION
SUBJECT	*BE*		
I	**am**	happy with my dog.	We use *am* with *I*.
The child He She The cat It That There	**is**	responsible. intelligent. lonely. happy. cute. a friendly cat. a dog in the yard.	We use *is* with *he, she, it, this, that*, and singular subjects (*the child, the cat*, etc.). We use *there is* with a singular noun.
We You Pets They Those There	**are**	hard working. home a lot. fun. good friends. cute kittens. schools for dogs.	We use *are* with *we, you, they, these, those*, and plural subjects (*pets, cats*, etc.). We use *there are* with a plural noun.

1.2 Contractions with *Be*

EXAMPLES		EXPLANATION
I am You are She is He is It is We are They are	**I'm** responsible. **You're** patient. **She's** happy. **He's** kind. **It's** necessary. **We're** busy. **They're** cute.	A contraction combines two words. We can make a contraction with the subject pronoun and *am, is,* or *are*. We put an apostrophe (') in place of the missing letter.
There is Here is That is	**There's** a pet store near my house. **Here's** an idea. Let's get a dog. **That's** a friendly cat.	We can make a contraction with *there is, here is,* and *that is*.
cat is dog is	The **cat's** hungry. Your **dog's** cute.	We can make a contraction with most singular nouns and *is*.
A fo**x** **is** a relative of a dog. A mou**se** **is** a small animal. Thi**s** **is** a cute cat.		We don't make a contraction with *is* if the word before ends in *s, se, ce, ge, ze, sh, ch,* or *x*.

EXERCISE 1 Listen to the conversation. Fill in the blanks with the words you hear. 🎧 1.2

A: I want a dog. My friend has a dog with new puppies. There _____are_____ nine puppies, and they
1.

need a home. The puppies _____are_____ two months old. They _____are_____ so cute. I want
2. 3.

one. Look—this _____is_____ a picture of my favorite puppy.
4.

B: Dogs _____are_____ a big responsibility.
5.

A: Mom, I _____am_____ nine years old now, and I _____am_____ responsible. I love dogs.
6. 7.

They _____are_____ so affectionate. They _____are_____ great friends. And dogs
8. 9.

_____are_____ fun.
10.

B: They _____are_____ expensive, too. For example, there _____is_____ the cost of food.
11. 12.

EXERCISE 2 Fill in the blanks with the correct form of *be* to finish the conversation from Exercise 1.
Use contractions wherever possible.

B: There __'re) is__ also vet bills.
1.

A: Vet bills?

B: Yes. A vet _____is_____ an animal doctor. Dogs need doctors just like we do. It __'s____
2. 3.

important to think about that, too.

A: But the puppies ___'are____ healthy.
4.

B: You _____are_____ healthy, too. But sometimes you _____are_____ sick and you need a
5. 6.

doctor. Also, your little brother _____is_____ only three years old. He _____is_____
7. 8.

afraid of dogs. Here __'is____ another problem: It _____is_____ summer now, so it
9. 10.

_____is_____ easy to take the dog out. But in winter, it _____is_____ so cold.
11. 12.

A: Please, Mom.

B: Let me think about it. I have to talk to Dad. We _____are_____ your parents, and we want to make
13.

the right decision.

A: Thanks, Mom.

1.3 Be—Use

EXAMPLES	USES
I **am** patient.	With a description (an adjective)
A vet **is** an animal doctor.	With a classification or definition of the subject
My dog **is** in the yard.	With a location
This dog **is** from Alaska.	With a place of origin
The dog **is** cold. It **is** cold outside.	With a reaction to the temperature (*hot, cold, warm*) and with weather. The subject for sentences about weather is *it*.
My dog **is** three (years old).	With age
The cat **is** hungry. I **am** afraid of dogs.	With a physical or emotional state: *hungry, thirsty, afraid*
There **are** toys for dogs. There **is** an animal hospital near my house.	With *there*, to show that something exists
It **is** ten o'clock now.	With time. The subject for sentences about time is *it*.
It **is** important to be responsible with a pet.	With certain expressions beginning with *it*

Note:

Some words that end in -ed are adjectives: *tired, married, worried, interested, bored, excited, crowded, located.*

> The pet shop is **located** on the corner.
> The children are **excited** about the new puppy.

EXERCISE 3 Fill in the blanks with the correct form of *be*. Then write **D** for description, **C** for classification, **L** for location, **O** for origin, **W** for weather, **A** for age, **P** for a physical or emotional state, **TH** for *there*, **T** for time, or **I** for expressions beginning with *it*. Use contractions wherever possible.

1. My dog _'s_ small. _D_

2. You _are_ home a lot. _L_

3. This dog _is_ friendly. _P_

4. There _are_ a lot of pets in the U.S. _TH_

5. It _is_ fun to own a pet. _P_

6. It _is_ hot today. _W_

7. The dog _is_ thirsty. _P_

8. The puppies _are_ three months old. _A_

9. It _is_ 7 a.m. _T_

10. I _am_ from Vietnam. _O_

11. Vietnam _is_ a country in Asia. _C_

1.4 Negative Statements with *Be*

EXAMPLES	EXPLANATION
The dog owner **is not** home now. She **isn't** home during the day. You **are not** ready for a pet. You **aren't** patient.	To make a negative statement with *be*, we put *not* after a form of *be*. The negative contractions are *isn't* and *aren't*.

We can make contractions in negative statements with most subject pronouns + a form of *be* or with a form of *be* + *not*. (Exception: *I am not*)

I am not	I'm not		—
you are not	you're not	OR	you aren't
he is not	he's not	OR	he isn't
she is not	she's not	OR	she isn't
it is not	it's not	OR	it isn't
we are not	we're not	OR	we aren't
they are not	they're not	OR	they aren't

Notes:

1. We can make contractions with most nouns:

   The dog is not friendly. = *The **dog's not** friendly.* = *The **dog isn't** friendly.*

2. Remember: We cannot make a contraction with certain words + *is*. (See 1.2.)

   This is not a good pet. = *This isn't a good pet.* (NOT: *This's not*)

EXERCISE 4 Fill in the first blank with the correct form of *be*. Then fill in the second blank with a negative form. Use contractions wherever possible. In some cases, more than one answer is possible. Write all possible answers.

1. Today <u>'s</u> my daughter's birthday. It <u>isn't</u> a holiday.

a.   b.

2. My daughter and I <u>am</u> at the pet shop. We <u>aren't</u> at home.

a.   b.

3. My husband <u>is</u> at work now. He <u>isn't</u> with me.

a.   b.

4. I <u>am</u> patient with dogs. I <u>am not</u> patient with cats.

a.   b.

5. This puppy <u>is</u> for my daughter. It <u>isn't</u> for my son.

a.   b.

6. My daughter <u>is</u> responsible. My son <u>isn't</u> responsible.

a.   b.

7. Dogs <u>are</u> good for protection. Cats <u>aren't</u> good for protection.

a.   b.

8. This <u>is</u> a small dog. It <u>isn't</u> a big dog.

a.   b.

9. There <u>are</u> a lot of puppies here. There <u>aren't</u> a lot of kittens here.

a.   b.

EXERCISE 5 Circle the correct words to complete the sentences. In some cases, both answers are possible, so circle both options.

1. My dog (**is**/are) sick.

2. (**She's not/She isn't**) young.

3. She (is/**'s**) 15 years old.

4. She (**isn't**/not) hungry.

5. This (**is**/**'s**) a serious problem.

6. My dog and I (am/**are**) at the vet.

7. (**I'm not**/I amn't) happy.

8. We (is/**are**) worried about the dog.

9. (**The vet's/The vet**) a good doctor.

10. There ('s/**are**) many dogs in the waiting room.

11. (**They aren't/They're not**) all sick.

12. There (are/**is**) one cat in the waiting room.

13. (**It's**/It) in a box.

14. The box (**is**/**'s**) small.

15. There (**are**/**'re**) pet magazines in the waiting room.

16. (Is/**It's**) important to have a healthy pet.

17. (**It's**/It) my turn with the vet now.

18. (**I'm**/I) next.

A father and his sons wait to see their dog's veterinarian.

1.5 Yes/No Questions and Short Answers with *Be*

Compare statement word order with *yes/no* question word order.

STATEMENT WORD ORDER	*YES/NO* QUESTION	SHORT ANSWER
I am patient.	**Am I** patient with pets?	Yes, you are.
You are happy.	**Are you** happy with the new dog?	Yes, I am.
The vet is kind.	**Is the vet** patient?	Yes, she is.
It is important to take the dog to the vet.	**Is it** important to give the dog exercise?	Yes, it is.
We are at the vet.	**Are we** in her office?	No, we're not.
Pets are fun.	**Are pets** interesting?	Yes, they are.
They are interested in a pet.	**Are they** interested in a bird?	No, they aren't.
Those are cute puppies.	**Are those** your puppies?	Yes, they are.
That is a friendly dog.	**Is that** your dog?	No, it's not.
There are dogs at the vet.	**Are there** birds at the vet?	No, there aren't.

Notes:

1. In a question, we put *am, is,* or *are* before the subject.
2. We use a contraction for a short *no* answer. We don't use a contraction for a short *yes* answer.

    Is your son responsible? No, he isn't. OR *No, he's not.*

    Is your daughter responsible? Yes, she is. (NOT: *Yes, she's.*)
3. We use a pronoun (*he, we, you,* etc.) in a short answer.
4. When the question contains *this* or *that*, the answer uses *it*, even for people.

    *Is that the vet? Yes, **it** is.*

Pronunciation Note: We usually end a *yes/no* question with rising intonation.

Is that your dog?

EXERCISE 6 Fill in the blanks to complete each item. Use contractions wherever possible.

1. **A:** _____ Is a bird _____ a good pet?

   B: Yes, it is. A bird is a very good pet.

2. **A:** _____ Are you _____ happy with your new kitten?

   B: Yes, I am. My new kitten is fun.

3. **A:** _____ Are they _____ interested in birds?

   B: No, he _____ isn't _____ . My son's interested in fish.

4. **A:** _____ Is there _____ a vet near here?

   B: Yes, _____ there is _____ . There's a vet on the next block.

5. A: _Is she_ in the yard?

   B: No, she _isn't_ . The dog is in the house.

6. A: _Are you_ ready for a dog?

   B: No, I'm not. _I am_ not home enough.

7. A: _Are you_ good with pets?

   B: No, you _aren't_ . You're not patient enough.

EXERCISE 7 Fill in the blanks to complete this conversation. Use contractions wherever possible. In some cases, more than one answer is possible.

A: _Is_ this your dog?
    1.

B: Yes, it _is_ .
    2.

A: He _is_ beautiful.
    3.

B: Thanks. But it's a "she."

A: _Is She_ friendly?
    4.

B: Yes, she _is_ .
    5.

A: She's so small. _she is_ a puppy?
         6.

B: No, she _isn't_ . _She's_ four years old.
    7.   8.

A: _Is it_ hard to take care of a dog?
    9.

B: No, it _isn't_ .
    10.

A: _Are you_ home a lot?
    11.

B: No, _I am not_ . _I am_ a student. But my parents _are_ home a
    12.   13.   14.

lot.

A: I love dogs, but I _am_ home very much, and I live alone. So that _is_ a
            15.   16.

problem.

B: Cats _are_ good pets, too. With a cat, it _is not_ necessary to be home a lot. I
        17.   18.

think a cat _is_ the perfect pet for you. _is that_ right?
        19.   20.

A: No, you _are not_ . I'm allergic to cats.
    21.

1.6 *Wh-* Questions with *Be*

Compare statement word order with *wh-* question word order.

AFFIRMATIVE STATEMENTS	AFFIRMATIVE *WH-* QUESTIONS
I am lost.	Where **am I**?
You are lonely.	Why **are you** lonely?
That is a nice dog.	What kind of dog **is that**?
The cat is old.	How old **is the cat**?
It is important to choose the right pet.	Why **is it** important to choose the right pet?
She is at work.	When **is she** at home?
There are a lot of dogs in my neighborhood.	How many dogs **are there** in your neighborhood?

NEGATIVE STATEMENTS	NEGATIVE *WH-* QUESTIONS
The dogs aren't friendly.	Why **aren't the dogs** friendly?
You aren't happy with the dog.	Why **aren't you** happy with the dog?

Notes:

1. Most question words can contract with *is*. The exceptions are *which is* and *how much is*.

   What's a vet?

   Where's your cat?

   Which is bigger, my dog or your dog?

2. After *what*, we can use a noun:

   what kind, what color, what country, what time

3. After *how*, we can use an adjective or adverb:

   how long, how hard, how old, how big, how much, how many

4. After *which*, we can use a noun:

   which dog, which vet, which animal

GRAMMAR IN USE

We ask different *wh-* questions to get information about specific topics.

Where	for a place	**A: *Where*** is your school?	**B:** *It's on Maple Street.*
Why	for a reason	**A: *Why*** are you here?	**B:** *Because I am a student.*
What kind	for a description	**A: *What kind*** of book is that?	**B:** *It's an English book.*
How old	for age	**A: *How old*** is Miguel?	**B:** *He's 18.*
When	for time	**A: *When*** is the concert?	**B:** *At 7 p.m./Tomorrow.*
How many	for number	**A: *How many*** students are here?	**B:** *15.*
How much	for amount	**A: *How much*** time is there?	**B:** *About ten minutes.*
How long	for length of time	**A: *How long*** is the flight?	**B:** *Two hours.*

EXERCISE 8 Fill in the blanks with the words you hear. 🎧 1.3

A: _____Is that_____ your dog?
   1.

B: No. It's my neighbor's dog.

A: _____What of kind of dog__ It's so cute.
   2.   is it

B: I think it's a mutt.

A: _____What is_____ a mutt?
   3.

B: It's a mixed breed dog.

A: My daughter wants a dog. But dogs are so expensive.

B: A mutt isn't so expensive.

A: _____Why isn't_____ expensive?
   4.

B: Because you can get a mutt at an animal shelter. Dogs aren't expensive there.

A: _____What is_____ an animal shelter?
   5.

B: It's a place for unwanted pets. Those animals need a loving family.

A: _____Are they Animal__ healthy?
   6.

B: Yes, they _____are_____. The vets check the animals' health.
   7.

A: Why _____are they__ so many unwanted pets?
   8.

B: There are a lot of unwanted pets because some people aren't responsible. They get a pet and then realize
   it's too much trouble to take care of it. What about your daughter? _____Is she_____
                                                                          9.
   responsible?

A: Yes, _____she is_____.
   10.

B: _____How older she_____?
   11.

A: She's almost 10 years old.

B: I love dogs, but it's not a good idea for our family.

A: _____Why isn't_____ a good idea?
   12.

B: We're all too busy.

EXERCISE 9 Fill in the blanks to complete the phone conversation.

A: Hello?

B: Hi, Betty. This is Lara. How ___are you___ ?
1.

A: I'm fine. I'm not home now.

B: Where ___are you now___
2.

A: I'm at the animal hospital with the cat.

B: You have two cats. Which cat ___is___ sick?
3.

A: Fluffy.

B: ___What is___ wrong with Fluffy?
4.

A: He isn't hungry or thirsty.

B: ___How old is___ ? Fluffy
5.

A: He's only four years old.

B: ___Are you___ alone?
6.

A: No, I'm not.

B: ___Who is___ with you?
7.

A: My daughter's with me.

B: Why ___she is not___ at school?
8.

A: She's on spring break now. She's very worried.

B: Why ___She's___ worried?
9.

A: Fluffy is tired all the time. Oh, I have to go. The vet is ready to see us now.

B: OK. Call me later.

ABOUT YOU Find a partner. Ask each other these questions and share your answers.

1. Are pets popular in your native country? What kind?

2. What's a popular name for dogs in your native culture?

3. What's a better pet in your opinion—a dog or a cat?

FUN WITH GRAMMAR

Race your classmates. Form two or three teams. Your teacher will write a statement on the board. Each team writes a *yes/no* question and a *wh-* question for the statement. The team to write two correct questions first wins a point.

Statement: *Sam is in Prague.*   Yes/No question: *Is Sam in Prague?*

Wh- questions: *Where is Sam?/Who is in Prague?*

Dung beetles keep the land healthy for grazing cattle.

BENEFICIAL BUGS[1]

Read the following article. Pay special attention to the words in bold. 🎧 1.4

Are you afraid of spiders? How about insects such as roaches, ants, or bees? If your answer is "yes," you are not alone. Most people **don't like** them—and for good reason. Insects and spiders **look** scary. They **have** lots of legs, and they **fly** or **move** fast. Also, some of them **bite**, and sometimes this **causes** pain or even illness. (Usually, a spider's bite **doesn't hurt**, though.)

Insects and spiders can be scary, but they aren't all bad. In fact, many **help** us. Here's how.

 They **feed** us.

Bees **do** a lot for us, for example. Everyone **knows** that bees **make** honey, which we **use** in food, drinks, and medicine. But bees also **pollinate**[2] plants. When they **do** this, it **gives** us many fruits and vegetables. In fact, the U.S. **uses** bees to grow about 30 percent of its crops[3].

 They **protect** our food.

Farmers **grow** crops for food, but many insects **eat** these plants. Luckily, we **have** ladybugs and spiders. They **kill** bad bugs and **protect** our food. A ladybug, for example, **eats** about 5,000 insects a year, and a spider **eats** about 2,000. Thanks to spiders and ladybugs, a farmer **doesn't need** to use as many pesticides.

 They **clean** the environment.

Many insects and spiders **eat** waste on the ground—for example, old food or dead animals and plants. On one street in New York City, spiders, ants, and roaches **consume** about 2,100 pounds (950 kilos) of food on the ground each year. That's the same as 60,000 hot dogs! Eating this food waste **cleans** the environment and **keeps** it healthy.

DID YOU **KNOW?**
Spiders and insects are members of the largest group of animals on Earth (called *arthropods*). For every one person, there are 1.4 billion insects and millions of spiders. Luckily, many are small, and they **don't live** very long.

---

[1] bug: an informal word for *insect*
[2] to pollinate: to give material from one plant to another so that the plant reproduces and makes seeds and fruit
[3] crops: plants that we grow for food

COMPREHENSION Based on the reading, write T for *true* or F for *false*.

1. ___T___ Spiders and insects are a type of animal. There are more of them on Earth than people.

2. ___F___ Farmers dislike bees because they kill plants.

3. ___F___ Spiders and insects don't like human food.

THINK ABOUT IT Discuss the questions with a partner or in a small group.

1. How do the following help people? Explain with an example from the reading.

   bees   spiders   ladybugs   ants and roaches

2. Are you afraid of spiders and insects? Did the reading change your feelings about them?

1.7 The Simple Present Affirmative Statements—Form

A simple present tense verb has two forms: the base form and the *-s* form.

EXAMPLES			EXPLANATION
SUBJECT	**BASE FORM**	**COMPLEMENT**	
I You We They Many people	**dislike**	insects.	We use the base form of the verb when the subject is *I, you, we, they,* or a plural noun. **NOTE:** *People* is a plural noun.
SUBJECT	**-S FORM**	**COMPLEMENT**	
He She It The child Everyone	**dislikes**	insects.	We use the *-s* form of the verb when the subject is *he, she, it,* or a singular noun. **NOTE:** *Everyone* is a singular noun.

Notes:

1. *Have* is an irregular verb. The *-s* form is *has.*

   Insects **have** six legs. A spider **has** eight legs.

2. We use the *-s* form in the following expression: It **takes** (time) to do something.

   It **takes** time for bees to make honey.

3. We use the *-s* form after an *-ing* subject (gerund).

   Eating food waste on the ground **cleans** the environment.

EXERCISE 10 Complete the sentences with the base form or the *-s* form of the verb given. Then listen and check your answers. 🎧 1.5

Amazing Ants

Ants _____ *live* _____ in a large group called a *colony*. Usually, the colony _____ *have* _____
1. live   **2. have**

one queen. She _____ *lays* _____ eggs. Female "worker" ants _____ *find* _____ food and
3. lay   **4. find**

_____ *protect* _____ the group. Male ants _____ *have* _____ one main function in the colony: to
5. protect   **6. have**

mate with the queen.

Many people _____ *thinks* _____ that the queen is the group's leader, but she isn't. No single
7. think

ant _____ *control* _____ the colony. Instead, each ant _____ *doing* _____ its part to help the colony,
8. control   **9. do**

and the group _____ *fix* _____ any problems together. For example, when a worker ant
10. fix

_____ *goes* _____ out to find food, she usually _____ *bring* _____ it back by herself. But sometimes
11. go   **12. bring**

an object is large, and the worker ant can't carry it alone. So she _____ *sends* _____ a chemical
13. send

message to other ants, and they _____ *come* _____ to help her. Then everyone _____ *carries* _____
14. come   **15. carry**

the large object together. Working as a group _____ *make* _____ the difficult task easier. People
16. make

can learn a lot from these little animals.

1.8 The Simple Present—Use

EXAMPLES	USES
Some insects **bite**. Everyone **knows** that bees **make** honey. The U.S. **uses** bees to grow 30 percent of its crops.	To talk about general truths, habits, or customs
A spider **eats** about 2,000 insects a year. I **see** ants in the kitchen all the time.	To show regular activity or repeated action

Ants work together to
solve problems.

EXERCISE 11 Fill in the blanks with the base form or the -s form of a verb in the box. You will use the verbs *catch* and *make* twice.

catch	have	hope	know	make	see✓	take

1. You probably _____ *see* _____ spiders' webs all the time.

2. A spider's web _____ *make* _____ insects for the spider to eat. Everyone _____ *catch* _____ this.

3. Making a new web _____ *take* _____ about an hour.

4. A spider _____ *knows* _____ its web from silk.

5. This silk is very strong. Some people _____ *make* _____ fishing nets from it, and they _____ *catchs* _____ fish.

6. In the future, scientists _____ *hope* _____ to make clothes from spider silk.

7. Spider silk also _____ *has* _____ the ability to stop bleeding in humans.

1.9 The Simple Present—Negative Statements

EXAMPLES	EXPLANATION
The girl **likes** ladybugs. She **doesn't like** spiders. A bee sting **hurts**. A spider bite **doesn't hurt** as much.	We use *doesn't* + the base form with *he, she, it,* or a singular subject. **Compare:** likes doesn't **like** hurts doesn't **hurt** *Doesn't* is the contraction for *does not.*
Many insects **live** for only a few hours. They **don't live** very long.	We use *don't* + the base form with *I, you, we, they,* or a plural subject. **Compare:** like don't **like** live don't **live** *Don't* is the contraction for *do not.*

EXERCISE 12 Fill in the blanks with the negative form of the underlined verb.

1. A spider <u>makes</u> a web. An insect _____ *doesn't make* _____ a web.

2. A spider <u>has</u> eight legs. An insect _____ *hasn't* _____ eight legs. It has six.

3. Most spiders <u>have</u> eight eyes. Insects _____ *haven't* _____ eight. They have two.

4. An ant <u>lives</u> in a colony. It _____ *doesn't live* _____ alone.

5. Pesticides <u>kill</u> many bugs, but they _____ *doesn't kill* _____ many spiders.

6. My brother <u>likes</u> spiders. I _____ *doesn't like* _____ them at all!

7. Elena and Carlos are entomologists. She <u>studies</u> bees. He _____ *doesn't study* _____ bees. He specializes in ants.

8. We <u>know</u> many bees are dying today. We _____don't know_____ why.

9. Some people raise bees for honey. It <u>takes</u> time, but raising bees _____doesn't take_____ a lot of work.

10. Some insects <u>bite</u> people. But bees _____doesn't bite_____. They sting.

EXERCISE 13 Fill in the blanks with the correct negative form of a verb in the box. Use each verb only once.

break	die	have	kill	know
like	live	make	see	want

1. Most spiders _____don't live_____ very long—only about a year.

2. Many people _____don't like_____ spiders because they look scary.

3. My sister is afraid of spiders, but I _____don't know_____ why.

4. A typical spider has eight eyes, but it _____doesn't see_____ very well.

5. Take my advice: If you _____don't want_____ spiders in your house, keep your home clean.

6. Using pesticides _____doesn't kill_____ most spiders. Instead, try vinegar. It kills most bugs.

7. Unlike many spiders, a tarantula _____doesn't make_____ a web. It makes a hole in the ground.

8. In a famous story, a dangerous spider bites a man, but he _____doesn't die_____. He lives and becomes the superhero Spider-Man.

9. A spider's web _____doesn't break_____ easily because it is very strong.

A tarantula is a large spider with a hairy body and legs.

10. We _____don't have_____ any more time today to talk about these eight-legged animals.

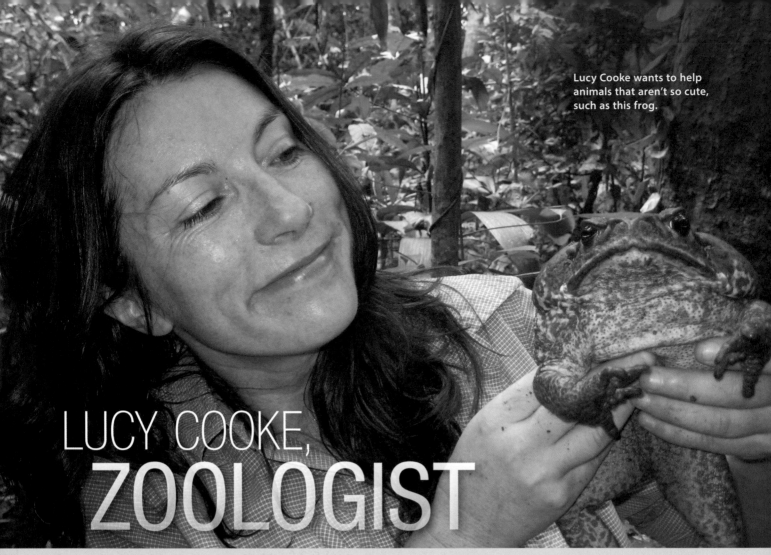

Lucy Cooke wants to help animals that aren't so cute, such as this frog.

LUCY COOKE, ZOOLOGIST

Read the following article. Pay special attention to the words in bold. 🎧 1.6

Which animal **do** you **prefer** to see? A baby panda, a toad, or a snake? Most people choose the baby panda. Why **do** people **choose** this animal? Most people like cute, furry animals with big eyes, like the panda. These animals get a lot of attention. Why **don't** people **like** snakes and toads? They're just not cute like pandas.

Lucy Cooke wants people to respect all animals. Who is Lucy Cooke? Why **does** she **want** to show people the importance of other animals? Cooke is a zoologist, a scientist who studies animals. She worries about the future of all animals. Scientists need money to study and protect these animals, but they get less money for toads and snakes than for pandas.

"There are so many television shows about koala bears and kittens," Cooke says. To get people interested in less popular animals, Cooke writes stories about them in a blog. She also makes videos about them and puts them online. People love her videos. They are fun to watch.

Cooke is especially interested in frogs and other amphibians[1]. Some of these are in danger of disappearing. She wants to save these animals. Why **does** she **want** to save these animals? Other animals depend on them for food. If we save frogs, we save other animals, too.

Do you **know** about the flying frog in Borneo? It has wings. It lives in the treetops and goes from tree to tree without going down to the ground. **Do** you **know** about the poison[2] dart frog? It is only one centimeter long. But it has enough poison to kill ten people.

Scientists need research money to protect all animals. Cooke's videos and blog make people aware of all kinds of animals.

---

[1] amphibian: an animal that can live on land or in water
[2] poison: a substance that harms or kills people or animals

COMPREHENSION Based on the reading, write T for *true* or F for *false*.

1. __T__ Cooke makes videos about animals.
2. __F__ The Borneo frog goes to the ground to get food.
3. __F__ Cooke writes a blog about animals.

THINK ABOUT IT Discuss the questions with a partner or in a small group.

1. Do you think it is important to protect all animals? Why or why not?

2. What are some unpopular animals? Why are they unpopular?

1.10 The Simple Present—Questions

Compare statements, *yes/no* questions, and short answers.

STATEMENT	*YES/NO* QUESTION & SHORT ANSWER	EXPLANATION
Cooke **studies** animals. She **writes** a blog.	**Does** she **study** frogs? Yes, she **does**. **Does** she **write** about pets? No, she **doesn't**.	For *yes/no* questions with *he, she, it,* or a singular subject, we use *Does* + subject + base form.
People **like** cute animals. Koala bears **get** attention.	**Do** people **like** insects? No, they **don't**. **Do** pandas **get** attention? Yes, they **do**.	For *yes/no* questions with *I, we, you, they,* or a plural subject, we use *Do* + subject + base form.

Note:

Compare *yes/no* questions and short answers with *be* and other simple present verbs:

> **Is** *Cooke a zoologist? Yes, she* **is**.   **Does** *Cooke research amphibians? Yes, she* **does**.

Compare statements and *wh-* questions.

STATEMENT	*WH-* QUESTION	EXPLANATION
Cooke **studies** frogs. She **makes** videos.	How **does** Cooke **study** frogs? Why **does** she **make** videos?	For *wh-* questions with *he, she, it,* or a singular subject, we use *wh-* word + *does* + subject + base form.
Some frogs **live** in trees. Some frogs **have** wings.	Where **do** other frogs **live**? Why **do** these frogs **have** wings?	For *wh-* questions with *I, we, you, they,* or a plural subject, we use *wh-* word + *do* + subject + base form.
Cooke **doesn't study** plants. Borneo frogs **don't live** on the ground.	Why **doesn't** Cooke **study** plants? Why **don't** Borneo frogs **live** on the ground?	For negative *wh-* questions, we use *wh-* word + *don't* or *doesn't* + subject + base form.

Note:

Compare *wh-* questions with *be* and other simple present verbs:

> *What kind of animals* **are** *you interested in?*   *Why* **aren't** *people interested in some animals?*
>
> *What kind of animals* **do** *you* **like**?   *Why* **don't** *people* **like** *some animals?*

EXERCISE 14 Listen to the conversation. Then write T for *true* or F for *false*. 🎧 1.7

1. __T__ Search and rescue dogs help find people after a disaster.
2. __F__ They rely on their excellent eyesight.
3. __F__ Small dogs make the best rescue dogs.

EXERCISE 15 Listen to the conversation again. Fill in the blanks with the words you hear. 🎧 1.7

A: There's a program on TV tonight about search and rescue dogs. __Do you want__ to watch it with me?
1.

B: I __know__ about guide dogs. But I __don't know__ anything about search and
2.   3.

rescue dogs. What __does__ search __mean__ ?
4.   5.

A: Search __mean__ "look for."
6.

B: __How does you__ search?
7.   speed

A: S-E-A-R-C-H.

B: What __do I__ these dogs __do__ ?
8.   9.

A: When there is a disaster, like an earthquake, they __help__ the workers find missing people.
10.

They __save__ people's lives.
11.

B: How __do__ they __do__ that?
12.   13.

A: They __have__ a great sense of smell. They can find things that people can't.
14.

B: __Do they need__ a lot of training?
15.

A: Yes, they __do__ .
16.

B: What kind of dogs __they use__ ?
17.

A: They usually __use__ large, strong dogs. Labrador retrievers or golden retrievers are often
18.

search and rescue dogs. Let's watch the program together tonight.

B: What time __is it begin__ ?
19.

A: At 9 p.m.

B: __Does__ your dog __want__ to watch the program with us?
20.   21.

A: Ha! I __don't__ think so. My dog is lazy. She just __like__ to eat, play, and sleep.
22.   23.

EXERCISE 16 Fill in the blanks to complete the conversation. Use context clues to help you.

A: Do you _____ like _____ animals?
1.

B: Yes, I _____ do _____. In fact, I like animals very much, especially dogs.
2.

A: _____ do you have _____ a dog?
3.

B: No, I don't have a dog, but my sister has two Labradors. I love to play with them when I visit her.

A: If you love dogs, why _____ you don't have _____ a dog?
4.

B: Because my landlord _____ doesn't allow _____ dogs.
5.

A: That's too bad. _____ does _____ he allow cats?
6.

B: Yes, he _____ does _____.
7.

A: Why _____ he allow _____ cats but not dogs?
8.

B: He says dogs make a lot of noise. I have a cat, but I have to find a new home for her. _____ do you _____
9.
you know anyone who wants a cat?

A: No, I _____ don't know _____. Sorry. Why _____ you don't want _____ your cat?
10.   11.

B: I want my cat, but my girlfriend doesn't.

A: Why _____ She doesn't want _____ your cat?
12.

B: She's allergic to cats.

A: That's a problem.

ABOUT YOU Choose Part 1 to interview a student who has a dog, or Part 2 to interview a student who has a cat. Then report what you learned to another student.

PART 1

1. your dog/big
   A: *Is your dog big?*
   B: *Yes, she is.*

2. your dog/sleep a lot (how many hours)
   A: *Does your dog sleep a lot?*
   B: *Yes, she does.*
   A: *How many hours does she sleep?*
   B: *She sleeps about fifteen hours a day.*

continued

3. how old/your dog   *how old is your dog?*

4. it/a male or a female   *Does it a male or Femal?*

5. what/your dog's name   *what is your dog's name?*

6. what/your dog/eat   *what does your dog eat?*

7. how often/you/take your dog out   *how often does you take y*

8. your dog/do tricks (what kind)   *what kind you do tricks*

9. your dog/have toys (what kind)   *Does your dog have your dog toys*

10. your dog/friendly

11. your dog/bark a lot (when)   *when Does you dog bark alot*

12. why/you/like dogs   *why do you like dogs*

PART 2

1. how old/your cat

2. it/a male or a female

3. what/your cat's name

4. your cat/eat special food (what kind)

5. your cat/friendly

6. your cat/sit on your lap a lot

7. your cat/have toys (what kind)

8. your cat/sleep with you (where)

9. why/you/like cats

EXERCISE 17 Circle the correct words to complete the conversation.

A: We're late. Hurry. The train is ready to leave.

B: Let's go . . . (on the train) . . . Why (*that dog is*/*is that dog*) on the train? (*Are*/*Do*) they allow dogs
on trains?
1.   2.

A: Not usually. But that's not an ordinary dog. That's a guide dog. It's a dog that helps people
with disabilities.

B: How (*do they help*/*they help*) people?
3.

A: They (*help*/*helps*) blind people move from place to place, on foot and by public transportation.
4.

B: (*Are*/*Do*) they need a lot of training?
5.

A: Yes, they (*are*/*do*).
6.

B: Where (*do*/*are*) they get their training?
7.

A: They get their training at special schools. There are guide dogs for the blind, the deaf, and people in wheelchairs.

B: Why (are you/you are) such an expert on guide dogs?
8.

A: My cousin is blind. He has a guide dog.

B: Then you know a lot about guide dogs.

A: Yes, I (am/do). A guide dog (need/needs) to concentrate.
9.   10.

B: When (are/do) they play?
11.

A: They (play/plays) when the owner (take/takes) off the dog's harness. Then the dog (know/knows) its
12.   13.   14.

work is finished.

B: It's amazing what a dog can do.

1.11 *Wh-* Questions with a Preposition

EXAMPLES	EXPLANATION
A: What does Lucy Cooke write **about**? **B:** She writes about animals in danger. **A:** What are these animals in danger **of**? **B:** They're in danger of disappearing.	In conversation, most people put the preposition at the end of the *wh-* question.
A: Where does Lucy Cooke **come from**? **B:** She comes from England. **A:** Where **is** she **from**? **B:** She's from England.	For place of origin, we use *be from* or *come from*.
A: What time does the program begin? **B:** It begins **at** 9 p.m.	We omit *at* in a question about time.

GRAMMAR IN USE

Putting the preposition before a question word is grammatically correct, but very formal. When the preposition comes at the beginning, we use *whom,* not *who.* This formal style is rarely used in everyday speech.

    FORMAL: **With whom** does the dog play?

    INFORMAL: **Who** does the dog play **with**?

EXERCISE 18 Complete each question using the underlined words as clues.

1. Lucy Cooke <u>comes from</u> England. What city _____does_____ she _____come from_____ ?

2. <u>I'm interested in</u> pandas. What animals _____do_____ you _____Interested in_____?

3. What _____Does_____ Lucy Cooke _____writes About_____? She <u>writes</u> a blog <u>about</u> animals in danger.

4. Who _Does studies with_____ ? She <u>studies</u> animals <u>with</u> other zoologists.

5. She <u>travels to</u> other countries. Which countries _____does she travel?_____

6. Cooke <u>worries about</u> certain animals. Which animals _____does she worries about_____ ?

7. I <u>want to learn</u> more <u>about</u> tree frogs. What animals _does you want_ you ~~want to le~~ _____want to learn about?_____

1.12 Questions about Meaning, Spelling, Cost, and Time

WH- WORD	DO/DOES	SUBJECT	VERB (BASE FORM)	COMPLEMENT
What	does	*puppy*	mean?	
How	do	you	spell	*puppy*?
How	do	you	say	*puppy* in Spanish?
How much	does	a puppy	cost?	
How long	does	it	take	to train a puppy?

EXERCISE 19 Fill in the blanks to complete the conversation.

A: _____Do you have_____ a pet?
                    1.

B: Yes. I have a new kitten.

A: I don't know the word *kitten*. What _____does it mean_____ ?
                                         2.

B: *Kitten* means "baby cat."

A: Oh. What's his name?

B: Romeo.

A: How _____do you spell it_____ ?
             3.

B: R-O-M-E-O. _____How_____ any pets?
                  4.
        do you

A: Yes, I do. I have a bird.

B: What kind of bird _____does you have_____ ?
5.

A: I have a bird that talks. I don't know the word in English.

How _____do you say_____ *loro* in English?
6.

B: Parrot. So you have a parrot.

A: Yes. His name is Chico.

B: How old _____doe he is_____ ?
7.

A: He's almost 20 years old.

B: How long _____do they live_____ ?
8.

A: They live a long time. Some live up to 80 years.

B: How much _____does it cost_____ ?
9.

A: It depends on what kind you get. But they usually cost between $175 and $1,000.

B: Wow! _____How much does_____ parrots affectionate?
10.

A: Oh, yes. They're very affectionate. Chico sits on my shoulder all the time.

B: What _____does he eat_____ ?
11.

A: He eats fruit, vegetables, rice, nuts, and seeds.

B: _____does he talak_____ a lot?
12.

A: Yes. He talks a lot.

B: What _____words he say does_____ ?
13.

A: He says, "Good-bye," "Hello," "I love you," and many more things. He speaks Spanish and English.

B: How long _____does it take_____ to teach a parrot a word?
14.

A: My parrot is very smart. It takes a few weeks to teach him one word.

FUN WITH GRAMMAR

Role-play a conversation. You have five minutes to write and practice a conversation with a partner about his or her job. It can be a real job, or you can choose from the ideas below. Use information questions and *wh-* questions to ask what your partner does, where he/she works, if he/she likes the job, and why/why not. The pair with the most original conversation wins.

    dolphin trainer   *fashion blogger*   *race car driver*   *video game tester*
    A: Why do you like to train dolphins?
    B: Dolphins are more fun to work with than people.

Bottlenose DOLPHINS

Read the following article. Pay special attention to the words in bold. 🎧 1.8

Bottlenose dolphins are very popular animals. We **often** see them in aquariums, sea parks, TV shows, and movies. Because of the shape of their nose, they look like they **always** have a smile on their faces.

Bottlenose dolphins live in warm climates. They live underwater, but they **rarely** stay there for more than seven minutes. Humans are involuntary[1] breathers. We don't **usually** think about breathing. But dolphins have to remember to breathe. One side of their brain is **always** active. This means they **never** fully sleep.

Dolphins have an excellent sense of hearing. They use clicking sounds to find food. The sound echoes[2] back and tells them where the food is.

Bottlenose dolphins are social animals. They **usually** swim in groups of 10 to 15. Together they hunt[3] for food. They **sometimes** hunt with fishermen near their fishing boats. **Once in a while** a dolphin hunts alone. **Sometimes** a dolphin gets lost. Each dolphin has a unique[4] whistle, so it uses its whistle to call out to the group.

Bottlenose dolphins **usually** live about 40 to 50 years.

---

[1] involuntary: done without thinking
[2] to echo: to be repeated by bouncing off a surface
[3] to hunt: to search for
[4] unique: one of a kind; not like anything else

COMPREHENSION Based on the reading, write T for *true* or F for *false*.

1. ___T___ Bottlenose dolphins are involuntary breathers.

2. ___F___ Bottlenose dolphins usually hunt alone.

3. ___T___ The whistle of the bottlenose dolphin helps it find other dolphins.

THINK ABOUT IT Discuss the questions with a partner or in a small group.

1. What is a "social animal"? In addition to dolphins, what other animals are social?

2. Why do you think dolphins are popular?

1.13 Frequency Words with the Simple Present

EXAMPLES	EXPLANATION
Dolphins **never** fully sleep. They **always** come up for air. They **sometimes** hunt with fishermen.	We use the simple present with frequency words to show a regular activity.
Whenever a dolphin gets lost, it uses sound to find its group.	*Whenever* shows a regular activity. It means "any time."

FREQUENCY WORDS	FREQUENCY
always	100%
usually/generally	↑
often/frequently	
sometimes/occasionally	
rarely/seldom/hardly ever	↓
never/not ever	0%

GRAMMAR IN USE

Hardly ever is more informal than *rarely* or *seldom*. We use it a lot in speaking.

FORMAL: I **rarely** go to the movies.

INFORMAL: I **hardly ever** go to the movies.

EXERCISE 20 Fill in the blanks with a phrase from the box.

always come	is always	are never✓	usually live	sometimes get	usually think

1. Dolphins ___are never___ completely asleep.

2. Dolphins ___always come___ up for air.

3. They ___sometimes get___ lost.

4. People don't ___usually think___ about breathing.

5. The dolphin's brain ___is always___ active.

6. Dolphins don't ___usually live___ more than 50 years.

ABOUT YOU Fill in the blanks with an appropriate frequency word to talk about your native country or culture. Find a partner and compare your answers.

1. People in my native culture _____ *rarely* _____ have cats in the house.

2. Dogs in my native culture _____ *sometime* _____ sleep with their owners.

3. Dogs are _____ *always* _____ part of the family.

4. Cats are _____ *always* _____ part of the family.

5. People _____ *often* _____ feed pet food to cats and dogs.

6. People _____ *hardly ever* _____ travel with their pets.

7. People _____ *never* _____ take dogs into restaurants.

8. Blind people _____ *sometime* use dogs to help them.

9. People are _____ *usually* _____ kind to animals.

EXERCISE 21 Look again at the sentences in the exercise above. Does the frequency word come before or after the verb? Write *B* for *before* or *A* for *after*.

1. _B_   4. ____   7. ____

2. _B_   5. _A_   8. ____

3. ____   6. ____   9. ____

1.14 Position of Frequency Words

EXAMPLES	EXPLANATION
A dolphin's brain **is always** active.	A frequency word can come after the verb *be*.
A dolphin **rarely stays** under water for more than seven minutes.	A frequency word can come before other verbs.
Sometimes a dolphin gets lost. A dolphin **sometimes** gets lost. Dolphins **usually** swim in groups. **Usually** dolphins swim in groups.	*Sometimes* and *usually* can come close to the verb or at the beginning of the sentence.

Note:

Always and *never* are rarely at the beginning of the sentence.

> I'm **always** interested in animal TV programs. (NOT: Always I'm interested . . .)
>
> Fish **never** live on land. (NOT: Never fish live . . .)

EXERCISE 22 Rewrite the sentence, adding the word given.

1. A guide dog stops at an intersection. (*always*)

   <u>A guide dog always stops at an intersection.</u>

2. Dogs like to play. (*often*)

   <u>Dogs often like to play.</u>

3. Lucy Cooke is excited about animals. (*always*)

   <u>Lucy cook is always "</u>

4. Dolphins hunt with fishermen. (*sometimes*)

   <u>Some Dolphins hunt</u>
   time

5. Dolphins come up for air. (*always*)

   <u>Always dolphins come up</u>

6. People go to sea parks to see dolphins. (*sometimes*)

   <u>Sometimes People go to sea</u>

7. Sea parks are crowded in the summer. (*always*)

   <u>Sea Parks are always</u>

8. A dolphin hunts alone. (*rarely*)

   <u>A dolphin hunts rarely</u>

9. A dolphin is awake. (*always*)

   <u>A dolphin is always</u>

10. A dolphin leaves its group. (*hardly ever*)

    <u>A dolphin hardly ever leave its group</u>

11. Dogs are happy to see their owners. (*always*)

    <u>Always Dogs are</u>

12. Cats are friendly to strangers. (*rarely*)

    <u>Cats are rarely</u>

1.15 Questions about Frequency

Yes/No Questions with *Ever*

DO/DOES	SUBJECT	EVER	VERB		SHORT ANSWER
Do	you	ever	sleep	with your cat?	No, I **never** do./No, **never**.
Does	the teacher		talk	about her dog?	Yes, she **often** does./Yes, **often**.

BE	SUBJECT	EVER		SHORT ANSWER
Are	dogs	ever	lonely?	Yes, they **sometimes** are./Yes, **sometimes**.
Is	your cat		home alone?	Yes, she **often** is./Yes, **often**.

Notes:

1. In a short answer, the frequency word comes between the subject and the verb.
2. The verb after *never* is affirmative.
   Does your cat ever drink milk?
   *No, she **never drinks** milk.*

EXERCISE 23 Answer the questions with a short answer and the frequency word given.

1. Do dogs ever bark? (*sometimes*)

   Yes, they sometimes do.

2. Do people ever travel with their dogs? (*sometimes*)

   Yes Sometime

3. Do fish ever make noise? (*never*)

   No they never do.

4. Do birds ever make noise? (*always*)

   Yes they Do always.

5. Do parrots ever live for more than 20 years? (*usually*)

   Yes they usually
   do

6. Do dogs ever live for more than 20 years? (*hardly ever*)

   Yes they do

7. Does a dolphin ever swim alone? (*sometimes*)

   Yes

8. Are parrots ever affectionate? (*sometimes*)

9. Do dolphins ever hunt in groups? (*usually*)

_____

10. Are pets ever lonely? (*sometimes*)

_____

1.16 Questions with *How Often*

EXAMPLES	EXPLANATION
How often do you take your dog out? I take her out **three times a day.** **How often** do you take your cat to the vet? I take my cat to the vet **twice a year.**	We use *how often* when we want to know about the frequency of an activity. We answer with a frequency expression.
Once in a while, a dolphin gets lost. A dolphin gets lost **once in a while.** **Every seven minutes**, a dolphin needs air. A dolphin needs air **every seven minutes.**	A frequency expression can come at the beginning or at the end of a sentence. When it comes at the beginning of the sentence, we sometimes separate it from the rest of the sentence with a comma.

Note:

Some frequency expressions are:

• every (other) day/week/month/year
• several/many/a few/five times—a day/week/month/year
• once/twice—a day/week/month/year
• from time to time
• once in a while

EXERCISE 24 Fill in the blanks to complete each item.

1. **A:** How _____*often*_____ do you take your dog to the vet?

   B: I take her to the vet _____*once*_____ a year, in April.

2. **A:** Do guide dogs _____*every*_____ play?

   B: Yes. They usually play when they finish their work.

3. **A:** Do dolphins _____*always*_____ swim in groups?

   B: Yes. They usually swim in groups.

4. **A:** _____*How*_____ often do dolphins come up for air?

   B: They come up for air _____*every*_____ seven minutes.

5. **A:** _____ do you put your dog in a pet hotel?

   B: I never _____*do it*_____.

continued

6. **A:** _How often_ does your dog want to go out?

   B: She wants to go out three times _a day_.

7. **A:** Does your dog _every night_ sleep with you?

   B: Yes. My dog sleeps with me _every night_ night.

8. **A:** _Once_ in a while, I take my dog to a dog park. What about you?

   B: I hardly _to_ go there. It's too crowded.

EXERCISE 25 Fill in the blanks to complete the conversation. Use contractions wherever possible.

A: I know you love dogs. _Do you have_ a dog now?
                                          1.

B: No, I _don't_. But I have two cats. I don't have time for a dog.
              2.

A: Why _you don't have_ time for a dog?
             3.

B: Because I'm not at home very much. I work in the day and go to school in the evening.

A: How _do you mange_? it
              4.

B: I have class three nights a week. I love dogs, but dogs need a lot of attention.

A: Cats need attention, too.

B: When I'm not home, sometimes my sister comes to play with them.

A: _How_ often does she come?
         5.

B: Two or three times _a_ week. What about you? _do you have_ any pets?
                            6.   7.

A: I have several tropical fish.

B: How _much does it cost_
             8.

A: Some tropical fish cost more than $100.

B: Wow! How many fish _do you have_? 9.

A: I have about 14 or 15. My favorite is my Oranda.

B: How _do you spell_ Oranda? 10.

A: O-R-A-N-D-A. It's a kind of goldfish.

B: You spend a lot of money for a boring pet.

A: Fish _is not_ boring. It _is_ interesting to look at them. And 11. 12.

they _are_ easy to take care of. When I go to work, they _often_ 13. 14.

get lonely, like dogs and cats.

B: Yes, but they _aren't_ affectionate like dogs and cats. 15.

A: They _do_ make noise like dogs do, so neighbors never complain about fish. One thing 16.

isn't easy: cleaning the fish tank.

B: _How often_ clean the tank? 17.

A: About once _a week_. I usually clean the tank every Saturday. 18.

B: Do you _ever_ forget to clean it? 19.

A: No, I _always_ do. I can see when it needs to be cleaned. 20.

B: _do you_ get a new fish? 21.

A: Not very _often_. They can live for many years. 22.

SUMMARY OF UNIT 1

The Simple Present with *Be*

	WITH *IS*	WITH *ARE*
Affirmative Statement	Your dog **is** smart.	Dolphins **are** smart animals.
Negative Statement	It **isn't** big.	They **aren't** afraid of fishermen.
Yes/No Question	**Is** it friendly?	**Are** dolphins fish?
Short Answer	No, it **isn't**.	No, they **aren't**.
Wh- Question	What kind of dog **is** it?	How smart **are** they?
Negative *Wh-* Question	Why **isn't** it friendly?	Why **aren't** they afraid of fishermen?

The Simple Present with Other Verbs

	BASE FORM	-*S* FORM
Affirmative Statement	My friends **have** a dog.	She **likes** birds.
Negative Statement	They **don't have** a cat.	She **doesn't like** cats.
Yes/No Question	**Do** they **have** a bird?	**Does** she **like** small birds?
Short Answer	No, they **don't**.	Yes, she **does**.
Wh- Question	What kind of dog **do** they **have**?	Why **does** she **like** birds?
Negative *Wh-* Question	Why **don't** they **have** a cat?	Why **doesn't** she **like** cats?

Frequency Words and Expressions

FREQUENCY WORDS	FREQUENCY	FREQUENCY EXPRESSIONS
always	100%	once in a while
usually/generally	↑	from time to time
often/frequently		every day
sometimes/occasionally		once a year
rarely/seldom/hardly ever	↓	several times a day
never/not ever	0%	every other month

Questions and Answers with Frequency Words

QUESTION	ANSWER
Does he **ever** take his dog to the park?	Yes, he often does.
How often does he feed his dog?	Twice a day.

REVIEW

Circle the correct words to complete the conversation.

A: Your dog ((is)/are) very friendly.
1.

B: Yes, he (love/loves) people. His name is Buddy.
2.

A: How (do you spell/you spell) Buddy?
3.

B: B-U-D-D-Y. He's a therapy dog.

A: What (a therapy dog does/does a therapy dog do)?
4.

B: He (make/makes) sick people feel better.
5.

A: How (does a therapy dog make/is a therapy dog make) sick people feel better?
6.

B: People (feel/feels) happy when they're with a nice dog. Buddy and I (often visit/visit often) patients in the
7.   8.

hospital. Everyone at the hospital (love/loves) him.
9.

A: How (does a dog become/a dog becomes) a therapy dog?
10.

B: First, the owner (need/needs) to answer a few questions such as these: "(Is your dog likes/Does your dog like)
11.   12.

people?" or "Does he (have/has) a calm personality?" But that's not enough.
13.

(Always the dog/The dog always) needs training.
14.

A: How much (costs the training/does the training cost)?
15.

B: (It's cost/It costs) about $500.
16.

A: (How long it takes/How long does it take) to train the dog?
17.

B: That (depend/depends) on the dog.
18.

A: (Are/Do) the dog owners make money?
19.

B: No. We (work/are work) as volunteers.
20.

A: How (often/ever) (do you visit/you visit) the hospital with Buddy?
21.   22.

B: (We once a week go/Once a week we go) to the hospital. For more information, check the TDI website.
23.

A: What (means TDI/does TDI mean)?
24.

B: (It's mean/It means) "Therapy Dogs International."
25.

A: (Do you ever/Do ever you) get tired of working with sick people?
26.

B: No, I (don't never/never do). I have to go now. Buddy (needs/is needs) water.
27.   28.

A: How (does you know/do you know) that?
29.

B: His tongue is out. That's dog talk for "(I/I'm) thirsty."
30.

FROM GRAMMAR TO WRITING

PART 1 Editing Advice

1. Don't use *have* with age. Don't use *years* without *old*.

   The dog ~~has~~ 10 years.   (is)   (old)

2. Don't use *have* with *hungry, thirsty, hot, cold,* or *afraid.*

   The dog ~~has~~ thirsty. She wants water.   (is)

3. Don't forget the verb *be*. Remember that some words that end in *-ed* are adjectives, not verbs.

   We ^ excited about our new puppy.   (are)

4. Use the correct question formation.

   Why ~~your sister doesn't~~ like dogs?   (doesn't your sister)

   Why ~~Lucy Cooke studies~~ animals?   (does Lucy Cooke study)

5. Don't use *be* with another present verb.

   We~~'re~~ have a new cat.

6. Use the *-s* form when the subject is *he, she, it,* a singular noun, *everyone,* or *family.*

   The cat sleep ^ all day.   (s)

   Everyone love ^ the new puppy.   (s)

   My family want ^ a cat.   (s)

7. Use *doesn't* when the subject is *he, she, it,* a singular noun, or *family.*

   He ~~don't~~ have a pet.   (doesn't)

   My family ~~don't~~ like cats.   (doesn't)

8. Use the base form after *does.*

   My brother doesn't ~~has~~ a pet.   (have)

   How does a dolphin ~~gets~~ air?

9. Use regular question formation for *spell, mean, cost,* and *take.*

   What ~~means "obey"~~?   (does "obey" mean)

   How ^ spell "dolphin"?   (do you)

   How much ~~costs~~ ^ a parrot?   (does) (cost)

   How long ^ it takes ^ to train a guide dog?   (does)

10. Use the correct word order with frequency words.

    ~~Never my dog~~ sleeps with me.   (My dog never)

11. Don't put longer frequency expressions between the subject and the verb.

    She ~~all the time~~ plays with her cat. ^   (all the time)

PART 2 Editing Practice

Some of the shaded words and phrases have mistakes. Find the mistakes and correct them. If the shaded words are correct, write C.

The relationship between people and pets in the U.S. is sometimes strange to me.
1. *C*

I surprised that Americans thinks of their pets as part of the family. I'm have a new American
2. **3.** **4.**

friend, Marianne. She live alone, but she's has a dog, Sparky. Marianne treats him like a child.
5. **6.** **7.**

I not very interested in him, but always she wants to show me pictures of him on her phone.
8. **9.**

She thinks everyone want to see them, but I think she wrong. She often buy toys for him,
10. **11.** **12.**

especially on his birthday. He has 12 years old, so she spends a lot of money on vet bills,
13. **14.**

too. How much cost a visit to the vet? At least $100!
15.

She have several coats for him for the winter weather, but he don't like to wear them. So when
16. **17.**

they go outside in winter, he has cold. She buys sometimes expensive food for him. (He likes
18. **19.** **20.** **21.**

steak.) She sometimes calls him on the telephone when she not home and talks into the answering
22. **23.** **24.**

machine which she keeps just for this purpose. Sparky always sleeps in bed with her.
25.

Once a month, she takes him to a dog groomer. What means "dog groomer"? This is a
26. **27.**

professional who gives Sparky a bath and cuts and paints his nails. Nothing cost too much
28.

money when it comes to Sparky.

Sometimes I'm think American dogs live better than most people in the world.
29.

WRITING TIP

When you write about an animal, introduce it by making a statement with *be* + an adjective to describe it:

> The zebra **is a social** animal.

When you write about the animal's behavior, use the simple present. Choose the correct form:

> A zebra **runs** very quickly./Zebras **live** in grasslands.

To describe animal behavior, use frequency words and expressions:

> Zebras **often** move around to find fresh grass.

PART 3 Write

Read the prompts. Choose one and write a paragraph about it.

1. Look for a Lucy Cooke video online. Watch the video and describe the behavior of the animal. What does this video teach you about the animal? (Provide your teacher with a link to the video.)
2. Describe the behavior of an animal you know about. This can be a pet or a wild animal.

PART 4 Edit

Reread the Summary of Unit 1 and the editing advice. Edit your writing from Part 3.

ACROSS
GENERATIONS

Grandmothers attend a school trip in South Korea with their classmates, who are also their grandchildren.

In youth we learn; in age we understand.
MARIE VON EBNER-ESCHENBACH

IRIS APFEL:
STILL GOING STRONG

Read the following article. Pay special attention to the words in bold. 🎧 2.1

Many people in the United States retire in their sixties, but not fashion icon[1] Iris Apfel. Born in 1921 in New York City, Apfel is now in her late nineties. But unlike many people her age, she **isn't relaxing** at home. Instead, she **is creating** a new line of clothing and jewelry. She**'s planning** a fashion show, too. And she**'s traveling** all over the world. "I**'m working** harder than ever," she says, "but I**'m having** so much fun."

For many years, Apfel was an interior designer[2]. Now she**'s working** in fashion. Her style is unique. She**'s** always **wearing** colorful clothing, jewelry, and large black glasses. On the street, people **are** constantly **approaching**[3] her and **taking** her photo.

On Instagram, Apfel has over a million followers, but she is worried about social media. She thinks it**'s ruining** fashion. People **are copying** each other, Apfel says. Everything **is becoming** the same everywhere—in New York, Hong Kong, Paris. It's boring, Apfel believes. When things are different, then they are interesting.

Don't follow others, Apfel tells people. "Be your own person"—in fashion and in life. Ask yourself: "**Am** I **doing** the right thing for *me*?" This can be about your clothing choices, or even the subject you**'re studying** in school. Apfel lives her life this way. And at almost one hundred years old, she **is** still **going strong**.

---

1 icon: a person who is well known and important
2 interior designer: a person who decorates the inside of a home or other building
3 to approach: to come close to someone

Iris Apfel's style is unique. Here, she is wearing black and white with red accessories, and, as always, her famous large black glasses.

COMPREHENSION Based on the reading, write T for *true* or F for *false*.

1. __F__ Iris Apfel is in her sixties, and she is planning to retire soon.

2. __F__ A lot of people like Iris Apfel's style.

3. __F__ Iris Apfel likes social media. In her opinion, it is improving fashion.

THINK ABOUT IT Discuss the questions with a partner or in a small group.

1. The last sentence of the reading says that Iris Apfel "is still going strong." What does the expression "still going strong" mean? Why does this expression describe Ms. Apfel?

2. Do you think it's a good idea for people to work into their sixties and beyond? Why or why not?

2.1 The Present Continuous—Form

For the present continuous, we use a form of *be* (*am, is, are*) + verb + *–ing*.

SUBJECT	BE (AM, IS, ARE)	VERB + -ING	
I	am	working	hard.
Iris/She	is	traveling	all over the world.
Social media/It	is	ruining	fashion.
Some people/They	are	taking	Ms. Apfel's photo.
You	are	learning	about Iris Apfel.

Notes:

1. We can make a contraction with the subject pronoun and a form of *be*. Most nouns can also contract with *is*.

   I'm *having so much fun.*

   She's *traveling all over the world.*

   Iris Apfel's *creating a new clothing line. Her* ***team's*** *helping her.*

2. To form the negative, we put *not* after *am/is/are*. In many cases, we can make a negative contraction in two ways:

   She is not relaxing. = ***She isn't*** *relaxing. =* ***She's not*** *relaxing.*

   You are not working. = ***You aren't*** *working. =* ***You're not*** *working.*

3. For *I am not,* there is only one contraction:

   I am not traveling. = ***I'm not*** *traveling.*

4. We do not repeat the *be* verb after *and* or *or*.

   She ***is traveling*** *and* ***planning*** *a fashion show.*

5. We can put an adverb between *be* and the verb + *–ing*.

   She's <u>still</u> ***going*** *strong.*

6. The present continuous is also called the present progressive.

EXERCISE 1 Fill in the blanks with the present continuous form of the words given. Use correct spelling and capitalization. Make contractions when possible.

A: What are you doing?

B: _____I'm looking_____ at something on Instagram.
　　　1. I/look

A: Yeah, what?

B: _____We're learning_____ about Iris Apfel in class, right? Well, there is this married couple, Alisa
　　　2. we/learn

and Min Soo. They're 70, and _____they are traveling_____ around the U.S. on their bikes.
　　　　　　　　　　　　　　　　3. they/travel

A: _____You are kidding_____ me!
　　　4. you/kid

B: No, I'm serious. _____they are trying_____ to visit every state park in the U.S.
　　　　　　　　　　　5. they/try

A: Wow, that's cool. So where are they now?

B: _____they are hiking_____ Yosemite National Park, in California. Look at this photo.
　　　6. they/hike

A: _____it is snowing_____. It's so beautiful!
　　　7. it/snow

B: I know. _____they are taking_____ classes in the park, too. _____Min Soo is learning_____ to paint,
　　　　　　　　8. they/take　　　　　　　　　　　　9. Min Soo/learn

and _____Alisa is studying_____ photography.
　　　10. Alisa/study

A: So how can they do this? Do they have a lot of money?

B: No, _____they are spending_____ only 80 dollars a day. _____they aren't staying_____ in hotels.
　　　　　11. they/spend　　　　　　　　　　　　　　12. they/not stay

_____they are using_____ home-sharing sites.
　　　13. they/use

A: That's great. I love that _____age isn't stopping_____ them from doing new things, just like Iris Apfel!
　　　　　　　　　　　　　　　14. age/not stop

EXERCISE 2 Read the items. Then listen and fill in the blanks with the words you hear. 🎧 2.2

1. Today, many older people _____are starting_____ new careers later in life. They _____are starting_____

and _____doing_____ nothing.

2. For example, for years, 70-year-old Judy Pearlman was an engineer. These days, _____she tutoring_____ high

school students in math.

3. "_____I am_____ really _____enjoying_____ my new job," Pearlman says. "_____I am not making_____

a lot of money, but _____I am helping_____ people. I like that."

4. The work is hard sometimes, but Judy _____isn't_____. "_____I am learning_____ a lot," she says,

"and that's a good thing."

2.2 The Present Continuous—Use

EXAMPLES	EXPLANATION
Iris Apfel **is talking** with two people. They **are taking** her photo.	We use the present continuous to describe an action in progress at this moment.
These days, Ms. Apfel **is working** in fashion. "I'm working** harder than ever," she says.	We use the present continuous to show a long-term action that is in progress. It may not be happening at this exact moment.
A lot of people on social media **are copying** each other. More retired people **are starting** a second career.	We use the present continuous to describe a trend. A trend is a behavior that many people are doing at this time. It describes a change in behavior from an earlier time.

GRAMMAR IN USE

We use the present continuous to describe the actions in an image.

> In this photo, my friends and I **are hanging out** at the beach. This is Jeff. He **is learning** to surf. Martina **is making** a sandcastle.

The present continuous is also used to describe action in a piece of art such as a painting or a drawing.

EXERCISE 3 Fill in the blanks with the present continuous form of one of the verbs from the box. Use each verb only once. You will not use all the verbs.

happen	exercise	lift	not swim
not take	ride	take	visit ✓

1. Jack _'s visiting_ a new gym. He _is taking_ a tour.

2. Some people _are exercising_ in the main room.

3. A woman _is riding_ an exercise bike.

4. A man _is not taking_ weights.

5. In a yoga class, Jack sees his friend Naomi. But she _is lifting_ the class. She's the instructor.

6. There's a pool, but people _are not swimming_ in it today.

EXERCISE 4 Are these things happening at this point in time in the United States, in the world, or in another country you know about? Explain your ideas to a partner.

1. Fewer senior citizens are retiring.

2. The world is becoming a safer place.

3. Everyone is spending more time on social media.

4. More people in their twenties are traveling.

continued

5. A lot of people are losing their jobs.

6. Fewer people in their twenties are buying cars.

7. More women are starting businesses.

8. Kids are growing up faster than before.

9. More young adults are living with their parents longer.

10. People are living longer.

11. Fewer people are smoking.

12. Fewer people are voting in elections.

ABOUT YOU Find a partner and discuss your answers to these questions.

1. What kinds of things are you doing in your free time these days?

2. What classes are you taking this semester?

3. What are you doing at work this month?

2.3 Questions with the Present Continuous

Compare statements, *yes/no* questions, short answers, and *wh-* questions.

STATEMENT	YES/NO QUESTION AND SHORT ANSWER	WH- QUESTION AND ANSWER
You **are studying** at Cornell.	**Are** you **studying** full time? Yes, I **am**.	What **are you studying**? I**'m studying** interior design.
They **are living** in New York.	**Are** they **going** to school? No, they**'re not**.	What **are they doing** in New York? They**'re working** at the U.N.
Iris **isn't relaxing** at home.	**Is** she **traveling**? Yes, she **is**.	Why **isn't** she **relaxing**? She **isn't relaxing** because she**'s working**.

Notes:

1. We sometimes leave a preposition at the end of a question.

   *What **are you listening** to?*   *I**'m listening** to a podcast on second careers.*

2. In spoken English, we often give a short answer to a *wh-* question. The short answer to a *why* question often starts with *because*.

   What are you studying?   *Computer science.*

   Why are you studying that?   *Because it pays well.*

3. When the question is "What ... doing?" we usually answer with a different verb. The short answer starts with the *-ing* word.

   ***What** are they **doing** in New York?*   ***Working** at the U.N.*

EXERCISE 5 Use the words given to make a *yes/no* question. Fill in the second blank to complete the short answer.

1. those students/interview

   A: _____Are those students interviewing_____ Iris Apfel?

   B: Yes, _____they are_____. Ms. Apfel is visiting their school today.

2. you/plan

   A: _____Are you planning_____ for your next vacation?

   B: Yes, _____I am_____. I'm thinking about visiting Costa Rica.

3. Alisa/take

   A: _____Is Alisa taking_____ a painting class?

   B: No, _____she isn't_____. She's studying photography.

4. social media/ruin

   A: _____Is social media ruinning_____ fashion?

   B: No, _____It isn't_____. It's making fashion more interesting.

5. Iris Apfel/still live

   A: _____Is she still living_____ in New York City?

   B: Yes, _____She is_____. She loves it there.

6. Alisa and Min Soo/stay

   A: _____Are they staying_____ in Yosemite long?

   B: No, _____they aren't_____. They're only there for three days.

7. I/ask

   A: _____Am I asking_____ too many questions?

   B: No, _____your n't_____. You can ask as many questions as you want.

8. you/write

   A: _____Are you writing_____ down this information?

   B: No, _____I am n't_____. I can check the website later.

EXERCISE 6 Read each statement and write a question about it using the word in parentheses. Then think of a short answer to the question.

1. Some older people are starting new careers. (*when*)

   <u>When are some older people starting new careers?</u>   Later in life.

2. Iris Apfel is wearing a colorful outfit in this photo. (*what*)

   <u>What is wearing Iris Appel in this pictuer.</u>

3. Jack is learning to paint. (*where*)

   _____

4. I'm taking an interesting class. (*what*)

   _____

5. My grandparents are visiting Mexico. (*who*)

   _____

6. People are living longer nowadays. (*why*)

   _____

7. My sister is applying to college. (*where*)

   _____

8. In this photo, we're not smiling. (*why*)

   _____

9. My parents aren't planning to retire. (*why*)

   _____

10. I'm doing an internship. (*where*)

    <u>Where are you</u>

11. My brother isn't working now. (*why*)

    <u>why isn't brothe</u>

12. I'm eating a sandwich for lunch. (*what*)

    _____

EXERCISE 7 Fill in the blanks with the present continuous to complete the conversation between a career coach (speaker A) and a retired firefighter (speaker B). Use contractions wherever possible.

A: So, I understand that __you're looking__ for part-time work.
　　　　　　　　　　　　　　　　1. you/look

B: Yes, I am.

A: Great. I work with a local community center. It has many part-time job openings right now.

__you're working__ at the moment?
2. you/work

B: No. I retired from the fire department six months ago.

A: Oh? Two retired firefighters __are working__ for us now.
　　　　　　　　　　　　　　　　3. work

B: Really? What kind of things __are they doing__ ?
　　　　　　　　　　　　　　　4. they/do

A: _____ a CPR¹ class. _____ people with their taxes.
　　　　　5. one/teach　　　　　　　　　　　　**6.** another/help

B: I can do those things. How many hours __are they work__ ?
　　　　　　　　　　　　　　　　　　　7. they/work

A: Twenty hours a week. The community center needs another CPR teacher.

B: Great, but __is it hiring__ right away?
　　　　　　　8. the community center/hire

A: Yes. Why?

B: __I am p__ to take a short trip.
　　　9. I/plan

A: That's not a problem. Where are you going?

B: Florida. My good friend Marcos __is living__ there now.
　　　　　　　　　　　　　　　　10. live

A: __what is he doing__ in Florida? Is he retired, too?
　　11. what/he/do

B: Yes, but he enjoys cooking, so __he is making__ online cooking tutorials. Two thousand
　　　　　　　　　　　　　　　12. he/make

__people are__ his channel now!
13. people/watch

---

¹ CPR: a method used to help a person who isn't breathing

Digital Natives and Digital Immigrants

Read the following article. Pay special attention to the words in bold. 🎧 2.3

They're everywhere: in coffee shops, on the train, in restaurants, at work. They**'re texting**; they**'re tweeting**; they**'re googling**; they**'re checking** social media; they**'re taking** selfies; they**'re listening** to music. And yes, they**'re** even **working**. They're always connected. These are the "digital natives."

Born at the end of the twentieth century and the beginning of the twenty-first century, digital natives **don't know** life without technology. The first generation of digital natives **is** now **entering** the workforce and **changing** the way we work. More and more younger people **are working** from home, in coffee shops, or anyplace. They**'re bringing** their personal equipment into the workplace, too. They **switch** back and forth between their social and professional lives. They **don't see** the need to separate the two.

Some older people **are adapting** well to technology. Some people call them "digital immigrants." Others **are having** trouble. Some **are refusing** to use any new technology. Older people often **think** that technology **is growing** too fast. Look at the older people around you. **Do** they **have** smart phones? **Do** they **have** earbuds in their ears? **Are** they **texting**? Many older people **prefer** to share information with a small group of friends. Digital natives **share** information globally[1].

The younger generations **want** high-tech devices that do everything: take pictures, send texts and photos, provide music and videos, and connect them with friends around the world. What **does** the older generation **want** from technology? In many cases, Grandma and Grandpa just **want** a device that **connects** them to family and friends. They **like** to see pictures of grandchildren. Some even **love** to have a video chat with family.

As more and more technology **is entering** every aspect of our lives, the digital divide between generations **is widening**.

---

[1] globally: throughout the world

A digital immigrant is improving his computer skills with help from a digital native.

COMPREHENSION Based on the reading, write T for *true* or F for *false*.

1. _T_ Many digital natives are always connected.
2. _F_ Digital natives separate their personal and professional lives.
3. _F_ Digital immigrants usually want a device that does many things.

THINK ABOUT IT Discuss the questions with a partner or in a small group.

1. Do you think being connected all the time is positive or negative? Explain.

2. Do you agree that the digital divide between generations is widening? Or are digital immigrants starting to catch up with digital natives? Explain with examples.

2.4 Contrasting the Simple Present and the Present Continuous

Form

THE SIMPLE PRESENT	THE PRESENT CONTINUOUS
Grandma **uses** email.	Marc **is sending** a message.
She **doesn't use** a smart phone.	He **isn't making** a phone call.
Does she **use** the Internet? Yes, she **does**.	**Is** he **sending** a message to his friend? Yes, he **is**.
When **does** she **use** the Internet?	How **is** he **sending** a message?
Why **doesn't** she **use** a smart phone?	Why **isn't** he **sending** a message to his friend?

Use

EXAMPLES	EXPLANATION
People **use** their phones to text. I sometimes **send** photos to my grandmother. Older people **prefer** to talk on the phone.	We use the **simple present** for: • a general truth. • a habitual activity. • a custom.
I'm **getting** a text message right now. My grandfather **is learning** about technology. Technology **is growing** quickly.	We use the **present continuous** for: • an action that is in progress now. • a longer action in progress at this general time. • a recent trend.
My grandparents **live** in a retirement home. My sister **is living** in a dorm this semester.	We use *live* in the simple present to talk about a person's home. We use *live* in the present continuous to talk about a temporary, short-term residence.
A: What does she do (for a living)? **B:** She's an English teacher. **A: What is she doing now?** **B:** She's texting her grandson.	"What does she do?" asks about a job or profession. "What is she doing?" asks about an activity now.

EXERCISE 8 Fill in the blanks with the simple present or the present continuous form of the verb given.

1. Conversation between a grandmother and grandson:

   A: You _'re eating and working_ on your essay at the same time.
   a. eat and work

   B: That's not a problem, Grandma.

   A: What _are you eating_? Is that a hamburger?
   b. you/eat

   B: No, it isn't. It's a veggie burger. I never _eat_ meat.
   c. eat

   A: You don't eat enough. Look at you. You're so thin.

   B: I _am trying_ to lose weight.
   d. try

   A: You always _eat_ in front of your computer. Take a break.
   e. eat

   I _am making_ soup now. When it's ready, please come to the table.
   f. make

   B: But I _am working_ on something important now.
   g. work

   A: How is that possible? You _'re eating and listening_ to music, too.
   h. eat and listen

   B: I always _listen_ to music when I _am_.
   i. listen   j. work or study

   A: Whenever I _work_, I _____ on my work.
   k. work   l. concentrate

   I _do not do_ other things at the same time.
   m. not/do

   B: You _do_ the world of young people. We often multitask.
   n. not/understand

   A: You're right. I don't.

2. Conversation between two brothers:

   A: _Are you sleeping_? Wake up. It's almost time for class.
   a. you/sleep

   B: I'm so tired. I never _get_ enough sleep.
   b. get

   A: That's because you're always on your computer or phone. How many hours _do you_ _____
   c. you/sleep

   a night?

   B: About four or five.

   A: That's not enough. You _need_ more sleep. Turn off your computer
   d. need

   and phone at night, and get some sleep.

   B: I never _____ my devices. I always _want_
   e. turn off   f. want

   to know when I get a message.

A: That's ridiculous! Let's go get breakfast. Mom _____is making_____ pancakes.
 g. make

B: I _____don't_____ breakfast. I just _____ coffee.
 h. not/want i. drink

A: That's not good. You _____ to live a healthier life.
 j. need

3. Conversation between two friends:

A: What _____does your_____ for a living?
 a. your mother/do

B: She's retired now.

A: _____Is she_____ old?
 b. she/be

B: No. She's only 58.

A: What _____does she do_____ with her free time?
 c. she/do

B: A lot of things. In fact, she _____doesn't_____ any free time at all.
 d. not/have

She _____is taking_____ a course at the art center this semester. Right now
 e. take

she _____is painting_____ a picture of me.
 f. paint

2.5 Action and Nonaction Verbs

EXAMPLES	EXPLANATION
He **is texting** his friend. I **am listening** to music.	Some verbs are action verbs. These verbs express physical or mental activity.
Young people **know** a lot about technology. Many people **have** a smart phone now. **Do** you **remember** a time without cell phones?	Some verbs are nonaction verbs. These verbs express a state, condition, perception, or feeling, not an action. We do not usually use the present continuous with nonaction verbs. We use the simple present even if we are talking about now.
She's **looking at** the text message. I want to learn about technology, but it **looks hard**. Your photo **looks like** a selfie.	Some verbs can express an action or a perception. When they express an action (for example, *look at*), they are action verbs. When they express a perception (for example, *look* + adjective or *look like*), they are nonaction verbs.
I'm **looking** at my cell phone. I **see** a text from my father. She **is listening** to music. She **hears** her favorite song.	*Look* and *listen* are action verbs. *See* and *hear* are nonaction verbs.
Grandma **is thinking about** getting an e-reader. She **thinks that** technology is a good thing.	When we think *about* or *of* something, *think* is an action verb. When *think* shows an opinion about something, it is a nonaction verb.
My grandfather **is having** a hard time with technology. He's **having** lunch with his friends now. Grandma **has** free time now. She **has** five grandchildren. I can't visit her now. I **have** a cold.	When *have* means to experience something or to eat or drink something, it is an action verb. When *have* shows possession, relationship, or illness, it is a nonaction verb.

continued

Note:

Some common nonaction verbs are verbs that show:

- Perception: *smell, taste, look, sound,* followed by an adjective or *like*
- Feelings and desires: *like, dislike, love, hate, hope, want, need, prefer, agree, disagree, care about, expect, matter*
- Mental states: *believe, know, hear, see, notice, understand, remember, think that, suppose, recognize*
- Other nonaction: *mean, cost, spell, weigh*

EXERCISE 9 Circle the correct words to complete the conversation.

A: Listen, Marco, (*I'm thinking*/*I think*) about getting a new computer. Can you help me choose?
1.

B: Sure, Grandma. How about on Saturday?

A: Saturday's good. What's that noise? It (*sounds*/*is sounding*) like rock music (*comes*/*is coming*) from
2.   3.

your pocket.

B: It's my cell phone. It's my new ringtone. (*I receive*/*I'm receiving*) a text message now. It's a message from
4.

Dad. See?

A: It (*looks*/*is looking*) like Greek to me. What does it say?
5.

B: (*He tells*/*He's telling*) me to come home early. (*He wants*/*He's wanting*) to give me another driving lesson.
6.   7.

(*I learn*/*I'm learning*) to drive, you know.
8.

A: When (*I have*/*I'm having*) something to say, (*I use*/*I'm using*) the phone.
9.   10.

B: (*I prefer*/*I'm preferring*) to text. (*It saves*/*It's saving*) time. You can text me, too, Grandma.
11.   12.

A: (*It looks*/*It's looking*) hard. Let me try to send a note to Grandpa. "Jim. Where are you? See you later."
13.

B: (*You're writing*/*You write*) so slowly. And (*you use*/*you're using*) whole words. Use abbreviations, like this:
14.   15.

"where r u c u later." Don't use punctuation. (*You need*/*You're needing*) to write fast.
16.

A: You know I'm an English teacher, and (*I don't like*/*I'm not liking*) to write without punctuation.
17.

B: Text messages don't need punctuation.

A: (*I don't think*/*I'm not thinking*) I can do it.
18.

B: But (*you send*/*you're sending*) email every day.
19.

A: That's different. (*I write*/*I'm writing*) slowly, and (*I check*/*I'm checking*) my spelling.
20.   21.

B: You're so old-fashioned!

A: No, I'm not. This month (*I study*/*I'm studying*) photo editing at the senior center.
22.

(*I make*/*I'm making*) a digital family album.
23.

B: That's great, Grandma! I'm proud of you.

EXERCISE 10 Fill in the blanks with the simple present or the present continuous form of the verb given.

1. **A:** My grandfather is a volunteer. Twice a week he _____*helps*_____ in the local school.
   a. help

   B: That's great! My grandmother _____*working*_____ part-time in a bookstore. She _____*loves*_____
   b. work **c. love**

   books. She usually _____*rides*_____ her bike to work. She _____*likes*_____ the exercise.
   d. ride **e. like**

   A: Where is she now? _____*Is she working*_____?
   f. she/work

   B: Right now she's on vacation. She _____*is visiting*_____ her sister in Florida.
   g. visit

2. **A:** Can I borrow your dictionary?

   B: I'm sorry. I _____*am using*_____ it now. Where's your dictionary?
   a. use

   A: I never _____*bring*_____ it to class. It's too heavy.
   b. bring

   B: _____*do you expect*_____ to use my dictionary all the time? You _____*need*_____
   c. you/expect **d. need**

   a dictionary app for your phone.

   A: I _____*don't have*_____ a smart phone.
   e. not/have

3. **A:** What _____*is the teacher saying*_____? She _____*is talking*_____ too fast, so
   a. the teacher/say **b. talk**

   I _____*don't understand*_____ her.
   c. not/understand

   B: I don't know. I _____*am not listening*_____. I _____*am texting*_____ a friend.
   d. not/listen **e. text**

   A: I _____*think*_____ you should pay attention in class.
   f. think

   continued

4. **A:** What _are you writing_?
a. you/write

   B: I _am writing_ an essay about my grandparents. I _love_
   b. write   c. love

   them very much.

   A: _Do they live_ with you?
   d. they/live

   B: No, they don't. They live in Pakistan. They _visit_ us once a year.
   e. visit

   A: How _do you_ ? By email?
   f. you/communicate

   B: We usually _do_ a video chat once a week. But right now their computer
   g. do

   is not working , so we _are using_ the phone.
   h. not/work   i. use

5. **A:** _Do you see_ that guy over there? Who is he?
   a. you/see

   B: That's my technology teacher.

   A: He _is wearing_ jeans and running shoes. And he _has_ an
   b. wear   c. have

   earring in his ear. He _looks_ like a student.
   d. look

   B: I _know_ . Everyone _thinks_ he's a student. But he's a very
   e. know   f. think

   professional teacher.

6. **A:** My parents _are planning_ to put Grandma in a nursing home. Mom _thinks_
   a. plan   b. think

   she'll receive better care there.

   B: It _sounds_ like a difficult decision.
   c. sound

   A: It is. Mom _doesn't know_ what else to do. Grandma _falls sometimes_
   d. not/know   e. sometimes/fall

   B: Maybe she _needs_ a cane or a walker.
   f. need

   A: Her memory is bad, too. She _never remembers_ where she puts things.
   g. never/remember

   B: Can I call you back later? I _am hearing_ my other phone. My son _is calling_ me.
   h. hear   i. call

FUN WITH GRAMMAR

Categorize. Work with a partner. Sort the words below into three columns: *action verbs, nonaction verbs,* and *both*. Then write a sentence for each verb that can be used in the present continuous. Be careful: some words can be both action and nonaction verbs but have a different meaning in the present continuous. The team with the most correct sentences wins.

listen	be	believe	have	hear	help	recognize	taste
know	learn	look	mean	ask	need	see	think

THE FUTURE
POPULATION OF THE UNITED STATES

Read the following article. Pay special attention to the words in bold. 🎧 2.4

The population of the United States is growing slowly. Today it's about 328 million. By 2050, it**'s going to be** about 400 million. This is not a big increase, but one group is growing very fast—the elderly. The 65-and-over population **will** more than **double** by 2050. The 85-and-over population **will** more than **triple**.

There are two reasons for this increase of older Americans. First, the "baby boomers" are getting old. Baby boomers are people born between 1946 and 1964. During that time, a very large number of babies were born. The oldest are now entering their senior years. Many more **will** soon **be** elderly. As these people retire, young people **are going to have** many more job opportunities. In fact, there**'s going to be** a shortage[1] of workers to take their place. The number of jobs in health care **will increase**. There **will be** many jobs for pharmacists, physical therapists, and home health aides.

There is another reason for the increase in older Americans: life expectancy is increasing. Some scientists predict that half the babies born in 2007 **will live** to be 104 years old. But according to Dr. Harrison Bloom of the Longevity Center of New York, many young people **won't reach** this age because they don't have a healthy lifestyle. Or, if they do live a long time, they**'re going to need** a lot of medical help.

When today's young people retire at age 65 or 70 they**'ll have** a lot of years ahead of them. They need to think about how they**'ll spend** their later years. If they want to have good health later, they need to think about it now.

---

[1] shortage: a state of not having enough

COMPREHENSION Based on the reading, write T for *true* or F for *false*.

1. ___F___ There will be a shortage of jobs in health care in the future.

2. ___T___ The biggest growth in population will be in people over 85.

3. ___F___ The baby boomers will live longer than younger generations.

THINK ABOUT IT Discuss the questions with a partner or in a small group.

1. What are some reasons that the current generation might not have a healthy lifestyle? How could young people improve their lifestyles?

2. Do you think it is a good idea to prepare to live a long time? Why or why not?

2.6 The Future with *Will*

EXAMPLES	EXPLANATION
The number of older people **will increase** in the future. My grandfather **will be** 85 next week.	We use *will* + the base form for the future.
I'll be 72 years old in 2050. **We'll** retire at age 65.	We can contract *will* with the subject pronouns. The contractions are *I'll, you'll, he'll, she'll, it'll, we'll,* and *they'll.*
The population **will not decrease.** I **won't retire** soon.	To form the negative, we put *not* after *will*. The contraction for *will not* is *won't.*
You**'ll probably have** a long retirement.	We can put an adverb between *will* and the main verb.

Compare statements, *yes/no* questions, short answers, and *wh-* questions.

STATEMENT	YES/NO QUESTION AND SHORT ANSWER	WH- QUESTION
She **will help** her parents.	**Will** she **help** her parents? Yes, she **will.**	How **will** she **help** her parents?
You **will retire** soon.	**Will** you **retire** next year? No, I **won't.**	When **will** you **retire**?
There **won't be** enough health workers.	**Will** there **be** a lot of jobs? Yes, there **will.**	Why **won't** there **be** enough health workers?

EXERCISE 11 Listen to the conversation between a 60-year-old mother and her 29-year-old daughter. Then write T for *true* or F for *false*. 🎧 2.5

1. ___T___ The woman's retired friends say she won't have any free time.

2. ___F___ The daughter won't be in New York in August.

3. ___F___ The grandfather will appreciate an email on his birthday.

EXERCISE 12 Listen to the conversation again. Fill in the blanks with the words you hear. 🎧 2.5

A: Tomorrow _____ will be _____ my last day of work.
1.

B: What _____ will you do _____ with all your free time?
2.

A: Our retired friends all say I _____ won't have _____ any free time. They say
3.

_____ I'll have _____ plenty of things to do.
4.

B: So, _____ what will you do _____ first?
5.

A: Dad and I are planning to travel.

B: _____ Where will you go _____ first?
6.

A: To the Grand Canyon.

B: That's great! How long _____ will you be _____ there?
7.

A: For about two weeks. Then _____ we'll visit _____ Grandpa in Nevada.
8.

B: I'm sure _____ he will be _____ happy to see you.
9.

A: _____ He will be _____ 85 at the end of August. _____ We'll be _____ there for his
10.   11.

birthday.

B: What _____ will you do _____ with the dog?
12.

A: Can you take care of her for us while we're gone?

B: Sorry. I _____ won't be _____ here the first week in August.
13.

A: Why _____ won't you be _____ here?
14.

B: I'm going to New York. _____ You'll need _____ to find someone else to take
15.

care of the dog.

A: _____ I'll ask _____ my neighbor. Maybe _____ she'll _____ it. Don't forget to send
16.   17.

Grandpa a birthday card.

B: _____ I'll send _____ him an email on his birthday.
18.

A: You know Grandpa. He doesn't use his computer much.

B: All right. _____ I'll send _____ him a card then.
19.

A: I'm sure _____ he'll appreciate _____ it.
20.

EXERCISE 13 Fill in the blanks with *will* and one of the verbs from the box. You may use the same verb more than once.

| spend | have | increase | triple | live✓ | need | move | find | be |

1. Today's generation _____ will live _____ longer.

2. The population of old people _____ will increase

3. The over-85 population _____ will triple _____ by 2050.

4. _____ Will have _____ young people _____ will find _____ more job opportunities?

5. Many young people _____ will find _____ jobs in health care.

6. Some older people _____ will move _____ into retirement housing.

7. How _____ will _____ you _____ spend _____ your retirement years?

8. Why _____ will _____ we _____ need _____ more health care workers?

9. How old _____ will _____ you _____ be _____ in the year 2050?

2.7 The Future with *Be Going To*

EXAMPLES	EXPLANATION
People **are going to live** longer. We **are going to need** more pharmacists in the future.	We can use a form of *be* + *going to* + the base form to express future time.
I'm **not going to work** after retirement. He **isn't going to retire** soon.	To form the negative, we put *not* after *am, is,* or *are*.
We're **going to go** to the Grand Canyon. We're **going** to the Grand Canyon.	We often shorten *going to go* to *going*.

Compare statements, *yes/no* questions, short answers, and *wh-* questions.

STATEMENT	YES/NO QUESTION AND SHORT ANSWER	WH- QUESTION
We **are going to travel**.	**Are** we **going to travel** by car? Yes, we **are**.	When **are** we **going to travel**?
She **is going to work** as a nurse.	**Is** she **going to work** at a hospital? No, she **isn't**.	Where **is** she **going to work**?
You **aren't going to send** Grandpa a present.	**Are** you **going to send** an e-card? Yes, I **am**.	Why **aren't** you **going to send** Grandpa a present?

Pronunciation Note:

In informal speech, *going to* before another verb often sounds like "gonna." In academic and formal English, we don't write "gonna."

> I'm not "gonna" work after retirement.

EXERCISE 14 Fill in the blanks with *be going to* and one of the verbs from the box. You may use the same verb more than once.

need	spend	study	be	live	find	become	double	have

1. Many people _are going to live_ to the age of 100.

2. Young people _are going to have_ a lot of job possibilities.

3. I _am going to be_ a nurse because it _is going to be_ easy to find a job.

4. Some people _are going to have_ a long retirement.

5. Some old people _are going to need_ a lot of medical help.

6. _Are_ you _goin to sutdy_ to be a physician's assistant?

7. Younger people _are going to find_ jobs in health care.

8. By 2050, the population of people over 65 _are going tu doub.le_

9. _Are_ your grandparents _going to live_ with your family?

10. You need to think about how you _are you ging to spend_ your retirement years.

11. In the future, there _is going to be_ a shortage of workers.

12. _Am_ I _going to live_ to be 100?

EXERCISE 15 Fill in the blanks with *be going to* and the words given to complete the conversation between two co-workers.

A: I'm so excited. I _'m going to retire_ at the end of this year!
   1. retire

B: That's wonderful news. What _are you going to_ next?
   2. you/do

A: I don't really know yet. I _am going to_ new things.
   3. explore

B: What _are you going to explore_?
   4. you/explore

A: I think I have a talent for art. I _am going to take_ art classes.
   5. take

B: _Are going to work_ part-time?
   6. you/work

A: No way! I want to have fun.

B: Is your husband happy about your retirement?

A: Yes. He _is going to retire_, too.
   7. retire

B: But you're not that old.

A: I'm 58 and he's 56. Our children <u>are not going to need</u> us much anymore.

8. not/need

B: Why <u>are not they going to</u> you?

9. not/need

A: Our youngest son <u>is graduate</u> from college in June. And the other two are

going to — 10. graduate

already on their own. The oldest <u>is going to get</u> married next year, and the

11. get

middle one has her own apartment and a job.

B: I <u>am going to miss</u> you at work. It <u>isnt going to be</u> the same

12. miss — 13. not/be

without you.

A: I <u>am not going to miss</u> the boss and the long hours.

14. not/miss

2.8 Choosing *Will, Be Going To,* or Present Continuous for Future

EXAMPLES	EXPLANATION
The U.S. population **will be** 400 million by 2050. The U.S. population **is going to be** 400 million by 2050.	For a prediction about the future, we use either *will* or *be going to*. *Will* is more formal than *be going to*.
Grandpa **will be** 85 years old in August. Grandpa **is going to be** 85 in August.	For a fact about the future, we use either *will* or *be going to*.
A: I'm interested in health care. I **am going to become** a nurse. **B:** My sister's a nurse. I'**ll tell** her about your plan. Maybe she can give you some advice.	When we have a definite plan for the future, we use *be going to*. When we are thinking about the future at the moment of speaking, we use *will*.
A: I want to buy a cell phone. What kind should I buy? **B:** I'**ll help** you. I'**ll take** you shopping. **A:** You always say that. But you never have time. **B:** I'**ll make** time. I promise.	To make a promise or offer to help with no previous plan, we use *will*. The decision comes at the moment of speaking.
My grandmother **is moving** into a retirement home on Friday. I'**m helping** her move. The weather report says it'**s going to rain** on Friday, so the move won't be easy.	We can use the present continuous with definite plans for the near future. We don't use the present continuous if there is no plan. (*NOT*: It is raining on Friday.)

Note:

For a scheduled event, such as a flight, movie, or class, we often use the simple present.

> The semester **begins** in August.
>
> My nursing course **ends** next month.

EXERCISE 16 Listen to the conversation. Fill in the blanks with the words you hear. 🎧 2.6

A: I hear _you're retiring_ next month.
　　　　　　1.

B: Yes. Isn't it wonderful? ___I will be___ 65 in September.
　　　　　　　　　　　　2.

A: What ___are you ging to do___ after you retire?
　　　　　3.

B: ___I will am moving___ to Florida.
　　　4.

A: What ___are you going to do___ in Florida?
　　　　　5.

B: ___I am going to buy___ a sailboat. Maybe ___I'll learn to___
　　　6.　　　　　　　　　　　　　　　　　　　　7.
　by

to play golf. What about you?

A: I don't know. ___I am not going to___ any time soon. I'm only 45.
　　　　　　　　8.

B: I hope ___you will visit___ me in Florida.
　　　　　9.

A: Of course ___I will___ ! Do you need help packing?
　　　　　　10.

B: Yes. ___I am starting___ to pack this weekend.
　　　　11.

A: ___I will help___ you.
　　12.

B: Thanks. ___that will make___ my life a lot easier!
　　　　　13.

EXERCISE 17 Circle the correct words to complete the conversation. In some cases, both choices are possible. If so, circle both.

1. **A:** Do you want to go for a cup of coffee?

　B: Sorry. I don't have time. (*I'm going to visit*/*I'll visit*) my grandfather this afternoon.
　　　　　　　　　　　　　　　　　　　　a.

　(*I'm going to help*/*I'll help*) him with his computer. And I need to return some books to the library.
　　b.

　A: Give them to me. I'm going that way on my way home. (*I'll return*/*I'm going to return*) them for you. Do you
　　　　　　　　　　　　　　　　　　　　　　　　　　　　　c.

　want to get together for coffee tomorrow?

　B: I'm not sure. (*I'll text*/*I'm going to text*) you tomorrow to let you know.
　　　　　　　　d.

2. **A:** I have to go to the airport. My grandparents' plane (*is arriving*/*is going to arrive*) at four o'clock this
　　　　　　　　　　　　　　　　　　　　　　　　a.

　afternoon.

　B: (*I'll go*/*I'm going*) with you. (*I'll*/*I'm going to*) stay in the car while you go into the airport.
　　　b.　　　　　　　c.

　A: Thanks.

　B: How long (*are they going to stay*/*are they staying*)?
　　　　　　　　d.

continued

A: *(They'll come/They're coming)* because *(my sister's graduating/my sister will graduate)* on Sunday.

After the graduation, *(they'll/they're going to)* visit my cousins in Denver.
    g.

3. **A:** My mother's so happy. *(She's going to retire/She'll)* retire next month.
    a.

    B: Are you *(going to have/having)* a party for her?
    b.

    A: Yes. Do you want to come to the party?

    B: What's the date?

    A: June 16.

    B: I have to check my calendar. *(I'm going to/I'll)* let you know later.
    c.

2.9 The Future + Time or *If* Clause

TIME OR *IF* CLAUSE (SIMPLE PRESENT)	MAIN CLAUSE (FUTURE)	EXPLANATION
When I **retire**,	I'm **going to start** a new hobby.	Some sentences have a time or *if* clause and a main clause. We use the future in the main clause; we use the simple present in the time or *if* clause.
If I **am** healthy,	I'**ll continue** to work.	
MAIN CLAUSE (FUTURE)	**TIME OR *IF* CLAUSE (SIMPLE PRESENT)**	
He'**ll move** to a warm climate	as soon as he **retires**.	
My parents **are going to travel**	if they **have** enough money.	

Note:

If the time or *if* clause comes before the main clause, we use a comma to separate the two parts of the sentence. If the main clause comes first, we don't use a comma.

> *If they have enough money, they're going to travel.*
> *They're going to travel if they have enough money.*

EXERCISE 18 Choose the correct words to complete the conversation. In some cases, both choices are possible. If so, circle both choices.

A: What *(are you doing/will you do)* later today?
    1.

B: After class *(will be/is)* over, I'm going to drive my grandfather to the airport.
    2.

A: Where *(is he going/will he go)*?
    3.

B: To Hawaii to play golf.

A: That's great! How old is he?

B: *(He's going to/He'll)* be 78 next month.
    4.

A: He's pretty old.

B: He's in perfect health. (*He's getting*/*He'll get*) married in two months.
5.

A: That's great! What are you and your family (*doing*/*going to do*) when (*he's*/*he'll be*) no longer able to take
6.   7.
care of himself?

B: We never think about it. He's in great health. I think he's (*outliving*/*going to outlive*) us all.
8.

A: But (*he's probably going to need*/*he'll probably need*) help when (*he'll get*/*he gets*) older.
9.   10.

B: If (*he'll need*/*he needs*) help, (*he has*/*he'll have*) his wife to take care of him.
11.   12.

A: My grandparents are in their sixties now. But when (*they're*/*they'll be*) older, they're going to live with my
13.
parents. In our country, it's an honor to take care of our parents and grandparents.

B: That sounds like a great custom. But I think older people should be independent. I'm glad that Grandpa
doesn't depend on us. And when (*I'm*/*I'll be*) old, (*I'm going to take*/*I'm taking*) care of myself. I don't
14.   15.
want to depend on anyone.

A: (*You'll change*/*You're changing*) your mind when (*you're*/*you'll be*) old.
16.   17.

ABOUT YOU Think about a specific time in your future (when you graduate, when you get married, when you have children, when you find a job, when you return to your native country, when you retire, etc.). Write three sentences to tell what will happen at that time. Find a partner who is close to your age. Compare your answers to your partner's answers.

1. When I have children, I won't have as much free time as I do now.

2. When I retire, I'm going to start a new hobby.

3. _____

4. _____

5. _____

FUN WITH GRAMMAR

Role-play a conversation. You have five minutes to write and practice a conversation with a partner about next weekend. Include the weather forecast, definite plans, and scheduled events. When you role-play the conversation, your teacher and classmates will listen for the various uses of the future and count them. The pair with the most correctly used statements in the future wins.

    A: Hey, Gina. What are you doing this weekend?
    B: Oh hi, Steve. Actually, I have big plans. First, I'm going to . . .

SUMMARY OF UNIT 2

SIMPLE PRESENT

For general truths	Many people **retire** in their sixties. Most young people **have** smart phones.
For regular activities, habits, customs	Jack **plays** golf twice a week. I **always** visit my grandparents on the weekend.
With a place of origin	My grandfather **comes** from Mexico. My grandmother **comes** from Peru.
In a time clause or in an *if* clause of a future statement	When she **retires**, she'll start a new hobby. If Grandma **needs** help, she'll live with us.
With nonaction verbs	I **care** about my grandparents. Your grandfather **needs** help now. My grandfather **prefers** to live alone now.
For scheduled events	The plane **leaves** at 8 p.m. tonight.

PRESENT CONTINUOUS (WITH ACTION VERBS ONLY)

For an action happening now, at this moment	My friend **is texting** me now. She**'s sending** me her photo.
For a long-term action in progress at this general time	Judy **is earning** money by tutoring students. Jack is retired now. He **is starting** a new career.
For a trend in society	The population of the U.S. **is getting** older. Americans **are living** longer.
For a definite plan in the near future	She **is retiring** next month. She **is going** on a long trip soon.
With a descriptive state	Mary **is standing** over there. She **is wearing** jeans and a T-shirt.

FUTURE

	WILL	BE GOING TO
For a plan		He **is going to retire** in two years.
For a fact	The number of old people **will increase**.	The number of old people **is going to increase**.
For a prediction	There **will be** more jobs in health care.	There **are going to be** more jobs in health care.
For a decision made at the time of speaking, usually with a promise or an offer	I promise I**'ll take care of** you when you're old.	

REVIEW

Circle the correct words to complete the conversation. If both answers are correct, circle both choices.

A: Hi, Maya.

B: Hi, Liz. How are you?

A: Fine. What (*are you doing*/*you are doing*)? (*Do*/*Are*) you want to go out for a cup of coffee?
    1.   2.

B: (*I'm not having*/*I don't have*) time now. (*I pack*/*I'm packing*). (*We're moving*/*We're going to move*) next
    3.   4.   5.

Saturday.

A: Oh, really? Why (*are you*/*you are*) moving? You (*have*/*are having*) such a lovely apartment now.
    6.   7.

B: Yes, I know we do. But my father (*comes*/*is coming*) soon, so we're (*going to need*/*needing*) a bigger
    8.   9.

apartment.

A: When (*is he*/*he is*) going to come?
    10.

B: He (*leaves*/*'ll leave*) as soon as he (*gets*/*'ll get*) his visa. That (*is probably*/*will probably be*) in about four
    11.   12.   13.

months.

A: But your present apartment (*has*/*have*) an extra bedroom.
    14.

B: Yes. But my husband (*likes*/*is liking*) to have an extra room for an office.
    15.

He usually (*brings*/*is bringing*) a lot of work home. He doesn't (*likes*/*like*) noise when he works.
    16.   17.

A: (*Is your father*/*Your father is*) going to get his own apartment after he (*will find*/*finds*) a job?
    18.   19.

B: He's retired now. He's going to (*live*/*living*) with us. He (*isn't liking*/*doesn't like*) to live alone.
    20.   21.

A: (*Do you need*/*Are you needing*) help with your packing?
    22.

B: No, thanks. Bill and I are (*stay*/*staying*) home this week to finish the packing. And my sister
    23.

(*is helping*/*helps*) me now, too.
    24.

A: I'd like to help. (*I come*/*I'll come*) over next Saturday to help you move.
    25.

B: (*We're going to use*/*We use*) professional movers on Saturday. We (*aren't*/*don't*) want to bother
    26.   27.

our friends.

A: It's no bother. I (*want*/*'m wanting*) to help.
    28.

B: Thanks. I have to go now. (*I hear*/*I'm hearing*) Bill. (*He calls*/*He's calling*) me.
    29.   30.

He (*need*/*needs*) help in the basement. (*I call*/*I'll call*) you back later.
    31.   32.

A: That's not necessary. (*I see*/*I'll see*) you on Saturday. Bye.
    33.

FROM GRAMMAR TO WRITING

PART 1 Editing Advice

1. Always include a form of *be* in a present continuous verb.

   is
   She ʌ working now.

2. Don't use the present continuous with a nonaction verb.

   like
   I am ~~liking~~ my new hobby.

3. Include *be* in a future sentence that has no other verb.

   be
   You will ʌ busy when you retire.

4. Don't combine *will* and *be going to.*

   He will ~~going to~~ leave. OR He's going to leave.

5. Don't use the future after a time word or *if.*

   When I ~~will~~ retire, I'll have more free time.

   If I ~~will~~ have enough money, I'll travel.

6. Use a form of *be* with *going to.*

   is
   He ʌ going to help his grandfather.

7. Use the correct word order in questions.

   will you
   When ~~you will~~ retire?

   isn't she
   Why ~~she isn't~~ going to work part-time?

PART 2 Editing Practice

Some of the shaded words and phrases have mistakes. Find the mistakes and correct them. If the shaded words are correct, write C.

My grandfather is retired now, and he's not happy. He wakes up every day and says,

will I   *C*
"What I will do today?" On the other hand, my grandmother is very busy. My grandparents live
    1.   **2.**

                                                          C   *taking*
in a retirement village, and Grandma is learning how to draw. She's also take singing lessons,
                                                         3.   **4.**

is studying
and she studying photography. Next month, she going to take a trip to India with a group of older
        5.   **6.**

people. When Grandma will get back from India, she's going to make a photo slideshow of her
                        7.   **8.**

                        gets   *C*
trip.

Grandpa doesn't want to travel. He says, "What ~~I'm going to~~ [am I] do in India?" ~~I'm thinking~~ [I think] that

9.   10.

Grandpa ~~is needing~~ [needs] to find a hobby. Grandma always tells him, "You ~~will happy~~ if you find

11.   12. → will be happy

something to do." Will I ~~going to~~ have a hard time like Grandpa when ~~I will~~ retire? I'll think

13.   [Will I]   14.   15. C

about it when the time comes.

16. C

WRITING TIP

When you write, it's important to think about the verb forms you need to express your ideas.

If you choose prompt 1 below, you might start with a general statement such as "My generation uses more technology than my parents' generation." If your supporting examples are of past events, use the simple past. If your examples are of habitual or general actions, use the simple present.

For prompt 2, decide which verb forms are necessary to ask someone questions about current activities and about plans for the future.

      habitual actions: "How do you spend your time?"

      future plans: "What are you looking forward to?"

Remember that there are various future forms, depending on the context.

PART 3 Write

Read the prompts. Choose one and write a paragraph about it.

1. Write about the differences in generations and their use of technology. Use examples from your own life or the lives of people you know.
2. Interview a retired person. What is this person doing with his or her life now? What are this person's plans for the future?

PART 4 Edit

Reread the Summary of Unit 2 and the editing advice. Edit your writing from Part 3.

What is
SUCCESS?

Walt Disney, seen here working on figures for a Disneyland exhibit, was once fired from a newspaper job for not having any good ideas or imagination. The Walt Disney Company is worth an estimated $130 billion today.

Success consists of going from failure to failure without loss of enthusiasm.

WINSTON CHURCHILL

FAILURE and SUCCESS

Read the following article. Pay special attention to the words in bold. 🎧 3.1

What is success? What do we learn from failure[1]? When we try something new, failure is always a possibility. In the nineteenth century, many explorers **attempted** to reach the North Pole by land, but they **died** trying. Salomon Andrée **was** a Swedish engineer. He **wanted** to be the first person to arrive at the North Pole. He **knew** that travel over land **was** very dangerous. He **had** an idea. He **thought** he **had** the perfect way to reach the North Pole: by balloon. On a windy day in July 1897, Andrée and two other men **climbed** into the basket of a balloon. They **took** with them enough food for several months. When they **left**, people cheered and **waved**.

As soon as they **lifted** off, strong winds **hit** the balloon. Fog[2] **froze** on it, making it too heavy. The men **traveled** by balloon for 65 hours. **Were** they successful? **Did** they **arrive** safely? Unfortunately, no. They **landed** almost three hundred miles from the North Pole. No one **heard** from them again. Thirty-three years later, hunters **found** their frozen bodies, their cameras, and their diaries.

Failure is part of all exploration. Robert Ballard, a famous ocean explorer, says that success and failure go together. Failure helps us do things differently the next time. Mountain climber Peter Athans said, "I **learned** how *not* to climb the first four times I **tried** to summit[3] Everest."

In 1914, a polar explorer, Ernest Shackleton, **led** an expedition across Antarctica. His ship became trapped in the ice. However, he **brought** the 27 men on his team home safely. The expedition **was** a failure, but the rescue of his men **was** a success.

Failure helps us on our next try. Failure is a good teacher. Without failure, success would be impossible.

---

[1] failure: an activity or project that does not succeed
[2] fog: a heavy gray vapor near the ground that makes it difficult to see
[3] to summit: to reach the top of a mountain

Salomon Andrée and Knut Fraenkel look at their balloon after it crashed on ice. The photograph was taken by the third team member, Nils Strindberg.

COMPREHENSION Based on the reading, write T for *true* or F for *false*.

1. ___T___ Salomon Andrée was the first person to reach the North Pole.

2. ___T___ The weather caused problems with the balloon.

3. ___F___ Robert Ballard successfully climbed Mt. Everest.

THINK ABOUT IT Discuss the questions with a partner or in a small group.

1. What did Peter Athans mean when he said, "I learned how *not* to climb the first four times I tried to summit Everest."? Do you think he eventually climbed Everest?

2. Do you agree that without failure, success would be impossible? Do you have any examples from *your* life of failing at something before eventually succeeding?

3.1 The Simple Past—Form

EXAMPLES	EXPLANATION
Andrée's balloon **landed** far from the North Pole. Peter Athans **learned** from his mistakes.	Some simple past verbs are regular. Regular verbs end in *–ed*. land—landed learn—learned
They **had** bad weather. Hunters **found** the bodies.	Some simple past verbs are irregular. Irregular verbs do not end in *–ed*. have—had find—found
Shackleton's expedition **was** a failure. The men **were** safe.	The verb *be* is irregular. It has two forms in the past: *was* and *were*.

Notes:

1. Except for *be*, the simple past form is the same for all subjects.

   *I **had** an idea. **He had** an idea.*

2. The verb after *to* does not use the past form.

   *He wanted to **reach** the North Pole.*

EXERCISE 1 Listen to the article. Then write T for *true* or F for *false*. 🎧 3.2

1. _____ Robert Ballard became interested in the ocean when he was young.

2. _____ There were many unsuccessful attempts to find the *Titanic*.

3. _____ Robert Ballard was not successful in finding the *Titanic*.

EXERCISE 2 Listen again. Fill in the blanks with the words you hear. 🎧 3.2

The famous ship *Titanic* _____sank_____ in 1912. It _____rested_____ on the ocean
                                      1.   2.

floor for over 70 years. There _____were_____ many attempts to find it—all of them
                                         3.

unsuccessful. Oceanographer Robert Ballard _____decided_____ to look for it.
                                                        4.

continued

Ballard _____grew_____ up in California near the ocean. When he _____was_____

5.   6.

young, he _____become_____ interested in ocean exploration. He _____wanted_____ to find

7.   8.

the *Titanic*. He _____needed_____ money for his exploration. He _____gave_____ the

9.   10.

U.S. Navy for money, and they _____created_____ it to him. Ballard _____invited_____ a

11.   12.

submersible called the *Argo*. He _____was_____ a French research team to join his

13.

exploration. His team _____was_____ on a ship called the *Knorr* while the *Argo*

14.

_____stayed_____ underwater for many weeks. The *Argo* _____found_____ pictures to

15.   16.

Ballard and his team. On September 1, 1985, the *Argo* _____found_____ the *Titanic*.

17.

It _____was_____ the first view of the *Titanic* in 73 years.

18.

3.2 The Simple Past—Use

EXAMPLES	EXPLANATION
In 1897, Andrée **left** for the North Pole in a balloon.	We use the simple past with a single, short past action.
The balloon **traveled** for 65 hours.	We use the simple past with a longer past action.
Peter Athans **climbed** Mt. Everest seven times.	We use the simple past with a repeated past action.

EXERCISE 3 In Exercise 2, underline the regular verbs once and the irregular verbs twice. Circle the forms of the verb *be*.

EXERCISE 4 Write the base form of the verbs. Write *R* for a regular verb. Write *I* for an irregular verb. Write *B* for the verb *be*.

1. _____cheer_____ cheered _____R_____

2. _____be_____ were _____B_____

3. _____attempt_____ attempted _____R_____

4. _____think_____ thought _____I_____

5. _____die_____ died _____R_____

6. _____wave_____ waved _____R_____

7. _____freze_____ froze _____I_____

8. _____lift_____ lifted _____R_____

9. _____hear_____ heard _____I_____

10. _____learn_____ learned _____R_____

11. _____take_____ took _____I_____

12. _____leave_____ left _____I_____

13. _____climb_____ climbed _____R_____

14. _____bring_____ brought _____I_____

George Dawson learned to read and write when he was 98 years old.

NEVER
TOO LATE TO LEARN

Read the following article. Pay special attention to the words in bold. 🎧 3.3

George Dawson **was** a successful man. **Was** he famous? No, he **wasn't**. He **was** just an ordinary man who **did** something extraordinary.

George Dawson **lived** in three centuries—from 1898 to 2001. He **was** born in Texas, the grandson of slaves. At that time, there **were** fewer opportunities for African Americans[1]. Dawson **was** the oldest of five children. His family **was** very poor, so George **had** to work to help his family. He **started** working for his father when he **was** only four years old. As a result, he **didn't have** a chance to get an education. He **didn't learn** to read and write. He **signed** his name with an *X*.

When Dawson **was** 98 years old, he **decided** to go to school. He **wanted** to learn to read and write. He **went** to adult literacy[2] classes. The teacher **asked** him, "Do you know the alphabet?" When he **answered** "No," his teacher **was** surprised. Over the next few years, his teacher **taught** Dawson to read and write. Dawson **said**,

"Every morning I get up and I wonder what I might learn that day."

Richard Glaubman **read** an article about Dawson in the newspaper and **wanted** to meet him. Glaubman **helped** Dawson write a book about Dawson's life, called *Life Is So Good*. Dawson **was** 102 when the book was published. Dawson **wrote** about what makes a person happy. He **learned** from his father to see the good things in life. They **had** a close family, and George never **felt** lonely. Dawson says in the book, "People worry too much. Life is good, just the way it is."

Was George Dawson a success? He definitely **was**. He **enjoyed** life and **accomplished** his goal: learning to read and write.

---

[1] African American: an American whose ancestors came from Africa
[2] literacy: the ability to read and write

COMPREHENSION Based on the reading, write T for *true* or F for *false*.

1. ___T___ George Dawson was born a slave.
2. ___F___ Richard Glaubman helped Dawson write his book.
3. ___F___ Dawson learned to enjoy life from his father.

THINK ABOUT IT Discuss the questions with a partner or in a small group.

1. What kind of student do you think Dawson was?

2. Dawson's philosophy is that "People worry too much. Life is good, just the way it is." Do you live by this philosophy? Explain.

3.3 The Past of *Be*

EXAMPLES	EXPLANATION
Dawson **was** from a poor family. His grandparents **were** slaves.	The past of the verb *be* has two forms: *was* and *were*. I, he, she, it → **was** we, you, they → **were**
There **was** an article about Dawson in the newspaper. There **were** many changes in his lifetime.	After *there*, we use *was* or *were* depending on the noun that follows. We use *was* with a singular noun. We use *were* with a plural noun.
Dawson's life **wasn't** easy. Education and books **weren't** available to him as a child.	To make a negative statement, we put *not* after *was* or *were*. The contraction for *was not* is *wasn't*. The contraction for *were not* is *weren't*.
Dawson **was born** in 1898.	We use a form of *be* with *born*.
Dawson **was able to** live a happy life.	We use a form of *be* with *able to*.

Compare statements, *yes/no* questions, short answers, and *wh-* questions.

STATEMENT	*YES/NO* QUESTION AND SHORT ANSWER	*WH-* QUESTION
Dawson **was** poor.	**Was** he successful? Yes, he **was**.	How **was** he successful?
His grandparents **were** slaves.	**Were** they from the North? No, they **weren't**.	Where **were** they from?
Dawson **wasn't** unhappy.	**Was** he in school as a child? No, he **wasn't**.	Why **wasn't** he in school?

EXERCISE 5 Fill in the blanks to complete these affirmative and negative statements and questions.

1. George Dawson _____was_____ poor.

2. Dawson _____was_____ born in 1898.

3. At that time, there _____weren't_____ many opportunities for him.

4. His parents _____were_____ poor.

5. He _____wasn't_____ unhappy.

6. George Dawson wasn't able to write his name. Why _____wasn't_____ he able to write his name?

7. _____Was_____ he happy to go to school? Yes, he _____was_____.

8. How old _____was_____ he when he learned to read? He _____was_____ 98 years old.

9. _____Was_____ there slavery in the U.S. when Dawson was born? No, there wasn't.

10. _____Were_____ there a lot of opportunities for African Americans at that time? No, there weren't.

ABOUT YOU Find a partner and discuss your answers to these questions.

1. What do you think makes a person successful?

2. What personal goals do you have? What steps do you need to take to reach those goals?

3. Were your goals different when you were younger? Do you think your goals will change over time?

3.4 The Simple Past of Regular Verbs

EXAMPLES	EXPLANATION
Dawson **signed** his name with an *X*. He **learned** a lot from his father. Dawson **accomplished** his goal.	sign—sign**ed** learn—learn**ed** accomplish—accomplish**ed**

Note:

If the verb ends in an *e*, we add only –*d*.

> Dawson *decided* to get an education. He *died* in 2001.

GRAMMAR IN USE

A common error in speaking is to add a syllable to simple past verbs that end in a consonant. Remember—only the consonant sounds /d/ and /t/ add a syllable in the *-ed* form.

> *waited* = /we^y-tɪd/   *started* = /stɑr-tɪd/
>
> *lived* = /lɪvd/   NOT: /lɪ-vɪd/
>
> *laughed* = /læft/   NOT: /læ-fɪd/

EXERCISE 6 Fill in the blanks with the simple past form of one of the verbs from the box. In some cases, more than one answer is possible.

fail	ask	live	decide	discover	try
land	attend	want	attempt	learn	
die	occur	rescue	help	start	

1. Dawson _____ *lived* _____ from 1898 to 2001.

2. He ___ *started* ___ to work when he was four years old.

3. Many changes *occured* during his long life.

4. His teacher ___ *asked* ___ him, "Do you know the alphabet?"

5. He ___ *attened* ___ school when he was 98.

6. Richard Glaubman ___ *attempted* ___ Dawson write a book.

7. Salomon Andrée ___ *decided* ___ to explore the North Pole.

8. Many people ___ *tried* ___ to reach the North Pole by land, but they weren't successful.

9. Andrée ___ *wanted* ___ to use a balloon.

10. The balloon ___ *landed* ___ far from the North Pole.

11. Andrée and his men ___ *died* ___ .

12. In 1914, Ernest Shackleton ___ *failed* ___ when he tried to cross Antarctica.

13. He ___ *learned* ___ from his failure.

14. He ___ *rescued* ___ his men.

15. Robert Ballard ___ *discovered* ___ the *Titanic* on the ocean floor.

3.5 The Simple Past of Irregular Verbs

Many verbs are irregular in the past. An irregular verb does not use the *–ed* ending.

EXAMPLES	EXPLANATION
A teacher **taught** Dawson to read.	teach—taught
Dawson **had** a close family.	have—had
Andrée and his men **went** up in a balloon.	go—went

Notice the different kinds of changes to form the simple past of irregular verbs.

VERBS WITH NO CHANGE				FINAL *D* CHANGES TO *T*	
beat	fit	put	spit	bend—bent	send—sent
bet	hit	quit	split	build—built	spend—spent
cost	hurt	set	spread	lend—lent	
cut	let	shut			

VERBS WITH VOWEL CHANGES		VERBS WITH VOWEL CHANGES	
feel—felt	mean—meant	dig—dug	sting—stung
keep—kept	sleep—slept	hang—hung	strike—struck
leave—left	sweep—swept	spin—spun	swing—swung
lose—lost	weep—wept	stick—stuck	win—won
awake—awoke	speak—spoke	begin—began	sing—sang
break—broke	steal—stole	drink—drank	sink—sank
choose—chose	wake—woke	ring—rang	spring—sprang
freeze—froze		shrink—shrank	swim—swam
bring—brought	fight—fought	blow—blew	grow—grew
buy—bought	teach—taught	draw—drew	know—knew
catch—caught	think—thought	fly—flew	throw—threw
arise—arose	rise—rose	bleed—bled	meet—met
drive—drove	shine—shone	feed—fed	read—read
ride—rode	write—wrote	flee—fled	speed—sped
		lead—led	
sell—sold	tell—told	find—found	wind—wound
mistake—mistook	take—took	lay—laid	say—said
shake—shook		pay—paid	
swear—swore	wear—wore	bite—bit	light—lit
tear—tore		hide—hid	slide—slid
become—became	forgive—forgave	fall—fell	run—ran
come—came	give—gave	hold—held	sit—sat
eat—ate	lie—lay		
forget—forgot	shoot—shot	stand—stood	
get—got		understand—understood	

MISCELLANEOUS CHANGES			
be—was/were	go—went	hear—heard	see—saw
do—did	have—had	make—made	

Pronunciation Notes:

1. *Meant* rhymes with *sent*.
2. The past form of *read* is pronounced like the color red.
3. *Said* rhymes with *bed*.

*For an alphabetical list of irregular past verbs, see Appendix C.

EXERCISE 7 Fill in the blank with the simple past form of the verb given.

1. Andrée _____flew_____ to the Arctic in a balloon.
   fly

2. Andrée _____thought_____ he could reach the North Pole in a balloon.
   think

3. He and his men _____left_____ in July 1897.
   leave

4. Fog _____made_____ the balloon heavy.
   make

5. Strong winds _____hit_____ Andrée's balloon.
   hit

6. They _____had_____ problems with the weather.
   have

7. The *Titanic* _____sank_____ in 1912.
   sink

8. Robert Ballard _____grew_____ up near the ocean.
   grow

9. He _____become_____ an oceanographer.
   become

10. He _____found_____ the *Titanic* on the ocean floor.
    find

11. Earnest Shackleton _____led_____ an expedition to Antarctica.
    lead

12. He _____brought_____ all of his men home safely.
    bring

EXERCISE 8 Fill in the blanks with the simple past form of one of the verbs from the box. You may use the same verb more than once.

teach	write	begin	see	say	have	go	become

1. Dawson _____had_____ a hard life.

2. He _____began_____ to work for his father when he was four years old.

3. He _____saw_____ many changes in his lifetime.

4. He _____become_____ interested in reading when he was 98.

5. He _____went_____ to school when he was 98.

6. His teacher _____taught_____ him the alphabet.

7. Dawson _____said_____, "I wonder what I might learn today."

8. Dawson _____wrote_____ a book about his life.

FUN WITH GRAMMAR

Play a matching game. Work in groups of three. Choose 10 verbs from chart 3.5. Cut 20 evenly sized pieces of paper. Write the base form of the verbs on 10 of the papers and the matching irregular simple past forms on the other 10 papers. Place all of the papers face-down on a desk and mix the papers up. Take turns turning two cards over at a time to find a matching base form–past form pair. If you find a pair, you get to go again. The person with the most pairs wins.

Diana Nyad on her fifth attempt to swim between Cuba and Florida

IF AT FIRST
YOU DON'T SUCCEED

Read the following article. Pay special attention to the words in bold. 🎧 3.4

Diana Nyad was a professional swimmer. She was in her twenties when she decided to swim around Manhattan. The first time she tried, she **didn't succeed**. But she **didn't give** up. She tried again and swam the 28 miles in less than eight hours. Then she had another goal: to swim from Cuba to Florida, a distance of 110 miles. She swam 79 miles in 42 hours. She **didn't stop** to sleep. But she **didn't finish**. Jellyfish attacked her, and the weather threw her off course[1]. **Did** she **try** again? Yes, but not until 33 years later.

Jellyfish

Nyad retired from competitive swimming in her twenties. For the next 30 years, she **didn't swim** at all. She became a sportscaster[2] and a journalist. But she **didn't stop** all physical activity. She always kept in shape. Every Friday she took a 100-mile bike ride.

In 2007, when Nyad was 60 years old, her mother died. She started to think about her own life. In the 30 years that she **didn't swim**, she always thought about the possibility of trying again. She **didn't want** to die without achieving her goal. She started to train again. By the summer of 2011, she tried again—and failed again—after 29 hours in the water. She tried two more times—and failed to reach Florida each time. What kinds of problems **did** she **face**? There were attacks by jellyfish, bad weather, and breathing problems from asthma[3]. How **did** she **solve** the problem of jellyfish? For her fifth attempt, she wore a bodysuit and mask to protect against jellyfish stings. On August 31, 2013, after 53 hours of swimming, she reached the Florida shore, 35 years after her first attempt. Nyad achieved[4] what younger and stronger swimmers could not.

Nyad always tells people, "Never give up."

---

1. to throw off course: to send in an unintended direction
2. sportscaster: someone who gives news about sports on the TV or radio
3. asthma: a medical condition that causes difficulty in breathing
4. to achieve: to succeed in doing something

COMPREHENSION Based on the reading, write T for *true* or F for *false*.

1. ___T___ Nyad made four attempts to swim from Cuba to Florida before she was finally successful.

2. ___F___ She didn't do any hard physical activity for 30 years.

3. ___T___ The death of her mother made her think about her own life.

THINK ABOUT IT Discuss the questions with a partner or in a small group.

1. Think about the details of Diana Nyad's life and the successes and failures described in the article. Then write six adjectives to describe her.

2. Diana Nyad had three obstacles to completing her goal: jellyfish, bad weather, and asthma. Think of a big goal you have in your life. What obstacles do you have? How can you overcome them?

3.6 Negatives and Questions with the Simple Past

EXAMPLES	EXPLANATION
Diana **succeeded** on her fifth attempt. She **didn't succeed** on her first attempt. She **swam** around Manhattan in her twenties. She **didn't swim** from Cuba to Florida in her twenties.	For the negative of the simple past, we use *didn't* (*did not*) + base form for regular and irregular verbs (except *be*). succeeded—didn't succeed swam—didn't swim

Did Nyad **face** difficulties? Yes, she **did**.
 Did she **succeed** the first time? No, she **didn't**.
	For *yes/no* questions about the past, we use *did* + base form for regular and irregular verbs (except *be*).
	 For a short answer, we use:
	    Yes, + subject pronoun + *did*.
	    No, + subject pronoun + *didn't*.

What kind of difficulties **did** Nyad **face**? When **did** she **succeed**?	For *wh-* questions about the past, we use: *Wh-* word + *did* + subject + base form.

Compare statements, *yes/no* questions, short answers, and *wh-* questions.

STATEMENT	*YES/NO* QUESTION AND SHORT ANSWER	*WH-* QUESTION
Diana **swam** to Florida.	**Did** she **swim** around Manhattan? Yes, she **did**.	When **did** she **swim** around Manhattan?
She **didn't succeed** the first time.	**Did** she **succeed** the second time? No, she **didn't**.	When **did** she **succeed**? Why **didn't** she **succeed** the first time?

Note:

We don't use *did* with the verb *be*.

Compare: *Nyad **wasn't** successful her first time.*   *What **was** her goal?*

            *She **didn't reach** Florida on her first try.*   *What **did** she **want** to accomplish?*

EXERCISE 9 Fill in the blanks with the negative form of the underlined verbs.

1. Andrée and his men <u>landed</u> on ice. They _____didn't land_____ on the North Pole.

2. George Dawson <u>knew</u> how to do many things. He _____didn't know_____ how to read and write.

3. His father <u>taught</u> him many things. His father _____didn't teach_____ him to read or write.

4. He <u>had</u> the chance for an education when he was old. He _____didn't have_____ the chance when he was young.

5. He <u>wrote</u> a book about his life. He _____didn't write_____ it alone.

6. Diana Nyad <u>wanted</u> to swim from Cuba to Florida. She _____didn't want_____ to die without achieving her goal.

7. She <u>swam</u> a lot when she was young. She _____didn't swim_____ for many years.

8. Nyad <u>went</u> to Cuba. She _____didn't go_____ alone.

EXERCISE 10 Fill in the blanks to complete the conversation. Use context clues to help you.

A: _____Did you read_____ the Harry Potter books?
   1.

B: Yes, I _____did_____. I read all of them. I recently wrote a paper about
   2.
   the author, J.K. Rowling. She's the first author to become a billionaire from her writing. When she
   first started writing, she considered herself a failure. _____did you know_____ that?
   3.

A: No, I _____didn't know_____. But I'd like to know more. When
   4.
   _____did she write_____ the first Harry Potter book?
   5.

B: She wrote the first one in 1995. She always wanted to be a writer. But her parents
   _____didn't like_____ the idea. They thought she needed a "real" job.
   6.

A: Why _____didn't they think_____ that writing novels was a real job?
   7.

B: They were worried that it wouldn't pay the rent for her. She was very poor. She went on welfare.
   At that time in her life, she was very depressed.

A: Why _____did she go_____ on welfare?
   8.

B: She was divorced and a single parent. She _____didn't have_____ enough money to
   9.
   support her daughter. She was also very depressed because her mother died. She sent her Harry Potter
   novel to 12 publishers, but they all rejected her novel.

continued

A: Why _did the reject_ her novel?

          10.

B: They didn't think it would be successful. Finally a publisher agreed to publish it.

A: _Did they offer_ her a lot of money?

     11.

B: No, they _didn't_. They only offered her about $2,000. They printed only

          12.

one thousand copies.

A: That's not very many books. _did she accept_ their offer?

                       13.

B: Yes, she _did_. She was happy to accept it.

           14.

A: _Did they print_ more copies?

   15.

B: Yes, they _did_. They had to print more copies because so many people wanted

          16.

to read about Harry Potter. By 1999, her book went to the top of best-seller lists. When she wrote

the fourth book, the publisher printed lots of copies.

A: How many copies _did they Print_?

                 17.

B: They printed over five million copies.

A: Wow! She wasn't a failure. She was a real success.

B: Besides writing, Rowling does other things. For example, she spoke to the graduating class of

Harvard in 2008.

A: _Did she speak_ about her novels?

     18.

B: No, _she didn't_. She spoke about the benefits of failure. She said, "It is impossible to live

        19.

without failing at something."

FUN WITH GRAMMAR

Play *Alibi.* Your teacher will tell you the time and place of a robbery. Two students are the suspects and leave the room. As a class, think of questions to ask the suspects, e.g., *Where were you at the time of the robbery? Who was with you?* The two suspects create an alibi (proof that they were not at the scene of the crime at the time it took place) together. They should try to anticipate what questions the class will ask them and think of answers. Then the class will interview the suspects one at a time. If their answers match, they are innocent. If their answers don't match, they are guilty.

      Class: *Where were you at the time of the robbery?*

      Suspect 1: *I was at the Mexican restaurant down the street. Suspect 2 was with me.*

      Class: *What time did you leave the restaurant?*

      Suspect 1: *We left at around 9:30.*

Martin Luther King, Jr., giving his famous "I Have a Dream" speech in Washington, DC, U.S.

SUCCESS IN CHANGING LAWS

Read the following article. Pay special attention to the words in bold. 🎧 3.5

Today all people in the United States have equal rights under the law. But this was not always the case, especially for African Americans. Even though slavery in the United States ended in 1865, blacks continued to suffer discrimination[1] and segregation[2], especially in the South. Many hotels and restaurants **used to serve** white customers only. Many businesses **used to have** signs in their windows that said, "Blacks Not Allowed." Black children **used to go** to separate, and often inferior, schools. Many professions were for whites only. Even in sports, blacks could not join the major baseball leagues[3]; there **used to be** separate leagues for them. In many places in the South, buses **used to reserve** the front seats for white people. But that all changed.

One evening in December of 1955, Rosa Parks, a 42-year-old woman, got on a bus in Montgomery, Alabama, to go home from work. She was tired and sat down. When some white people got on the crowded bus, the bus driver ordered Ms. Parks to stand up. Ms. Parks refused. The bus driver called the police, and they arrested Ms. Parks.

Martin Luther King, Jr., a black minister living in Montgomery, Alabama, wanted to put an end to discrimination. When King heard about Ms. Parks's arrest, he told African Americans in Montgomery to boycott[4] the bus company. People who **used to ride** the bus to work decided to walk instead. As a result of the boycott, the Supreme Court outlawed[5] discrimination on public transportation.

About 100 years after the end of slavery, Congress passed the Civil Rights Act of 1964. This law officially gave equality to all Americans. The law made discrimination in employment and education illegal. King won the Nobel Peace Prize for his work in creating a better world.

Martin Luther King, Rosa Parks, and other brave people succeeded in changing unfair laws.

---

1 discrimination: unfair treatment, especially because of race, age, religion, etc.
2 segregation: separation of the races
3 league: a group of sports teams that compete against each other
4 to boycott: to refuse to do business with a company
5 to outlaw: to make an action illegal or against the law

COMPREHENSION Based on the reading, write T for *true* or F for *false*.

1. _F_ When slavery ended, blacks gained equality.

2. _T_ Rosa Parks refused to obey the law on the bus.

3. _T_ The bus boycott in Montgomery was successful in helping change the law.

THINK ABOUT IT Discuss the questions with a partner or in a small group.

1. What do you think made Rosa Parks protest the way she did on that day? What might she have been feeling?

2. What are some ways to protest that you know about? What are the pros and cons of each?

3.7 The Habitual Past with *Used To*

EXAMPLES	EXPLANATION
Black children **used to attend** separate schools. Many professions **used to be** for white people only. There **used to be** separate baseball leagues for black people.	We use *used to* + a base form to show a habit or custom over a past period of time. It refers to a custom that no longer exists.

Notes:

1. *Used to* is not for an action that happened once or a few times.

   Many restaurants **used to serve** white people only. (This happened over a period of time.)

   In 1955, Rosa Parks **refused** to stand up. (This happened one time.)

2. For negatives and questions, we omit the *d* in *used to*.

   Some restaurants **didn't use to** serve African Americans.

   Where **did** they **use to** eat?

EXERCISE 11 Fill in the blanks with *use(d) to* + one of the verbs from the box. You will use two of the verbs twice.

make	be✓	suffer	give up	ride	travel
consider	have	dream	wonder	support	

1. J.K. Rowling ___used to be___ poor. Now she's rich.

2. Rowling ___used to make___ billions of dollars. But she gave away a lot of her money.

3. She didn't ___use to consider___ herself a success. She thought she was a failure.

4. How did she ___use to support___ herself and her daughter when she was poor?

5. Peter Athans, who climbed Mt. Everest several times, ___used to have___ a lot of mistakes.

   Now he's much more experienced and careful.

6. People _used to wonder_ where the *Titanic* was. Thanks to Robert Ballard, now we know where it is.

7. Diana Nyad _used to dream_ of swimming from Cuba to Florida. She finally accomplished it.

8. Nyad _used to ride_ her bike 100 miles every Friday.

9. It _used to travel_ difficult to arrive at the North Pole. Now it's easy.

10. People _used to travel_ from Europe to the U.S. by ship. Now people fly across the ocean.

11. Black people in the South _used to be_ discrimination in hotels and restaurants.

12. Black people in the South _used to give up_ their seats on buses to white people.

13. Baseball teams didn't _used to have_ black players. But that changed in 1947.

ABOUT YOU Compare the situation in your country in the past with the situation in your country today. Discuss your answers with a partner.

1. _People used to have large families. Now most people have one or two children._

2. _____

3. _____

4. _____

ABOUT YOU Write sentences comparing the way you used to live with the way you live now. Discuss your answers with a partner. Use the ideas below for your sentences.

| school | job | hobbies | apartment/house | family | friends |

1. _I used to live with my whole family. Now I live alone._

2. _I didn't use to speak English at all. Now I speak English pretty well._

3. _I used to go school Now I have job_

4. _I didn't use to live in apartment Now I live in apartment._

5. _I used to live with my fathers family Now I live with my husband_

6. _____

7. _I used to have a lot friends Now I have kids_

8. _____

SUMMARY OF UNIT 3

THE SIMPLE PAST OF *BE*

Affirmative Statement:	Dawson **was** happy.
Negative Statement:	He **wasn't** rich.
Yes/No Question:	**Was** he from a large family?
Short Answer:	Yes, he **was**.
Wh- Question:	Where **was** he born?
Negative Wh- Question:	Why **wasn't** he in school?

THE SIMPLE PAST OF REGULAR VERBS

Affirmative Statement:	Andrée **wanted** to go to the North Pole.
Negative Statement:	He **didn't want** to go over land.
Yes/No Question:	**Did** he **want** to go by balloon?
Short Answer:	Yes, he **did**.
Wh- Question:	Why **did** he **want** to go to the North Pole?
Negative Wh- Question:	Why **didn't** he **want** to go over land?

THE SIMPLE PAST OF IRREGULAR VERBS

Affirmative Statement:	Dawson **felt** happy.
Negative Statement:	He **didn't feel** lonely.
Yes/No Question:	**Did** he **feel** good when he learned to read?
Short Answer:	Yes, he **did**.
Wh- Question:	How **did** he **feel** about his life?
Negative Wh- Question:	Why **didn't** he **feel** lonely?

THE HABITUAL PAST WITH *USED TO*

Affirmative Statement:	Black children **used to attend** separate schools in some places.
Negative Statement:	They **didn't use to attend** schools with white children.
Yes/No Question:	**Did** baseball teams **use to have** black players?
Short Answer:	No, they **didn't**.
Wh- Question:	Why **did** schools **use to segregate** students?

REVIEW

Fill in the blanks to complete the conversation. Use the words given and context clues to help you. Use contractions wherever possible.

A: There _____was_____ a good program on TV last night. __Did you see__ it?
1. be   2. you/see

B: No, I ____didn't____. What ___was it___ about?
3.   4. be

A: It was about successful people who ___failed___ at first.
5. fail

B: Who __did they talk__ about?
6. they/talk

A: One success was Bill Gates. Gates ___started___ a company with a friend when he

_____was_____ 17 years old.
8. be

B: What kind of company _did they start_ ?
9. they/start

A: They __built__ software to help regulate traffic. They __tried__ to sell it to the city,
10. build   11. try

but they __weren't__ successful.
12. not/be

B: Why __weren't they__ successful?
13. they/not/be

A: The software ___did___ well in the lab, but it __didn't do__ well when they showed it
14. do   15. not/do

to the city. Then Gates ___went___ to college, but he __didn't finish__. He
16. go   17. not/finish

___left___ before graduation.
18. leave

B: I __didn't know__ that. Why __did he leave__ college?
19. not/know   20. he/leave

A: He ___was___ very interested in computers, and he ___started___ Microsoft with his
21. be   22. start

friend. They __became__ successful. The program also talked about Thomas Edison. He
23. become

__invented__ many things. He ___made___ 1,000 attempts
24. invent   25. make

before he __succeeded__ with the light bulb. A reporter ___asked___ him
26. succeed   27. ask

how it ___felt___ to fail so many times. Edison ___replied___,
28. feel   29. reply

"I __didn't fail__ 1,000 times. The light bulb was an invention with 1,000 steps."
30. not/fail

B: I __used to think__ that successful people succeeded right away.
31. use to/think

I __didn't use to think__ of failure as a part of success.
32. not/use to/think

FROM GRAMMAR TO WRITING

PART 1 Editing Advice

1. Use *was/were* with *born*.

   was
   Dawson ˄ born in the South.

2. Don't use *was* or *were* with *die*.

   He ~~was~~ died in 2001.

3. Don't use a past form after *to*.

   swim
   Nyad decided to ~~swam~~ from Cuba to Florida.

4. Don't use *was* or *were* to form the simple past.

   accomplished
   She ~~was accomplish~~ her goal.

5. Use a form of *be* before an adjective. Remember, some *–ed* words are adjectives.

   was
   Dawson ˄ excited about going to school.

6. Don't use *did* with an adjective. Use *was* or *were*.

   weren't
   Andrée and his men ~~didn't~~ successful.

7. Form the past question correctly.

   didn't you
   Why ~~you didn't~~ read the article?
   did   write
   Why ˄ Dawson ~~wrote~~ a book?

8. Use the base form after *didn't*.

   He didn't learn~~ed~~ to read when he was a child.

9. Don't forget the *d* in *used to* in affirmative statements.

   d
   He use ˄ to live in the South.

10. Don't add the verb *be* before *used to* for habitual past.

    Nyad ~~is~~ used to be a sportscaster.

11. Use the correct past form.

    swam
    Nyad ~~swimmed~~ from Cuba to Florida.

PART 2 Editing Practice

Some of the shaded words and phrases have mistakes. Find the mistakes and correct them. If the shaded words are correct, write *C*.

     C   was
I recently read an article about Jackie Robinson. He were the first African American to play on
       1.   **2.**

a major league baseball team, the Brooklyn Dodgers. Major league baseball teams use to have only
                                                        used to
                                                      3.

white players. Blacks were used to have their own teams.
                    used to
                      4.

was

Robinson born in 1919 in the South. His family was very poor. When he was just a baby, his
left **5.** ~~**6.**~~ _move_   _was_

father leaved the family, and his mother decided to moved the family to California. When he were in
7. **8.** **9.** **10.**

high school and college, he interested in several different sports. After junior college, he went to the
was **11.** **12.**

University of California, where he was won awards in baseball, basketball, football, and track. He
13.

didn't finished college. He taked a job as athletic director of a youth organization. Then he enter the
14. **15.** _took_ **16.** → _entered_

U.S. Army in 1942. After he left the Army in 1944, he accepted an offer to be the athletic director at a
17.

college in Texas. In 1945, the Kansas City Monarchs, an African American baseball team, sended him an
18. _sent_

offer to play professional baseball. In 1947, the Brooklyn Dodgers offered him a contract. The manager
19.

of the team knowed that Robinson would face racial discrimination. He didn't wanted Robinson to fight
20. _knew_ _didn't want_ **21.**

back. Some people in the crowds yelled racial insults to him. Even some of his teammates objected to
22. **23.**

having an African American on their team. Robinson didn't surprised. He knew this would happen.
wasn't **24.** **25.**

Some other teams threatened not to play against the Dodgers. How the manager of the team reacted?
26. _did_ **27.** _react_

The manager, Leo Durocher, supported Robinson. He sayed that he would rather keep Robinson than
28. **29.** _said_

some of them. In one game, when people yelled racial insults at Robinson, the team captain come over
30. _came_

and putted his arm around Robinson to show his support.
Put **31.**

Robinson succeeded in breaking the racial barrier. He become the highest paid player in
32. **33.** _became_

Dodgers history. But more importantly, he opened the door for other African American athletes in
34.

professional sports. He retired from baseball in 1957. He was died in 1972.
35. **36.**

WRITING TIP

When writing about someone's life story, we use simple past forms. We often begin with information about when and where a person was born. Then it is common to provide details of his or her life chronologically; for example, the person's childhood, schooling, accomplishments, etc., in the simple past. Question forms may be used to bring attention to a particular detail, for example *Was George Lawson a success? He definitely was.*

PART 3 Write
Read the prompts. Choose one and write a paragraph about it.

1. Write about an ordinary person who did something extraordinary (like George Dawson). It can be someone you read about or someone you know.
2. Write about a time when you failed at something. What did you learn from your failure?

PART 4 Edit
Reread the Summary of Unit 3 and the editing advice. Edit your writing from Part 3.

WEDDINGS

Newlyweds Qu Shen and Liu Ge pose for
wedding photos at the fire station where he
works as a firefighter in Shangluo, Shaanxi
Province of China.

A great marriage is not when the 'perfect couple' comes together. It is when an imperfect couple learns to enjoy their differences.

DAVE MEURER

A Traditional American WEDDING

Read the following article. Pay special attention to the words in bold. 🎧 4.1

Many young couples consider **their** wedding to be one of the most important days of **their** lives. They often spend a year planning for **it**: finding a place, selecting a menu, buying a wedding dress, ordering invitations and sending **them** to friends and relatives, selecting musicians, and more.

The bride chooses **her** bridesmaids[1] and maid of honor[2], and the groom chooses **his** groomsmen and best man. The bride and groom want to make this day special for **themselves** and for **their** guests. Sometimes the bride and groom use a professional wedding planner so they don't have to do everything by **themselves**.

When the day arrives, the groom doesn't usually see the bride before the wedding. It is considered bad luck for **him** to see **her** ahead of time. When the wedding begins, the groom and groomsmen enter first. Next, the maid of honor and bridesmaids enter. When the bride finally enters in **her** white dress, everyone turns around to look at **her**. Often the **bride's** father or both of **her** parents walk **her** down the aisle to the groom.

During the ceremony, the bride and groom take vows[3]. They promise to love and respect each other for the rest of their lives. The groom's best man holds the rings for **them** until they are ready to place **them** on each **other's** fingers. At the end of the ceremony, the groom lifts the **bride's** veil and kisses **her**.

There is a dinner and dance after the ceremony. The bride and groom usually dance the first dance alone. Then guests join **them**.

Before the bride and groom leave the party, the bride throws **her** bouquet over **her** head, and the single women try to catch **it**. It is believed that the woman who catches **it** will be the next one to get married.

The newlyweds[4] usually take a trip, called a honeymoon, immediately after the wedding.

---

[1] bridesmaid: one of a group of women (a good friend or close relative of the bride) who is part of the wedding ceremony
[2] maid of honor: one special woman (a good friend or close relative of the bride) who helps the bride during the wedding ceremony
[3] vow: a promise
[4] newlywed: a recently married person

A groom and his groomsmen

COMPREHENSION Based on the reading, write T for *true* or F for *false*.

1. __T__ Some people use a wedding planner to help plan for the wedding.
2. __F__ The bride usually enters with the groom.
3. __F__ All the women try to catch the bouquet.

THINK ABOUT IT Discuss the questions with a partner or in a small group.

1. Are you familiar with American wedding customs? Are they similar to traditions in your culture?
2. Describe the perfect wedding. It can be a wedding you have been to or a wedding you imagine for yourself.

4.1 Overview of Possessive Forms and Pronouns

EXAMPLES	EXPLANATION
Your wedding was beautiful. **Her** mother looks happy.	A possessive adjective shows ownership or relationship.
You attended my wedding, and I attended **yours**.	A possessive pronoun also shows ownership or relationship.
The **bride's** dress is white.	A noun has a possessive form.
They sent **me** an invitation.	An object pronoun follows the verb.
They want to make the wedding special for **themselves** and their guests.	Some pronouns are reflexive.

EXERCISE 1 Listen to the conversation between a bride-to-be and a professional wedding planner. Then write T for *true* or F for *false*. 🎧 4.2

1. __F__ The bride's mother suggested this wedding planner.
2. __F__ Planning a wedding is actually pretty simple.
3. __T__ The wedding planner costs between $1,000 and $3,500.

EXERCISE 2 Listen to the conversation again. Fill in the blanks with the words you hear. 🎧 4.2

A: My friend gave ___me your___ contact information. She said she used ___your___ services
      _{1.}   _{2.}

when she got married last year. My fiancé and ___I___ are planning ___our___
                                                                _{3.}   _{4.}

wedding now, and we want to know how ___you___ can help ___us___.
                                                    _{5.}   _{6.}

B: Some people try to plan ___their___ wedding ___themselves___, but the results are often not
                                            _{7.}   _{8.}

so good. So I'm glad you contacted ___me___. I can help ___you___ plan the perfect
                                                  _{9.}   _{10.}

wedding. Planning a wedding by ___yourselves___ is stressful. It's ___your___ special day,
                                                  _{11.}   _{12.}

and I want ___you___ to enjoy ___it___. There are a lot of little details in planning
                                                  _{13.}   _{14.}

a wedding, and it's my job to take care of ___them___ for ___you___.
                                                                _{15.}   _{16.}

continued

A: My ___cousin's___ mother helped ___her___ plan ___her___ wedding, but
17.   18.   19.

she was so busy that she didn't enjoy ___it___ very much. My cousin told
20.

___me___ that ___her___ wedding day was stressful for ___her___ and
21.   22.   23.

___her___ fiancé. I need help, but ___our___ budget is limited. How much is this
24.   25.

going to cost ___us___ ?
26.

B: That depends. If you want ___my___ services for every step, it will be about $3,500. If you make
27.

___your___ own arrangements and want ___my___ services for the two weeks before
28.   29.

the wedding and on the wedding day, ___my___ fee is about $1,000. I have a list of all the
30.

things I can do for a wedding. Please look at ___it___ and give ___me___ a call if
31.   32.

___you___ have any questions. I would be happy to explain ___your___ options.
33.   34.

4.2 Possessive Forms of Nouns

NOUN	RULE	EXAMPLES
Singular nouns: bride groom	Add apostrophe + *s*.	The **bride's** dress is white. The **groom's** tuxedo is black.
Plural nouns ending in –*s*: parents guests	Add apostrophe only.	She got married in her **parents'** house. The **guests'** coats are in the coat room.
Irregular plural nouns: men women	Add apostrophe + *s*.	The **men's** suits are black. The **women's** dresses are beautiful.
Names that end in –*s*: Charles	Add apostrophe + *s*.	Do you know **Charles's** wife?
Inanimate objects: the church the dress	Use *the* _____ *of the* _____.	New Hope is **the name of the church.** **The front of the dress** has pearls.
Time words: today this month	Add apostrophe + *s*.	**Today's** weddings are very expensive. **This month's** assignment is easy.

Note:

Sometimes you will see only an apostrophe when a name ends in –*s*.

Do you know **Charles'** wife?

EXERCISE 3 Fill in the blanks to make the possessive form of the noun given.

1. The _____ *bride's* _____ grandfather looks very handsome.
   _{bride}

2. The _____ *bridesmaids'* _____ dresses are blue.
   _{bridesmaids}

3. They invited many guests to the wedding. Did they invite the _____ *guests'* _____ children?
   _{guests}

4. The _____ *women's* _____ dresses are very elegant.
   _{women}

5. _____ *Ross's / s'* _____ sister is a bridesmaid.
   _{Ross}

6. _____ *Today's* _____ newspaper has the _____ *newlyweds'* _____ photo.
   _{Today}   _{newlyweds}

7. Do you know the _____ *children's* _____ names?
   _{children}

EXERCISE 4 Fill in the blanks with the two nouns given. Put them in the correct order. Use the possessive form of one of the nouns, except with inanimate objects.

1. _____ *The bride's name* _____ is Lisa.
   _{name/the bride}

2. _____ *The door of the church* _____ is open.
   _{the door/the church}

3. _____ *The bride's grandmother* _____ came to the wedding from London.
   _{the bride/grandmother}

4. _____ *The date of the wedding* _____ is June 1.
   _{the wedding/the date}

5. _____ *The bride's mother* _____ is crying.
   _{the bride/mother}

6. _____ *The men's tuxedos* _____ are black.
   _{the men/tuxedos}

7. _____ *The color of the limousine* _____ is white.
   _{the limousine/color}

8. _____ *The girls' dresses* _____ are pretty.
   _{dresses/girls}

9. Some people get married in their _____ *parents' house* _____.
   _{house/parents}

10. What is _____ *the cost of the wedding* _____?
    _{wedding/the cost}

11. _____ *The guests' gifts* _____ are put on a table in the reception room.
    _{the guests/gifts}

12. _____ *the groom's* _____ helped him get ready before the ceremony.
    _{the groom/brother}

4.3 Possessive Adjectives

EXAMPLES	EXPLANATION	
I love **my** wife. Where did you buy **your** gift? He chose **his** brother to be **his** best man. She's wearing **her** sister's dress. It's a big restaurant with **its** own reception hall. We planned **our** wedding for over a year. They bought **their** rings at a jewelry store.	Subject Pronoun I you he she it we they	Possessive Adjective my your his her its our their
My sister loves **her** husband. **My brother** loves **his** wife.	A possessive adjective refers to the noun before it. Be careful not to confuse *his* and *her*. Not: My sister loves *his* husband. Not: My brother loves *her* wife.	
The **bride's mother's** dress is blue.	We can use two possessive nouns together.	
My brother's wife didn't attend the wedding.	We can use a possessive adjective (*my*) before a possessive noun (*brother's*).	

Note:

Don't confuse:

- *your* vs. *you're (you are)*.
- *their* vs. *they're (they are)*.
- *its* vs. *it's (it is)*.

EXERCISE 5 Fill in the blanks with a possessive adjective.

1. I love _____ my _____ parents.

2. I have one sister. _____ my _____ sister got married five years ago.

3. She loves _____ his _____ husband very much.

4. He's an accountant. He has _____ his _____ own business.

5. They have one child. _____ their _____ son's name is Jason.

6. My sister and I visit _____ our _____ parents once a month. They live two hours away from us.

7. My sister said, "My car isn't working this week. Let's visit them in _____ your _____ car."

8. I agreed, but then my car wouldn't start. _____ its _____ battery had died.

EXERCISE 6 Fill in the blanks with a possessive adjective.

A: My sister, Nicole, is getting married next month.

B: Will your parents have the wedding at _____their_____ home?
1.

A: Oh, no. They live in an apartment. _____their_____ apartment is too small. My sister invited more
2.

than 200 guests. The wedding is going to be at a church. Afterwards, there's going to be a reception

nearby. The church has _____its_____ own reception hall.
3.

B: Did she already buy _____her_____ dress?
4.

A: Dresses are so expensive. We wear the same size, so my sister's going to wear _____my_____
5.

dress. Nicole and _____her_____ fiancé, Kevin, want to save money for _____their_____
6.   7.

honeymoon. They're going to Paris.

B: Wow! Paris is beautiful—and expensive.

A: Yes, it is. But Kevin's aunt lives there. They're going to stay at _____her_____ apartment.
8.

B: Isn't she going to be at her apartment?

A: No. _____his_____ aunt is coming here for _____their_____ wedding. She's going to stay here
9.   10.

an extra week to give Kevin and Nicole _____her_____ apartment.
11.

B: That's great! I'm sure they will enjoy _____their_____ honeymoon in Paris.
12.

4.4 Possessive Pronouns

We use a possessive pronoun to avoid repetition of a possessive adjective and noun.

EXAMPLE	EXPLANATION		
We had our wedding in a church. They had **theirs** in a garden. (*theirs* = their wedding)	**Possessive Adjective**		**Possessive Pronoun**
Her dress is white. **Mine** is blue. (*Mine* = My dress)	my		mine
Their wedding was big. **Ours** was small. (*Ours* = Our wedding)	your		yours
	his		his
	her		hers
	its		—
	our		ours
	their		theirs
The groom's parents look happy. The **bride's** do, too. (*bride's* = bride's parents)	After a possessive noun, we can omit the noun to avoid repetition.		

EXERCISE 7 Circle the correct words to complete the conversation.

A: I heard your brother got married last month. How was the wedding? Was it anything like your wedding? I

remember (*your*/**yours**) very well.
       1.

B: (**My**/*Mine*) wedding was very different from my (*brother*/**brother's**). (**His**/*Hers*) was a very formal
       2.   3.   4.

wedding in a church. (*My*/**Mine**) was very informal, in a garden.
                      5.

A: I enjoyed (**your**/*yours*) wedding. I prefer informal weddings. At most weddings, I have to get dressed up
               6.

in a suit and tie. At (*your*/**yours**), I wore comfortable clothes. Where did your brother and his wife go for
                      7.

(**their**/*theirs*) honeymoon?
       8.

B: They had a very different honeymoon from (*our*/**ours**). (**Our**/*Ours*) honeymoon was a two-day trip to
                                               9.   10.

Chicago. (**Their**/*Theirs*) was a two-week trip to Hawaii.
          11.

A: I remember your wife made (**her**/*hers*) own dress. You saved a lot of money.
                                12.

B: Yes. But my sister-in-law, Gina, bought (**hers**/*his*). Sarah made her dress for under $100. But
                                              13.

(*Gina*/**Gina's**) cost over $1,000.
       14.

A: The cost of a wedding isn't the most important thing. The most important thing is the happiness that

follows. My (**uncle's**/*uncle*) wedding cost over $30,000, but his marriage lasted only eight months.
          15.

B: That's too bad! (**My**/*Mine*) uncle had a short marriage, too. (**His**/*Hers*) only lasted a year.
                      16.   17.

A: Well, I hope your (*brother*/**brother's**) marriage is happy and long!
                        18.

ABOUT YOU Find a partner and discuss your answers to these questions.

1. What kind of clothes do a bride and groom wear in your native culture?

2. What kind of clothes do guests wear?

3. Do people use professional wedding planners in your country? Why or why not?

4.5 Questions with *Whose*

Whose + a noun asks a question about ownership or relationship.

WHOSE + NOUN	AUXILIARY VERB	SUBJECT	VERB	ANSWER
Whose dress	did	the bride	borrow?	She borrowed her sister's dress.
Whose flowers	are	those?		They're the bride's flowers.
Whose advice	will	the groom	take?	He'll take his mother's advice.

Note:

Don't confuse *whose* with *who's (who is)*.

> **Who's** that? That's the wedding planner.
>
> **Whose** mother is that? That's the bride's mother.

GRAMMAR IN USE

Whose can refer to possession of concrete objects (e.g., *Whose sweater is this? Whose computer did you use?*) as well as possession of abstract ideas (e.g., *Whose advice did you take in the end? Whose opinion matters to you the most?*). Even though you cannot touch the abstract ideas, they still belong to other people.

EXERCISE 8 Write a question with *whose*. The answer is given.

1. Whose flowers are these? _____

   They're the bride's flowers.

2. Whose car is that? _____

   That's my father's car.

3. Whose gifts are those? _____

   Those are the newlyweds' gifts.

4. Whose necklace is she wearing? _____

   She's wearing her sister's necklace.

5. Whose advice did the follow? _____

   They followed the wedding planner's advice.

6. Whose house did they use? _____

   They used their friend's house.

A DESTINATION Wedding

Read the following article. Pay special attention to the words in bold. 🎧 4.3

A year ago, Emily Reese and Josh Knoll got engaged[1]. The couple surfs, and one afternoon at the beach, Josh wrote "I love **you**. Will you marry **me**?" in the sand. "Of course, I told **him** yes," Emily laughs.

Later, Josh and Emily called their families. "When we told **them**, everyone was happy," Josh says. There was just one problem: Where would the couple get married?

"Josh's family is from Chicago," Emily explains. "They wanted **us** to have the wedding there. My family is in Miami, and they wanted **it** in that city. And Josh and I work in San Francisco."

Then the couple had an idea: have a destination wedding.

"We planned to honeymoon in Baja (Mexico) and go surfing," Josh explains. "So we said to **ourselves**, let's have the entire wedding in Baja on the beach."

Today, one in four couples in the U.S. has a destination wedding. The couple and their guests travel to an interesting place (in another city or country) for the event. Couples do **it** because it's fun, but there's another reason. The average American wedding costs around $35,000. Often, a destination wedding is several thousand dollars less, mainly because fewer people attend. The average number of guests at a destination wedding is 48, compared to 136. That's a big savings, especially for couples who pay for **it by themselves**.

Emily liked the idea for another reason. "I couldn't picture **myself** in a church in a formal dress," she says. "I wanted something casual and fun."

When Emily and Josh got married in Baja, only close family and friends came. "It was small, but we all enjoyed **ourselves**," Emily says. "Also, before the wedding, I didn't know Josh's sister. But she stayed in Baja for a few days, and I spent time with **her**. It was a great way to meet my new in-laws[2] and get to know **them**."

Top Destination Wedding Locations for Americans
Las Vegas, Nevada
Hawaii
Saint Thomas, U.S. Virgin Islands
Jamaica
The Bahamas
Mexico

---

[1] to get engaged: to agree formally that you will marry someone
[2] in-laws: your spouse's parents and siblings

COMPREHENSION Based on the reading, write T for *true* or F for *false*.

1. _____F_____ Josh and Emily are from the city of Chicago.
2. _____T_____ The average destination wedding costs about $35,000.
3. _____T_____ Emily was very happy with her wedding.

THINK ABOUT IT Discuss the questions with a partner or in a small group.

1. What are some advantages of a destination wedding? Can you think of any disadvantages?

2. Look at the list of popular places for destination weddings. What do most of them have in common? Add one more idea to the list.

4.6 Object Pronouns

The object pronouns are *me, you, him, her, it, us*, and *them*.

EXAMPLES	EXPLANATION
"I love **you**," Josh said. We saw the wedding photos. We liked **them**.	We use object pronouns after a verb.
Did Emily's parents pay for the wedding? No, Josh and Emily paid for **it**.	An object pronoun can follow a preposition (*at, with, of, about, to, from, in*, etc.).
He invited my family and **me** to the wedding. My family and **I** went to the wedding.	Be careful with subjects and objects connected with *and*. After a verb, we use an object pronoun. Before a verb, we use a subject pronoun.

Notes:

1. An object can be direct or indirect.

    *I love **you**.* (A direct object receives the action of the verb.)

    *Emily showed **me** the wedding photos.* (An indirect object answers *to whom* or *for whom*, in this case, "Who did Emily show the wedding photos **to**?")

2. We can use *them* for plural people and things.

    *Emily met **Josh's sisters**, and she liked **them**.*

    *These are **the wedding photos**. Let's look at **them**.*

3. Compare subject pronouns (in the first column) and object pronouns (in the last column):

I				me.
You				you.
He	went to the			him.
She	wedding.	Emily	invited	her.
We				us.
They				them.
It	was great.		loved	it.

EXERCISE 9 Fill in the blanks with an object pronoun that corresponds to the underlined word(s).

1. Did <u>you</u> receive the wedding invitation? Josh and Emily want _____you_____ to come.

2. Yes. I received <u>the invitation</u>. I put _____it_____ on my refrigerator.

3. At the wedding, <u>Emily</u> didn't arrive at the ceremony with Josh. He arrived before _____her_____.

4. During the ceremony, <u>Josh</u> promised to love Emily, and she promised to love _____him_____.

5. <u>Emily</u> wore <u>a veil</u>. At the end, Josh lifted _____it_____ to kiss _____her_____.

6. Josh and Emily got <u>hotel rooms</u> for their guests, and the couple paid for _____them_____.

7. <u>I</u> am going to give <u>the wedding toast</u>. Emily asked _____me_____ to do _____it_____.

8. You don't know <u>Josh's brothers</u>. I'll introduce you to _____them_____.

9. <u>We</u> sent Josh and Emily <u>a wedding gift</u>. They sent a note to thank _____us_____ for _____it_____.

EXERCISE 10 Fill in the blanks with the correct subject pronoun, object pronoun, or possessive adjective.

A: How was Josh and Emily's wedding?

B: _____It_____ was great.
        1.

A: How many guests were there?

B: About 40. I didn't count _____them_____ all.
                            2.

A: Their wedding was in Mexico, right? How did they pay for _____it_____?
                                                              3.

B: _____They_____ used some of their savings. Also, _____their_____ parents helped
        4.   **5.**

_____them_____, too.
    6.

A: Did Emily wear a traditional white dress?

B: No. The wedding was on the beach, so _____She_____ wore an informal sun dress, but she looked
                                          7.

beautiful in _____it_____.
            8.

A: I hope _____they_____ 'll be happy. Sometimes marriage isn't easy.
            9.

B: I agree with _____you_____. But I'm sure Emily and Josh will be happy. She loves
                  10.

_____him_____ and _____he_____ loves _____her_____ very much.
    11.   **12.**   **13.**

A: Did you take pictures at the wedding?

B: Yes. Do you want to see _____them_____? I have some on _____my_____ phone. Here's a
                              14.   **15.**

picture of Emily and _____me_____.
                    16.

A: Who's that older woman between the two of you?

B: Emily is my cousin, and that's _____*our*_____ grandmother. We were so happy she came to the
_____17._____

wedding. It was a long trip for _____*her*_____ because she lives in Australia.
_____18._____

A: _____*your*_____ grandmother looks so proud. Please tell Emily and Josh that I'm so happy for
_____19._____

_____*them*_____!
___20.___

EXERCISE 11 Circle the correct words to complete each sentence.

1. (*I*/I'm) have a wonderful fiancé, Katya.

2. I love (*her*/hers) very much, and she loves (*me*/my), too.

3. (*I*/I'm) so happy because (we/*we're*) going to get married.

4. (*Our*/We're) wedding will be in March.

5. My brother's wedding was small. (Our/*Ours*) is going to be big.

6. We invited all (*our*/ours) friends and relatives.

7. Some of (*them*/they) are coming from out of town.

8. (*They're*/Their) going to stay with relatives or in a hotel.

9. Katya has two sisters. (Hers/*Her*) sisters are going to be bridesmaids.

10. (*Their*/They're) dresses are blue.

11. There's one problem: Katya's father. (*I*/I'm) don't like (*his*/her) father very much.

12. I think (*he*/he's) doesn't like (my/*me*), either. (He's/*His*) very bossy.

13. But I like Katya's mother. (Hers/*Her*) mother is nice.

14. The wedding will be in a church. The church has (it's/*its*) own reception hall. (Its/*It's*) going to be a
beautiful wedding.

15. Katya and (me/*I*) are going to have our honeymoon in Hawaii. My parents gave Katya and (*me*/I) money
to help with the trip.

16. My fiancé and (me/*I*) will enjoy the wedding day with (*our*/ours) friends and family, and then (we/*we're*) going
to relax on the beach for a week!

4.7 Reflexive Pronouns

EXAMPLES	EXPLANATION
"I can't see **myself** in a formal wedding dress," Emily said. They enjoyed **themselves** at the wedding. We said to **ourselves**, let's have the wedding in Mexico.	We use a **reflexive pronoun** when the object refers to the subject of the sentence. A reflexive pronoun can follow a verb or a preposition.
She made the invitations **all by herself.** They paid for the wedding **by themselves.**	We add *(all) by* before a reflexive pronoun to mean "alone," "without help."

SUBJECT	VERB	REFLEXIVE PRONOUN	
I		myself	
You		yourself	
He		himself	
She	enjoyed	herself	at the wedding.
We		ourselves	
You		yourselves	
They		themselves	

GRAMMAR IN USE

We use reflexive pronouns in a few idiomatic expressions.

> **Help yourself** *(to more cake, to a drink, etc.).*
> **Make yourself** comfortable/at home.
> *If you don't believe me, come* **see for yourself.**
> *Relax and just* **be yourself.**

EXERCISE 12 It is now a year after Josh and Emily's wedding, and their relationship has changed. Read each one's story and fill in the blanks with a reflexive pronoun.

Emily's Story:

Now that we're married, I don't have time for _____myself_____ anymore. Josh and I
                                               1.

used to go out every weekend. Now, there's never any time. It's hard because I'm in law school

and Josh works for ____himself____ . (He just started a small software company.) We're
                        2.

both busy, but Josh rarely helps with the housework or bills. I have to do everything by

____myself____ . And I'm so tired. My friends are always saying, "You don't look well. You
      3.

need to take better care of ____yourself____ ." But how can I? I'm exhausted, and Josh
                                4.

thinks only of ____himself____ . I tell ____myself____ that things will get better, but
                    5.   6.

I'm not sure.

Josh's Story:

Emily never has time for me anymore. We used to do things together. Now I have to do everything by ___myself___ . She's always too busy or too tired. I try to help, but when I
7.

offer to do the housework, for example, she says "no" because she prefers to do everything

___herself___ . My dad tells me, "Josh, don't blame ___yourself___ ." But it's hard.
8. 9.

Our friends seem to enjoy ___themselves___
10.

I keep asking ___myself___ : Why can't Emily and I be happy?
11.

EXERCISE 13 Fill in the blanks with the correct object or reflexive pronoun.

Josh and Emily used to do a lot of things together. But now they are always too busy. Josh

works for ___himself___ ; Emily is in law school. On the weekend, instead of sharing
1.

household chores together, Emily does ___them___ by ___herself___ . When Josh
2. 3.

offers to help, Emily tells ___him___ "No, I'll do it ___myself___ ." And so Josh
4. 5.

goes out by ___himself___ or with others.
6.

Emily and Josh knew they had a problem, but they couldn't solve ___it___ by
7.

___themselves___ . So they went to see a marriage counselor. At first, Josh didn't want to go.
8.

He told Emily, "If you want to see a counselor, you can go by ___youself___ . I'm not going
9.

with ___you___ ." To this, Emily said, "Josh, if you love ___me___ , you'll
10. 11.

come." And so Josh agreed.

During their meeting, the counselor said, "Emily, you spend your weekends doing

housework. Can Josh help ___you___ ?"
12.

"Emily doesn't want ___me___ to help," Josh replied.
13.

"That's not true," Emily said. "I ask ___him___ to do the laundry, but he's always
14.

busy, so I have to do ___my it___ ."
15.

"OK, here's an idea," the counselor said. "Make a list of chores together. Then Josh, you take

some of ___them___ and Emily, you take some, too. You should make a schedule for
16.

___youselves___ , too: time for work and time for you to go out *together*. When you have your
17.

schedule, you have to follow ___it___ . Try this, and then let's meet again in a month.
18.

New Wedding Trends

Read the following article. Pay special attention to the words in bold. 🎧 4.4

Wedding traditions are changing. More and more couples are choosing to create a unique wedding experience for themselves and for their guests. In traditional weddings, a clergyperson[1] faces the bride and groom and **reads them their vows**. The bride and groom simply say, "I do" in response to the question of whether or not they agree to marry. But today, 43 percent of weddings are officiated by a friend or family member rather than a clergyperson. And more and more couples are writing their own vows and **saying them to each other** in their own words.

Following tradition, the bride and groom send their friends and relatives an invitation. But with today's busy schedules, the new norm is for the bride and groom to tell **their guests the date** at least five or six months in advance. They **send them "save-the-date" cards** so that their guests can make plans. Some couples are choosing to have a themed wedding—a central idea or style for their big day. Examples include a specific decade, a movie or television show, a book, a city, or a color. The cards give this information to guests so that they can dress appropriately.

Another new trend in weddings is to create a wedding based on the couple's ethnic background. For example, in an African-American wedding, some couples want to **show respect to their ancestors**[2] by jumping over a broom, a tradition from the time of slavery. The jumping of the broom symbolizes a new beginning by sweeping away the old and welcoming the new. Some African Americans use colorful clothing inspired by African costumes, rather than a white dress for the bride and a suit or tuxedo for the groom.

One thing stays the same. The newlyweds **send the guests thank-you cards** by mail to thank them for attending the wedding and for the gifts they gave.

An African-American couple jumps over a broom.

---

[1] clergyperson: a minister, rabbi, or other religious leader
[2] ancestor: the people from whom one is descended; great-grandparent, great-great-grandparent, etc.

COMPREHENSION Based on the reading, write T for *true* or F for *false*.

1. ___T___ More couples are choosing to have unique weddings.
2. ___T___ Both the couple and the guests need time to plan for a wedding.
3. ___T___ Jumping over a broom is part of some ethnic weddings.

THINK ABOUT IT Discuss the questions with a partner or in a small group.

1. Do you like the idea of modern weddings with an unusual theme, or do you prefer a more traditional celebration? Why?

2. What ethnic traditions have you seen in weddings? Which traditions would you like to have or did you have, at your wedding?

4.8 Direct and Indirect Objects

Some verbs can have both a direct and an indirect object. The order of direct objects (DO) and indirect objects (IO) depends on the verb we use. With some verbs, it can also depend on whether we use a noun or a pronoun as the object.
With some verbs, pronouns affect word order.

POSSIBLE WORD ORDER	VERBS			
He gave his wife a present. (IO/DO)	bring	hand	read	show
He gave a present to his wife. (DO *to* IO)	email	offer	sell	tell
He gave it to his wife. (DO *to* IO)	give	pay	send	write
He gave her a present. (IO/DO)				
He gave a present to her. (DO *to* IO)				
He gave it to her. (DO *to* IO)				

Note:
When the direct object is a noun, not a pronoun, we usually put the indirect object before the direct object. However, we sometimes put the direct object before the indirect object for emphasis or contrast.

> *He didn't send you the invitation. He sent the invitation to me.*

With some verbs, pronouns don't affect word order.

WORD ORDER = DO *TO* IO	VERBS			
He described the wedding to his friends. (DO *to* IO)	announce	introduce	recommend	say
He described it to them. (DO *to* IO)	describe	mention	repeat	speak
He described it to his friends. (DO *to* IO)	explain	prove	report	suggest
He described the wedding to them. (DO *to* IO)				

EXERCISE 14 Fill in the blanks with the words given. Put them in the correct order. Add *to* if necessary. In some cases, more than one answer is possible.

A: How was your cousin's wedding? Can you describe _____*it to me*_____ ?
　　　　　　　　　　　　　　　　　　　　　　　　　　　　　1. it/me

B: It was beautiful. The bride read ____*a lovely poem to*____, and then the groom read
　　　　　　　　　　　　　　　　　　2. a lovely poem/the groom　*the groom*

____*a poem to her*____, too.
　　　3. a poem/her

A: Did they get married in a church?

B: No. They got married in a beautiful garden. Why didn't you go? I thought they sent

____*an*_____*to you*_____ .
　　4. an invitation/you

A: They did. But I couldn't go. I wrote _____*to*_____, and I explained
　　　　　　　　　　　　　　　　　5. an email/them

_____*to*_____ . I had to take an important exam for college that day.
　　　6. my problem/them

But I sent _____*to*_____ .
　　　　　　　7. a present/them

B: I'm sure they'll appreciate it. It's too bad you couldn't go.

A: I'm sure I mentioned ____*it to you*____ a few weeks ago.
　　　　　　　　　　　　　　8. you/it

B: You probably did, but I forgot.

A: Do you have pictures from the wedding?

B: I took a lot of pictures. I'll email ____*them to you*____ tonight.
　　　　　　　　　　　　　　　9. you/them

A: Thanks.

4.9 *Say* and *Tell*

Say and *tell* have the same meaning, but we use them differently.

EXAMPLES	EXPLANATION
She **said** her name.	We say something: *say* + DO.
She **told** me her name.	We tell someone something: *tell* + IO + DO.
She **said** her name to me.	We say something to someone: *say* + DO *to* IO.
They **told** the musicians to start the music.	We tell someone to do something: *tell* + IO *to* + verb.
She **said** (that) she wanted a big wedding.	We say (that): *say* (+ *that*) + statement.
Tell the truth: do you love me?	We can use *tell the truth* or *tell a lie* without an indirect object.

EXERCISE 15 Fill in the blanks with the correct form of *say* or *tell*.

1. The bride _____*said*_____ , "I love you."

2. They _____*told*_____ us the date of the wedding.

3. You _____*told*_____ me the groom's name, but I forgot it.

4. ___Tell___ the truth: do you like the bride's dress?

5. The bride hates to ___say___ goodbye to her family.

6. During the ceremony, the bride and groom ___said___, "I do."

7. We ___told___ the band to play romantic music.

8. My neighbor wants to come to my wedding. I wasn't planning on inviting her, but I can't ___say___ no.

9. We ___told___ our daughter to economize on her wedding, but she ___said___ that she wanted a fancy wedding.

ABOUT YOU Find a partner and discuss your answers to these questions.

1. Are wedding customs changing in your native culture? How?

2. In your native culture, what kind of vows do the bride and groom make to each other?

FUN WITH GRAMMAR

Create a story. Work with a partner. First, unscramble each sentence below. Then put the story in order. The first team to complete the task, add a title, and tell the story to the class wins.

told/was/she/him/it/delicious
gave/she/a present/husband/her
dinner/her/instead/cooked/an anniversary/for/he
she/to him/explained/that it was/their anniversary/for
buy/he/her/didn't/a gift

Throwing rice at the newlyweds is traditional.

QUESTIONS and ANSWERS about American Weddings

Read the following questions and answers. Pay special attention to the words in bold. 🎧 4.5

Q: **Who pays** for the wedding?

A: Usually the bride and groom do, especially if they are working and earning money. In some cases, their parents help.

Q: **What's** a shower?

A: A shower is a party for the bride (sometimes the bride and groom) before the wedding. Guests give the couple gifts to help them start their new home. Typical gifts are cookware, linens¹, and small kitchen appliances.

Q: **Who hosts²** the shower?

A: Usually the maid of honor hosts the shower.

Q: **When do** they **have** the shower?

A: Usually the shower is two to six weeks before the wedding.

Q: **How long does** it **take** to plan a wedding?

A: Most couples plan their wedding for seven to twelve months.

Q: **When do** the couples **send** invitations?

A: They usually send the invitations about eight weeks before the wedding.

Q: When guests come in from out of town, **who pays** for their hotel?

A: They pay for the hotel themselves. However, the groom pays for his groomsmen, and the bride pays for her bridesmaids.

Q: **Whom does** the groom **choose** as his best man?

A: He usually chooses a brother or best friend. The groom chooses other close friends or male relatives as the groomsmen.

Q: **When do** the bride and groom **open** their gifts?

A: They open their gifts at home, not at the wedding.

Q: **How do** the guests **know** what the bride and groom need as gifts?

A: The bride and groom usually register for gifts at stores. They list the gift items they want and need for their new home. When the guests go to buy a gift, they check the registry in the store. However, money is the most popular gift.

Q: **How do** I **know** how much money to give?

A: Most guests spend about $100 on a gift. People who are closer to the bride or groom often spend more.

---

¹ linens: sheets, pillowcases, and towels
² to host: to invite and entertain guests

1. _____ In most cases, the bride's parents pay for the wedding.

2. _____ It takes about six weeks to plan for a wedding.

3. _____ A registry in a store lets guests know what kind of gifts the bride and groom want.

THINK ABOUT IT Discuss the questions with a partner or in a small group.

1. Which details about American weddings surprise you?

2. Imagine you are marrying an American man or woman. Which of the elements of an American wedding would you want to include? Which ones would you not include? Why?

4.10 Subject Questions

STATEMENT	SUBJECT QUESTION
The groom **paid** for the rings.	Who **paid** for the wedding dress?
The bride **has** a white dress.	Who **has** a blue dress?
Some women **plan** the shower.	Which women **plan** the shower?
Some people **send** money.	How many people **send** money?
The bride's mother **cried** at the wedding.	Whose mother **cried** at the wedding?

Notes:

1. Subject questions do not include *do, does,* or *did.*

   For the simple present:
   - We use the singular (-s) form after *who* and *which* + singular noun.
   - We use the base form after *which* and *how many* + plural noun.

2. *What happened* is a subject question. We answer with a different verb.

   What happened after the wedding?   Everyone **left**.

3. We often answer a subject question with a subject and an auxiliary verb.

   Who paid for the rings?   *The groom **did**.*

   Who likes a simple wedding?   *I **do**.*

4. Don't confuse *who's* (who is) and *whose.*

   Whose dresses are blue?   *The bridesmaids' dresses are blue.*

   Who's that woman?   *She's the bride's grandmother.*

EXERCISE 16 Read each statement. Then write a subject question with the words given.

1. Someone takes the bride to the groom. (*who*)

   Who takes the bride to the groom?

2. Someone holds the rings. (*who*)

   Who holds the rings.

continued

3. Someone's car has a "just married" sign. (*whose car*)

   Whose car has a just

4. Some couples have a destination wedding. (*how many couples*)

   how many couples have

5. One woman has a camera. (*which woman*)

   which woman has a

6. Some guests stay at a hotel. (*which guests*)

   which guest

7. Many people give money. (*how many people*)

   How many people

4.11 *Wh-* Questions

STATEMENT	WH- QUESTION
The groom **paid** a lot of money for the wedding.	How much **did** he **pay**?
The bride **has** a white dress.	What color dress **does** her mother **have**?
The bride **borrowed** her dress.	Whose dress **did** she **borrow**?
The bride and groom **chose** a restaurant for the wedding dinner.	Which restaurant **did** they **choose**?
The bride and groom **will go** on a honeymoon.	Where **will** they **go**?

Notes:

1. *Wh-* questions include *do, does, did,* and other auxiliary verbs.
2. In a question about the object, *whom* is very formal. Informally, many people use *who*.

   FORMAL: **Whom** did your brother marry?

   INFORMAL: **Who** did your brother marry?

EXERCISE 17 Read each statement. Then write a *wh-* question with the words given.

1. The wedding will be in a church. (*where*)

   <u>Where will the wedding be?</u>

2. I bought a nice gift. (*what*)

   what did you buy?

3. The bride's brother lives in another state. (*where*)

   Where does bride's brother.

4. I'm going to spend a lot of money. (*how much*)

   How much are you going to
   spent?

5. I received an invitation. (*when*)

When did you receive   invitation?

6. My brother needs to buy a new suit for the wedding. (*why*)

Why does your brother need to

7. They didn't invite our children. (*why*)

Why didn't they invite our children?

EXERCISE 18 Read each statement. Then write a question with the words given. Some are subject questions, and some are *wh-* questions.

1. The bride wears a white dress. (*what/the groom*)

What does the groom wear?

2. The bride enters last. (*who/first*)

Who enters first?

3. The bride throws the bouquet. (*when*)

When the bride throws the
does

4. Some women try to catch the bouquet. (*which women*)

which women does

5. The bride chooses women for bridesmaids. (*which women*)

Which wome does

6. The band plays music. (*what kind of music*)

What kind of music does the band play?

7. Someone dances with the bride. (*who*)

who dances with

8. The guests give presents. (*what kind of presents*)

what kind of " do they give?

9. Some people cry at the wedding. (*who*)

who cries at the "?

10. The guests go to dinner after the ceremony. (*where/after the dinner*)

Wher do the guests go after "

EXERCISE 19 Fill in the blanks to complete the questions in the conversation. Some are subject questions, and some are *wh-* questions. In some cases, more than one answer is possible.

A: How do you have time to work, go to school, and take care of a family?

B: I don't have to do everything myself.

A: Who _____helps you_____ ?
        1.

B: My husband helps me.

A: I usually cook in my house. Who _____cooks in your house_____ ?
        2.

B: Sometimes my husband cooks; sometimes I cook. We take turns.

A: I usually clean. Who _____cleans in your house_____ .
        3.

B: I usually clean the house.

A: How many _____children do you have_____ ?
        4.

B: I have five children.

A: How many _____go to school_____ ?
        5.

B: Three children go to school. The younger ones stay home.

A: Do you send them to public school or private school?

B: One of my sons goes to private school.

A: Which son _____goes to private_____ ?
        6.

B: The oldest does. He's in high school now.

A: It's hard to take care of so many children. How do you find the time to go to class?

B: As I said, my husband helps me a lot. And sometimes I use a babysitter.

A: I'm looking for a sitter. Who _____do you recommend_____ ?
        7.

B: I recommend our neighbor, Sasha. She's sixteen years old, and she's very good with our children.

A: Maybe she's too busy to help me. How many families _____does she work for_____ ?
        8.

B: I think she works for only one other family. I'll give you her phone number. If she's not busy, maybe

she can work for you, too.

EXERCISE 20 Fill in the blanks with *who, whom, who's,* or *whose.*

1. _____Who's_____ that woman over there?

   That's my mother-in-law.

2. ___Who (m)___ did you invite to the wedding?

   I invited all my friends and relatives.

3. _____Who_____ took pictures?

   My brother did. He borrowed a camera because his is broken.

4. _____Whose_____ camera did he borrow?

   He borrowed my aunt's camera. She has a fantastic camera.

5. _____Who's_____ your aunt?

   She's that woman over there.

ABOUT YOU Find a partner. Use the questions to talk about weddings and marriages in your native culture and country.

1. Who pays for the wedding?   *Groom's Paied for*

2. What happens at the wedding?

3. What happens after the wedding?

4. Do the guests bring gifts to the wedding?

5. What kind of gifts do they give?

6. Where do the bride and groom open the gifts?

7. How many people attend a wedding?

8. Where do people get married?

9. Do people dance at a wedding?

10. What color dress does the bride wear?

11. How long does a wedding last?

12. How do the bride and groom invite people? Do they send invitations?

13. Is there a shower before the wedding? Who hosts the shower? Who attends the shower?

14. Do the bride and groom send thank-you notes for the gifts?

SUMMARY OF UNIT 4

Possessive Forms and Pronouns

SUBJECT PRONOUN	OBJECT PRONOUN	POSSESSIVE ADJECTIVE	POSSESSIVE PRONOUN	REFLEXIVE PRONOUN
I	me	my	mine	myself
you	you	your	yours	yourself
he	him	his	his	himself
she	her	her	hers	herself
it	it	its	—	itself
we	us	our	ours	ourselves
you	you	your	yours	yourselves
they	them	their	theirs	themselves
who	whom	whose	whose	—

Order of Direct and Indirect Objects

EXAMPLE	EXPLANATION
I sent my grandmother the date. I sent her the date. I sent the date to my grandmother. I sent the date to her. I sent it to my grandmother. I sent it to her.	Some verbs have two possible word orders (*bring, give, send, show, tell, write*). Pronouns can affect the word order.
They announced their engagement to their parents. They announced it to them.	Some verbs have one possible word order (*announce, describe, explain, say, suggest*). Pronouns don't affect the word order.

Possessive Form of Nouns

SINGULAR NOUN	PLURAL NOUN	INANIMATE NOUN
the **bride's** dress my **father's** house the **child's** toy the **man's** hat **Charles's** wife **today's** topic	the **bridesmaids'** dresses my **parents'** house the **children's** toys the **men's** hats	the entrance of the building the name of the hotel

Questions

SUBJECT	WH-
Who **has** the rings? Which woman **wore** a red dress? How many people **came** to the wedding? What **happened** after the wedding? Who **will come** to the wedding?	Who(m) **do** you **know** at the wedding? Which women **did** you **meet**? How many people **did** they **invite**? What **did** they **serve** at the wedding? Who(m) **will** you **invite** to your wedding?

REVIEW

Circle the correct words to complete the conversation.

A: I know (**you**/your/you're) just got married. (**Tell**/Say/Tell to) me about (you're/you/**your**) wedding.
1.   2.   3.

B: (**It's**/It/Its) was a small wedding. Sara wanted a big wedding, but a big wedding is so expensive.
4.

(Hers/Her's/**Her**) parents wanted to pay for (**it**/its/it's). (Their/Their's/**Theirs**) was a big wedding
5.   6.   7.

because they have a big family. But we don't have a lot of money. We wanted to pay for it

(ourself/**ourselves**/oneself). We explained (them the situation/**the situation to them**/the situation them).
8.   9.

We showed (**them our budget**/to them our budget/our budget them), and they didn't insist on a large
10.

wedding. We just invited (**our**/ours/our's) immediate families: parents, grandparents, sisters, brothers,
11.

aunts, and uncles.

A: How many people (did attend/**attended**/did attended) the wedding?
12.

B: Fifty. Unfortunately (**Sara's grandfather**/grandfather Sara/grandfather of Sara) didn't come.
13.

A: Why not? What (was happened/did happen/**happened**) to (**him**/his/he)?
14.   15.

B: Nothing. (**His**/Her/Her's) grandfather lives in Peru. (His/He/**He's**) old and doesn't like to travel.
16.   17.

A: (**Your**/You're/Yours) grandparents are old, too, aren't they? Did they come?
18.

B: Yes, they did. (Mines/Mine/**My**) live nearby.
19.

A: Where (you got/you get/**did you get**) married?
20.

B: In a church. The (**name of the church**/the church name/the church's name) is St. John. We had a party
21.

afterwards at (**my uncle's house**/house my uncle/my uncle house). (He/He's/**His**) house is big. We even
22.   23.

saved money on the wedding dress because Sara borrowed one.

A: (**Whose**/Who's/Who) dress (**did she borrow**/she borrowed/borrowed she)?
24.   25.

B: She borrowed her cousin's dress. We saved money on photos, too. My uncle took pictures, and he gave

(them us/**us them**/them to us) digitally. We printed (they/**them**/its) and made an album. We went to
26.   27.

Miami for our honeymoon. Sara's uncle has a home there. He let (myself and Sara/**Sara and me**/Sara and I)
28.

use it. With the money we saved, we hope to buy a house soon.

A: (You're/Your/**You**) a wise man! When (Lisa and I/me and Lisa/**Lisa and me**) get married after we graduate,
29.   30.

I'd like to do the same thing. But I don't think Lisa will agree. She wants a big wedding.

B: Who (know/does know/**knows**)? Start to talk to (hers/**her**/she) about it now.
31.   32.

FROM GRAMMAR TO WRITING

PART 1 Editing Advice

1. Don't confuse contractions with possessive forms.

   You're ~~Your~~ late for the wedding. It's ~~Its~~ almost 6 o'clock.

   He's ~~His~~ married. His ~~He's~~ wife is a doctor. They're ~~Their~~ from California.

2. Don't confuse *his* and *her*.

   My sister loves her ~~his~~ husband. My brother loves his ~~her~~ wife.

3. Be careful to choose the right pronoun in compound subjects and objects.

   My mother and I ~~Me and my mother~~ planned the wedding.

   My parents gave my husband and me ~~I~~ $500.

4. Don't use an apostrophe to make a plural form.

   They invited many guests ~~guest's~~ to the wedding.

5. Don't use an auxiliary verb in a subject question.

   Who ~~does~~ help**s** the bride?

6. Put the apostrophe after the *-s* of a plural noun that ends in *-s*.

   My parents' ~~parent's~~ house is too small for the wedding.

7. Don't use *-s* in a possessive adjective. (A possessive adjective has no plural form.)

   Their~~s~~ parents live in Canada.

8. Use the correct word order with direct and indirect objects.

   They explained their wedding customs to me ~~me their wedding customs~~.

   Do you have the wedding present? Please give it to them ~~them it~~.

9. Don't confuse *say* and *tell*.

   She told ~~said~~ me about her wedding.

PART 2 Editing Practice

Some of the shaded words and phrases have mistakes. Find the mistakes and correct them. If the shaded words are correct, write *C*.

Sometimes we [C] have an unrealistic view of marriage. We think that it's [its] all about love and
                1.   2.

nothing else. Some women especially think of the wedding as the bride's special day and don't
                                                                       3.

think about the marriage that follows. [C]

My sister and I [Me and my sister] both wanted to get married. I got married when I was 27 years old. My [C]
        4.   5.

husband was 30. We both had good careers. By the time I got married, many of my friends were

already married. Some of them [they] had small children.
                               6.

120 Unit 4

My sister, Maya, got married right after high school. Ours parents wanted her to wait, but
[handwritten above: Our] *[7.]* *[8. c]*

she didn't want to. She was so in love with his boyfriend, Tony. My parent's were against it at
[handwritten above his: her] *[9.]* *[10. parents]*

first, and Tony's were, too, but they gave to them permission to get married. Mine sister wanted
[11.] *[12.]* *[13. My]*

to have a big wedding. But of course, Maya and Tony couldn't pay for it themself. Mom and Dad
[14. themselves]

said them they would pay for the wedding, but it would have to be small.
[15. told]

Maya and Tony really loved each other, but there marriage didn't last more than three years.
[handwritten above: their] *[16.]*

What went wrong? Maya and Tony didn't understand they're responsibilities as a married couple.
[17.] *[18. their]*

My parents told to them that marriage includes bills, laundry, and children, too. My father said,
[19.]

"If you're going to stay in school, you have to budget not only you're money but you time, too." He
[20.] *[21. your]* *[22. your]*

also warned they, "If you have kids while you're still in school, their going to need your attention.
[23. them] *[24.]* *[25. they're]*

Whose going to take care of them?" Tony and Maya soon had a baby girl.
[26. Who's]

Maya wants to stay in school, but she can't. My mother can't help her because she works
[27.]

full time. Tony loves her daughter. His a good father, and he works hard to support her, so he
[28. his] *[29. He's]*

can't finish college at this time. Theirs lives are so difficult now. I feel sorry for them. I'm happy
[30. Their] *[31.]*

my husband and me established ourselves as responsible adults before marriage.
[32. I] *[33.]*

If you compare my sister and I, you can see a big difference in our lives. Her life is very hard
[34. me]

as a single mother with no career. Its too bad my sister didn't listen to our parent's advice.
[35.] *[36.]*

WRITING TIP

When writing about differences between two things, it is important to use transition words to help connect ideas. Some examples are:

| although | however | instead | in contrast | on the other hand | but | yet |

Brides in the Unites States typically wear white wedding dresses. **In contrast***, brides in China often wear red.*

PART 3 Write

Read the prompts. Choose one and write a paragraph about it.

1. How is a typical wedding in your native culture different from a typical American wedding?
2. What are some problems many married people have today?

PART 4 Edit

Read the Summary of Unit 4 and the editing advice. Edit your writing from Part 3.

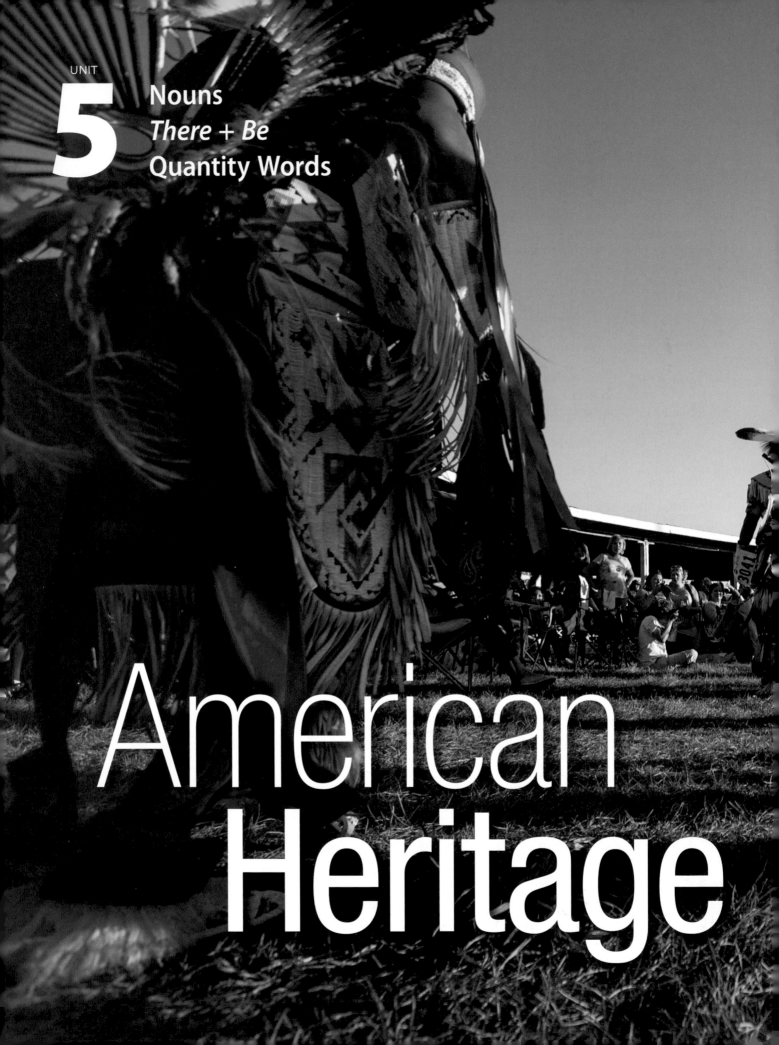

American Heritage

Treat the Earth well: it was not given to you by your parents, it was loaned to you by your children. We do not inherit the Earth from our Ancestors, we borrow it from our Children.

ANCIENT AMERICAN INDIAN PROVERB

Dancers wear traditional clothing during the annual pow wow at the Crow Indian Reservation, Montana, U.S.

The Macy's Thanksgiving Day Parade in New York has been an annual event since 1924. Each year it draws millions of spectators.

THANKSGIVING

Read the following article. Pay special attention to the words in bold. 🎧 5.1

Thanksgiving is a very special American holiday. On the fourth Thursday in November, **Americans** come together with their **families** and **friends** to share a special meal and give **thanks** for all the good **things** in their **lives**. Typical **foods** on Thanksgiving are turkey, sweet **potatoes**, mashed **potatoes** and gravy, stuffing, cranberry sauce, **green beans**, and pumpkin pie for dessert.

What is the origin of this great day? In 1620, a group of **Pilgrims** left England and came to America in search of religious freedom. There were 120 of them: **men**, **women**, and **children**. They started their new life in a deserted[1] American Indian village in what is now the state of Massachusetts. But half of them did not survive their first cold, hard winter. In the spring, two American **Indians**[2] found the **people** from England in very bad condition. They didn't have enough food, and they were in bad health. Squanto, an English-speaking American Indian, stayed with them for several **months** and taught them how to survive in this new land. He brought them deer meat and animal **skins**; he showed them how to grow corn and other **vegetables**; he showed them how to use **plants** as medicine; he explained how to use **fish** for fertilizer[3]—he taught

them many **skills** for survival in their new land. By the time their second fall arrived, the **Pilgrims** had enough food to get through their second winter. They were in better health. They decided to have a Thanksgiving feast[4] to celebrate their good fortune[5]. They invited Squanto and neighboring Indian **families** of the Wampanoag tribe to come to their dinner. The **Pilgrims** were surprised when 90 **Indians** showed up. The **Pilgrims** did not have enough food for so many **people**. Fortunately, the Indian chief sent some of his **people** to bring food to the celebration. They brought **deer**, **fish**, **beans**, squash, cornbread, **berries**, and wild **turkeys**. The feast lasted for three **days**. This was a short time of peace and friendship between the **Indians** and the **Pilgrims**.

Now on Thanksgiving, Americans eat some of the traditional **foods** from this period in American history.

---

[1] deserted: empty of people
[2] American Indians: the native people of America; American Indians are sometimes called Native Americans.
[3] fertilizer: something put into the earth to help plants grow
[4] feast: a large meal
[5] fortune: luck

COMPREHENSION Based on the reading, write T for *true* or F for *false*.

1. ___F___ American Indians helped the Pilgrims through their first winter in America.

2. ___T___ Squanto helped the Pilgrims learn about their new land.

3. ___F___ The Pilgrims invited 90 American Indians for a feast of Thanksgiving.

THINK ABOUT IT Discuss the questions with a partner or in a small group.

1. Reread the last line of the second paragraph. Why do you think there was a short time of peace between the Indians and Pilgrims? What do you think happened afterwards?

2. On Thanksgiving, Americans give thanks for all the good things in their lives. What things in your life are you thankful for?

5.1 Noun Plurals—Form

We use the plural to talk about more than one. To make regular noun plurals, we add -s or -es.

REGULAR NOUN PLURALS

WORD ENDING	EXAMPLE NOUN	PLURAL ADDITION	PLURAL FORM	PRONUNCIATION
Vowel	bee banana	+ s	bees bananas	/z/
ch *sh* *x* *s*	church dish box class	+ es	churches dishes boxes classes	/əz/
Voiceless consonants	snack month	+ s	snacks months	/s/
Voiced consonants	card pin	+ s	cards pins	/z/
Vowel + *y*	boy day	+ s	boys days	/z/
Consonant + *y*	lady story	~~y~~ + ies	ladies stories	/z/
Vowel + *o*	video radio	+ s	videos radios	/z/
Consonant + *o*	potato hero	+ es	potatoes heroes	/z/
Exceptions: altos, autos, avocados, photos, pianos, solos, sopranos, tuxedos				
f or *fe*	leaf knife	~~f~~ + ves	leaves knives	/z/
Exceptions: beliefs, chefs, chiefs, cliffs, roofs, sherriffs				

continued

IRREGULAR NOUN PLURALS

SINGULAR	PLURAL	EXAMPLES	EXPLANATION
man woman tooth foot goose	men women teeth feet geese	The **women** cooked the dinner. The **men** washed the dishes.	Vowel change
sheep fish deer	sheep fish deer	There are many **fish** in the lake.	No change in word
child mouse person	children mice people	The **children** set the table. We invited a lot of **people** to dinner.	Different word form

Notes:

1. The plural of *person* can also be *persons*, but *people* is more common.

2. The pronunciation of *woman* is /'wʊ-mən/. The pronunciation of *women* is /'wɪ-mən/. We hear the difference between singular and plural in the first syllable.

EXERCISE 1 Fill in the blanks with the words you hear. 🎧 5.2

1. _____Airports_____ are often crowded right before Thanksgiving.

2. ___People___ want to get home to their ___Families___.

3. On Thanksgiving, people eat a very big ___dinner___.

4. Before the big dinner, they often eat ___snacks___, such as ___nuts___ and potato ___chips___, while waiting for other ___guests___ to arrive.

5. The Thanksgiving meal usually includes turkey and sweet ___potatoes___.

6. The typical Thanksgiving meal contains more than 3,000 ___calories___.

7. Many ___cities___ have a parade on Thanksgiving morning. ___Thousands___ of people go to see the parade.

8. ___Children___ like to watch the parade.

9. After the meal, it is a typical ___tradition___ to watch professional football on TV.

10. Some ___families___ play a friendly game of football before or after the big meal.

EXERCISE 2 Write the plural form of each noun. If the plural ends in -s or -es, indicate if the pronunciation is /s/, /z/, or /əz/. If not, write Ø.

1.	hour	hours	/z/	13.	spice	spices	/əz/
2.	turkey	turkeys	/z/	14.	pie	pies	/z/
3.	cranberry	cranberries	/z/	15.	knife	knives	/z/
4.	potato	potatoes	/z/	16.	deer	deer	Ø
5.	child	children		17.	watch	watches	/əz/
6.	family	families	/z/	18.	tax	taxes	/əz/
7.	guest	guests	/s/	19.	pot	pots	/s/
8.	ship	ships	/s/	20.	goose	geese	Ø
9.	man	men		21.	dish	dishes	/əz/
10.	woman	women		22.	month	months	/s/
11.	apple	apples	/z/	23.	life	lives	/z/
12.	peach	peaches	/əz/	24.	plant	plants	/s/

EXERCISE 3 Fill in the blanks with the plural form of the words.

A: Who prepares the Thanksgiving meal in your family?

B: As usual, the ____women____ in my family do most of the cooking. But the ____men____
   1. woman   2. man

help, too. My husband usually makes the mashed ____potatoes____ and gravy. I always prepare the
                                                3. potato

turkey and stuffing. Even the ____children____ help. Last year, my son and daughter made the
                              4. child

cranberry sauce.

A: Did they use fresh ____cranberries____?
                        5. cranberry

B: Yes, they did. They just boiled them with sugar and added fruit.

A: What kind of fruit did they use?

B: They used ____apples____.
                6. apple

A: What do you make for dessert?

continued

B: I don't make the dessert. I always invite my next-door ___neighbors___. They bring several

___pies___ . They buy them at a bakery.
8. pie

A: It's nice when all the ___guests___ help with the preparation.
9. guest

B: I agree. I love Thanksgiving. The only thing I don't like is washing the ___dishes___ afterwards.
10. dish

A: Same here. After all that cooking, I like to put my ___feet___ up and relax by watching the
11. foot

football game.

5.2 Using the Plural for Generalizations

EXAMPLES	EXPLANATION
Football games last about three hours. **Sweet potatoes** are nutritious.	We can use the plural to make a generalization. We don't use the article *the* to make a generalization.

ABOUT YOU Make a generalization about the following nouns. Talk about holiday traditions in your country or native culture. You may talk about family members, schools, businesses, etc. Discuss your answers with a partner.

1. children _For Chinese New Year, children get money in red envelopes._

2. men _For Eid men usually go to mouge for pray_

3. women _In Eid women cook dosort._

4. games _In Eid children do alots of games._

5. grandparents ___

6. stores ___

7. schools ___

8. people ___

9. food ___

10. soccer games ___

5.3 Special Cases of Singular and Plural

EXAMPLES	EXPLANATION
The U.S. has more than 320 **million** people.	We use the singular form for exact numbers.
Millions of people go shopping the day after Thanksgiving.	We use the plural form for inexact numbers.
My grandfather is in his **seventies**. He was born in the **1940s**.	We use the plural form for an approximate age or year.
One of my **neighbors** brought a pie to our Thanksgiving dinner. One of the **men** helped with the dishes.	We use the plural form after the expression: *one of (the, my, his, her,* etc.).
Every **guest** brought something. Each **person** helped.	We use a singular noun after *every* and *each*.
We washed all the **dishes**.	We use a plural noun after *all*.
After dinner, the kids put on their **pajamas** and went to bed. We're wearing our best **clothes** today.	Some words have no singular form: *pajamas, clothes, pants, slacks, (eye)glasses, scissors.*
Let's watch the **news**. It's on after dinner. Let's not discuss **politics** during dinner. It's not a good subject.	Even though *news* and *politics* end in *-s*, they are singular.

EXERCISE 4 Fill in the blanks with the correct form of the word given.

1. Five _____ men _____ watched the football game.
   <small>man</small>

2. One of the ___ Children ___ helped make the cranberry sauce.
   <small>child</small>

3. Each __ student __ gave a presentation to the class.
   <small>student</small>

4. Ten __ million __ people pass through the airports before Thanksgiving.
   <small>million</small>

5. __ Millions __ of people travel for Thanksgiving.
   <small>million</small>

6. Every __ guest __ stayed to watch the game.
   <small>guest</small>

7. Thanksgiving is one of my favorite __ holidaies __.
   <small>holiday</small>

8. __ thousands __ of people saw the parade.
   <small>thousand</small>

9. My grandmother came for Thanksgiving. She's in her __ eighties __.
   <small>eighty</small>

10. The children should go to bed. Their __ pajamas __ are on the bed.
    <small>pajama</small>

11. English people started to come to America in the sixteen __ hundreds __.
    <small>hundred</small>

12. One __ hundred __ twenty Pilgrims came in 1620.
    <small>hundred</small>

Cranberry SAUCE

Read the following article. Pay special attention to the words in bold.

🎧 5.3

Cranberries are **a** very American **fruit**. They grow in the cooler **regions** of northeastern North America and are ready for harvest[1] in the fall. We see cranberry **juice** all year, but **packages** of fresh **cranberries** appear in **supermarkets** just before Thanksgiving.

American **Indians** introduced **cranberries** to the **Pilgrims** in 1621. The **Indians** used **cranberries** as **a food** and for different kinds of **medicines**. They also made **tea** from **cranberries** and used it to add color to their **jewelry**.

Cranberries are very sour, so a recipe for cranberry sauce uses **a lot of sugar** or **honey**. You prepare cranberry sauce by boiling **water** with **sugar** and then adding the **cranberries**. You continue cooking them until the **skins** pop[2] open. Before serving, you cool the mixture in the refrigerator. Some people add **pieces of fruit**, such as **apples** or **pears**, to the **cranberries**. Some people sprinkle chopped **walnuts** on top. This is the perfect side dish to go with **helpings of turkey**.

---

[1] harvest: a time for picking or gathering crops
[2] to pop: to break, burst

The Native American Superfood
Cranberries, **blueberries**, and Concord **grapes** are the three cultivated **fruits** that are native to North America. **Cranberries** in particular have **many** health **benefits**.

- **Cranberries** have **a lot of fiber** and **antioxidants**.
- **A glass of** cranberry **juice** may have up to a day's worth of Vitamin C.
- The **fruit** doesn't have **much sugar** or **many calories**. (**A cup of cranberries** has only 1 **teaspoon of** natural **sugar** and just 46 **calories**.)
- The **berries** are good for heart **health**.

COMPREHENSION Based on the reading, write T for *true* or F for *false*.

1. F Cranberries grow in all parts of the United States.

2. F The Indians used cranberries for medicine.

3. T The Pilgrims learned about cranberries from the American Indians.

THINK ABOUT IT Discuss the questions with a partner or in a small group.

1. What is a typical fruit in your country? How do people eat it?

2. Describe your favorite recipe that has fruits from your country. How is the dish made? When do you eat it?

5.4 Count and Noncount Nouns

A count noun is something we can count. It has a singular and plural form. A noncount noun has just one form.

EXAMPLES	EXPLANATION
We used one **apple** in the recipe. We used two **pears** in the recipe.	We use a count noun in the singular form or plural form. We can put *a, an,* or a number before a count noun.
Boil **water** and add **sugar**.	We use a noncount noun in the singular form only. We don't put *a, an,* or a number before a noncount noun.

There are several types of noncount nouns.

GROUP A: NOUNS THAT HAVE NO DISTINCT, SEPARATE PARTS. WE LOOK AT THE WHOLE.					
milk	coffee	yogurt	soup	butter	lightning
oil	tea	beef	bread	paper	thunder
water	juice	honey	meat	air	blood

GROUP B: NOUNS THAT HAVE PARTS THAT ARE TOO SMALL OR INSIGNIFICANT TO COUNT.			
rice	hair	sand	salt
sugar	popcorn	grass	snow

GROUP C: NOUNS THAT ARE CLASSES OR CATEGORIES OF THINGS. THE MEMBERS OF THE CATEGORY ARE NOT THE SAME.	
money or cash (nickels, dimes, dollars)	mail (letters, packages, postcards, flyers)
furniture (chairs, tables, beds)	homework (essays, exercises, readings)
clothing (sweaters, pants, dresses)	jewelry (necklaces, bracelets, rings)
fruit (apples, peaches, pears)	produce (oranges, apples, corn)

GROUP D: NOUNS THAT ARE ABSTRACTIONS.					
love	happiness	nutrition	patience	work	nature
truth	education	intelligence	poverty	health	help
beauty	advice	(un)employment	music	fun	energy
luck/fortune	knowledge	pollution	art	information	friendship

GROUP E: SOME FRUITS AND VEGETABLES ARE USUALLY NONCOUNT NOUNS.					
broccoli	celery	lettuce	kale	asparagus	spinach
corn	squash	cauliflower	grapefruit	cabbage	celery

Note:

Count and *noncount* are grammatical terms, but they are not always logical. *Rice* and *beans* are both very small, but *rice* is a noncount noun and *bean* is a count noun.

EXERCISE 5 Fill in the blanks with a noncount noun from the box.

advice	snow	freedom✓	friendship
health	work	corn	honey

1. The Pilgrims wanted to find _____freedom_____ in America.

2. They had poor ___health___ during their first winter in America.

3. The American Indians gave the Pilgrims a lot of ___advice___ about how to grow food.

4. Squanto taught them to plant ___corn___.

5. The first winter was hard. It was cold, and there was a lot of ___snow___.

6. Learning American agriculture was hard ___work___ for the Pilgrims.

7. In the beginning, there was ___friendship___ between the Pilgrims and the American Indians.

8. Cranberries are very sour, so the Indians added ___honey___.

5.5 Nouns That Can Be Both Count and Noncount

EXAMPLES	EXPLANATION
(NC) **Life** in America was difficult. (C) The Pilgrims had difficult **lives**. (NC) The Pilgrims had a lot of **trouble** their first winter. (C) The American Indians' **troubles** began when the Europeans arrived. (NC) I like to spend **time** with my family on the holidays. (C) My neighbors invited me for dinner many **times**. (NC) American Indians had **experience** with American winters. (C) The first winter for the Pilgrims was **a bad experience**.	The meaning or use of a noun determines whether it is count (C) or noncount (NC).
We put some **fruit** in the cranberry sauce. We prepare a lot of **food** for Thanksgiving. Oranges and lemons are citrus **fruits**. American Indians used cranberries as **a food** and as a dye.	When we talk about fruit or food in general, these words are noncount nouns. When we are referring to kinds or categories of food or fruit, these words are count nouns.
We ate some **pie** for dessert. We eat **turkey** on Thanksgiving. My friend brought three **pies** to the Thanksgiving dinner. One **turkey** is enough for the whole family.	When a noun refers to a part of the whole, it is a noncount noun. When a noun refers to the whole, it is a count noun.

EXERCISE 6 Decide if each noun given is count or noncount. If it is a count noun, change it to the plural form. If it is a noncount noun, do not change it.

1. The _____Pilgrims_____ wanted _____freedom_____.
   a. Pilgrim   **b.** freedom

2. American Indians have a lot of respect for _____nature_____.
   a. nature

3. They love _____trees_____, _____birds_____, and _____fish._____.
   a. tree   **b.** bird   **c.** fish

4. Thanksgiving is a celebration of _____peace_____ and _____.
   a. peace   **b.** friendship

5. On Thanksgiving, Americans eat a lot of _____food_____.
   a. food

6. Americans sometimes eat _____pie_____ for dessert.
   a. pie

7. Squanto gave the Pilgrims a lot of _____advice_____ about planting _____corn_____ and other
   a. advice   **b.** corn
   _____vegetable_____. He had a lot of _____ about the land.
   c. vegetable   **d.** knowledge

8. The Pilgrims didn't have any _____ with American agriculture.
   a. experience

9. On the first Thanksgiving, American Indians brought _____meat_____, _____beans_____,
   a. meat   **b.** bean
   _____bread_____, and _____berries_____.
   c. bread   **d.** berry

10. The Pilgrims celebrated because they had a lot of good _____fortune_____.
    a. fortune

11. American Indians use _____plants_____ for _____.
    a. plant   **b.** medicine

12. I would like more _____ about American _____holidays_____
    a. information   **b.** holiday

5.6 Units of Measure with Noncount Nouns

We don't usually put a number before a noncount noun. We use a unit of measure, which we can count—for example, two *cloves* of garlic.

BY CONTAINER	BY PORTION	BY MEASUREMENT	BY SHAPE OR WHOLE PIECE	OTHER
a bottle of water	a slice (piece) of	an ounce of sugar	a loaf of bread	a piece of mail
a carton of milk	bread	a teaspoon of salt	an ear of corn	a piece of furniture
a jar of pickles	a piece of meat	a cup of oil	a piece of fruit	a piece of advice
a bag of flour	a piece of cake	a pound of meat	a head of lettuce	a piece of
a can of soda (pop)	a strip of bacon	a gallon of milk	a bar of soap	information
a cup of coffee	a slice of pizza	a pint of cream	a clove of garlic	a work of art
a glass of water	a piece of candy	a scoop of ice cream	a stalk of celery	a homework
a bowl of soup		a pinch of salt	a candy bar	assignment
a tube of toothpaste			a stick of butter	a piece (sheet) of
				paper

Note:

We can use *a helping of* or *a serving of* for almost any food.

➤ *How many **helpings/servings of turkey** did you have?*

EXERCISE 7 Listen to this list of ingredients for stuffing. Fill in the blanks with the unit of measure for each ingredient. 🎧 5.4

1. A half _____cup_____ of chopped onions

2. One __stick__ of butter

3. Two __clove__ of garlic

4. Three __stalks__ of celery, chopped

5. Four __cups__ of dry bread, cut into cubes

6. One quarter __teaspoon__ of salt

7. One __tablespoon__ of dry parsley

8. One __cup__ of hot chicken broth

EXERCISE 8 Fill in the blanks with a specific quantity or unit of measure + *of*. Answers may vary.

1. We bought three ___loaves of___ bread for Thanksgiving.

2. Would you like a __glass of__ water with dinner? There's a pitcher on the table. Help yourself.

3. You'll need a __stick of__ butter to make the stuffing.

4. How many __clove of__ garlic are in the stuffing?

5. After dinner, we served a __cup of__ coffee to each guest.

6. Most guests ate a __piece of__ pie after dinner.

7. Can I have your recipe for cranberry sauce? I need a pencil and a __piece of__ paper to write it down.

8. Would you like a __piece of__ fruit after dinner? How about an apple or a tangerine?

9. I bought two __heads of__ lettuce to make a salad.

10. Let me give you a __piece of__ advice about Thanksgiving: There's a lot of food. Try to eat just a little of everything. If you eat too much, you won't feel good afterwards.

ABOUT YOU Find a partner. Talk about the food you eat on a holiday or special day. Describe the ingredients using specific quantities or units of measure.

5.7 A Lot Of, Much, Many

Notice which quantity words go with count (C) and noncount (NC) nouns.

	EXAMPLES	EXPLANATION
Affirmative	(C) You need **a lot of cranberries** for this recipe. (NC) We use **a lot of sugar** to make cranberry sauce.	We can use *a lot of* with both count and noncount nouns in affirmative statements.

Affirmative	(C) I am thankful for **many things**.
	(NC) We eat **a lot of food** on Thanksgiving.
		In affirmative statements, we use:
		  many with count nouns.
		  a lot of with noncount nouns.
		Much is rare in affirmative statements.

Negative	(C) The Pilgrims didn't have **many skills** in American agriculture.
	(NC) Today American Indians don't have **much land**.
		In negative statements, we use:
		  many with count nouns.
		  much with noncount nouns.

Negative	(C) The Pilgrims didn't have **a lot of skills** in American agriculture. (NC) Today American Indians don't have **a lot of land**.	We can use *a lot of* with both count and noncount nouns in negative statements.

Question	(C) Did you invite **many people** for dinner?
	(NC) Did you eat **much turkey**?
		In questions, we use:
		  many with count nouns.
		  much with noncount nouns.

Question	(C) Did you invite **a lot of guests** for Thanksgiving? (NC) Did you eat **a lot of turkey**?	We can use *a lot of* with both count and noncount nouns in questions.

Question	(C) **How many hours** did you cook the turkey?
	(NC) **How much time** did you spend on food preparation?
		In questions, we use:
		  how many with count nouns.
		  how much with noncount nouns.

Note:

With a quantity word, we can sometimes omit (leave out) the noun when we know what the noun is.

> *I usually drink **a lot of water**, but I didn't drink **a lot** today.* (We know that *a lot* refers to *water*.)

GRAMMAR IN USE

We use quantity words often in speaking and in writing, so it's a good idea to recognize which one to use in different situations. Notice how these words express different levels of formality.

FORMAL:	*many, much*	*We're having **many** problems at work.*
LESS FORMAL:	*a lot of*	*We're having **a lot of** problems at work.*
LEAST FORMAL:	*lots of*	*We're having **lots of** problems at work.*

EXERCISE 9 Circle the correct words to complete this conversation. In some cases, more than one answer is correct. If so, circle both options.

A: Did you prepare (*a lot of*/*many*) food for Thanksgiving?
  1.

B: No, I didn't prepare (*a lot*/*a lot of*). This year I didn't invite (*much*/*many*) people. I just invited my
  2.   3.

immediate family.

A: How (*much*/*many*) people are there in your immediate family?
  4.

B: Just seven. I bought a 12-pound turkey. It was more than enough.

A: I don't know how to prepare a turkey. Is it (*a lot of*/*many*) work?
  5.

B: Not really. But if it's frozen, it takes (*a lot of*/*much*) time to defrost it. Cooking it is easy.
  6.

A: Did you make (*many*/*a lot of*) other dishes, like sweet potatoes and cranberry sauce?
  7.

B: No. Each person in my family made something. That way, I didn't have (*much*/*a lot of*) work. But we had
  8.

(*many*/*a lot of*) work cleaning up.
  9.

A: Have you thought about using paper plates? That way, you won't have (*many*/*much*) work cleaning up.
  10.

B: I know (*many*/*much*) people do that, but I want my dinner to look elegant. For me, paper plates are for
  11.

picnics.

A: That's true. Also paper plates aren't very environmentally friendly. It's better to have (*a lot*/*a lot of*) dishes
  12.

to clean, especially with (*a lot*/*a lot of*) people to help.
  13.

B: Right! With help, it wasn't too (*much*/*many*) work.
  14.

FUN WITH GRAMMAR

Play a game with units of measure. Form two or three teams. Your teacher will say a noncount noun and one team member will go to the board and write the noun with a unit of measure (e.g., *water—a glass of water*; *art—a work of art*). For each correct answer, the team earns a point. Every student has a turn. The team with the most points wins.

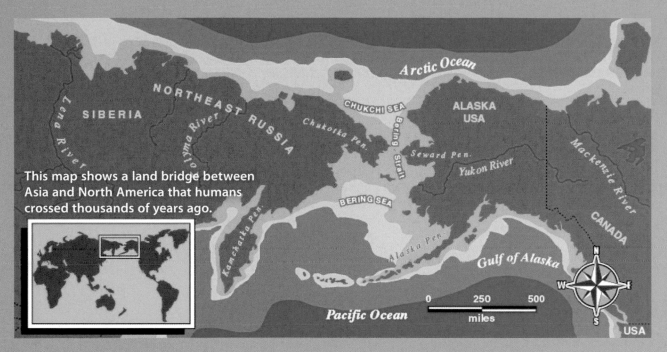

This map shows a land bridge between Asia and North America that humans crossed thousands of years ago.

The First Americans

Read the following article. Pay special attention to the words in bold. 🎧 5.5

Who were the first Americans? Long before Europeans came to America starting about 500 years ago, Indians lived in the Americas. We refer to these people as American Indians. Where did these people come from, and how did they get here?

Thousands of years ago, **there was** a land bridge connecting Eastern Siberia to Alaska. For many years, scientists believed that Siberians crossed this bridge about 16,000 years ago and spread out over the Americas.

In 1968, the skeleton of a young boy was found in Montana. Recently scientists tested the DNA[1] of this child's bones and learned that he lived 12,600 years ago. Scientists refer to his ancient Indian culture as Clovis culture, and to the boy as Clovis Boy. **Is there** a connection between Clovis Boy and Siberians? Definitely. Scientists compared the DNA from Clovis Boy with the DNA of a 24,000-year-old Siberian boy, and **there is** enough genetic[2] evidence to show that Clovis Boy's ancestors were from Siberia.

But even more interesting is this: **There is** a genetic connection between Clovis Boy and about 80 percent of native North and South Americans today.

There were many tools and other objects buried with the boy. At that time, **there were** large mammals, such as mastodons, mammoths, horses, and camels in America. These early Americans used the tools to hunt these animals. These animals became extinct[3] in America, maybe because the Clovis people over-hunted[4].

Even though **there was** a lot to learn from this boy's bones, American Indians wanted to make sure that he was buried again. They saw him as a connection to their ancestors. Shane Doyle, a member of the Crow tribe of Montana, was satisfied to find the connection of his people to Clovis Boy. But, says Doyle, "now it is time to put him back to rest again." Clovis Boy was buried again in June of 2014 in a tribal ceremony. The tools from the first burial are at the Montana Historical Society in Helena, Montana.

---

[1] DNA: the genetic information in cells
[2] genetic: related to the traits that are transmitted from parents to offspring
[3] extinct: no longer in existence
[4] to over-hunt: to hunt and kill too many of an animal

Stone tools found with Clovis Boy

COMPREHENSION Based on the reading, write T for *true* or F for *false*.

1. ____T____ Most American Indians came to America from Siberia.

2. ____F____ Clovis Boy is about 24,000 years old.

3. ____T____ Most of today's American Indians are genetically connected to Clovis Boy.

THINK ABOUT IT Discuss the questions with a partner or in a small group.

1. Look at the map on the previous page. Reread the second paragraph and discuss with a partner how people might have arrived at the Clovis Boy site in Montana.

2. Look at the photograph of Clovis tools. How do you think Clovis people used the tools?

5.8 *There* + a Form of *Be*

We use *there* + a form of *be* to introduce a subject into the conversation.

EXAMPLES	EXPLANATION
There is a connection between Clovis Boy and today's American Indians. **There was peace** between the American Indians and the Pilgrims at first.	We use *there is/was* to introduce a singular noun.
There are American Indian tribes in Montana. **There were Indians** in America before Europeans.	We use *there are/were* to introduce a plural noun.

Were there any tools with Clovis Boy?
Yes, **there were.**
 	
Were there other people with Clovis Boy?
No, **there weren't.**
	For *yes/no* questions, we put *be* before *there*.
	For an affirmative short answer, we use:
	    Yes, + *there* + form of *be.*
	
	For a negative short answer, we use:
	    No, + *there* + form of *be* + *not.*

How many tools **were there** with him? **There were** more than 100. How much time **is there** between now and Thanksgiving? **There are** about 28 days.	We often use *how many/how much* to ask a question with *there*. We put *be* before *there*.

Notes:

1. We can make a contraction with *there is: there's*. We don't make a contraction with *there are.*

2. If two nouns follow *there*, we use a singular verb if the first noun is singular. We use a plural verb if the first noun is plural.

   *There **was** a skeleton and tools at the burial site.*   *There **were** tools and a skeleton at the burial site.*

3. After we introduce a noun with *there*, we can use a pronoun (*they, it, she*, etc.) in place of the noun.

   *There is **information** in Clovis Boy's DNA.*   ***It's** very important to scientists.*

   *There were **tools** with Clovis Boy.*   ***They** give us information about his life.*

4. For the future, we use *there + will be.*

   *There **will be** a documentary about American Indians next week.*

   Will there be** a discussion after the movie? Yes, **there will.

5. In *How many* questions with a location, we sometimes omit *there*.

   How many tools were (there) at the Clovis Boy site?

EXERCISE 10 Listen to the conversation. Then write T for *true* or F for *false*. 🎧 5.6

1. _F_ There are about 12 million American Indians in the United States today.

2. _T_ The friendship and peace between Pilgrims and Indians during the first Thanksgiving did not last.

3. _F_ American Indians didn't want to speak their own language when they moved to reservations.

EXERCISE 11 Listen again. Fill in the blanks with words you hear. 🎧 5.6

A: How many American Indians ___are there___ in the United States today?
   _{1.}

B: ___It's___ about five million. But before the arrival of Europeans, ___there were___.
   _{2.}   _{3.}

many more.

A: How many ___were there___?
            _{4.}

B: ___There were___ at least 12 million. Some historians think ___there were___ up to
   _{5.}   _{6.}

18 million.

A: In this unit, ___It's___ an article about the first Thanksgiving. ___It's___ a
                _{7.}   _{8.}

beautiful story about peace. It says ___there was___ friendship between the Pilgrims and the
                                     _{9.}

American Indians.

B: Unfortunately, ___it___ didn't last. As more English people came to America,
                  _{10.}

___they___ started to take the land away from the Indians. In 1830, President Andrew Jackson
_{11.}

sent American Indians away from their lands. They had to live on reservations.

A: What's a reservation?

B: ___It's___ land given to the American Indians. American Indian children had to learn
   _{12.}

English. Often ___they___ weren't allowed to speak their own language. As a result,
               _{13.}

___there were___ very few American Indians today who speak the language of their ancestors.
_{14.}

A: How many reservations ___are there___ in the United States today?
                         _{15.}

B: ___There are___ about 300.
   _{16.}

EXERCISE 12 Fill in the blanks to complete each conversation. Use *there, is, are, was, were, it, they, not,* or a combination of these words. Use contractions wherever possible.

1. **A:** What's Siberia?

   B: _____It's_____ a region of Russia.
   a.

   A: How did people go from Siberia to Alaska thousands of years ago?

   B: Today _____there's_____ water between these two places. But thousands of years ago, there
   b.

   _____was_____ a land connection.
   c.

2. **A:** Where's Montana?

   B: _____It's_____ in the northwest of the United States.
   a.

   A: _____Are there_____ any reservations in Montana?
   b.

   B: Yes, there _____are_____ .
   c.

3. **A:** How many tribes _____are there_____ in the U.S. today?
   a.

   B: There _____are_____ about 560 tribes in the U.S. today. Some, like the Navajo tribe in the
   b.

   Southwest, are very big.

   A: How many people _____are there_____ in the Navajo tribe?
   c.

   B: There are about 300,000 members.

4. **A:** _____there's_____ a very small tribe in California. It's the Cahuilla tribe.
   a.

   B: How many members does _____it_____ have?
   b.

   A: In 2010, _____it_____ had only eleven members.
   c.

5. **A:** _____Is there_____ a reservation in every state?
   a.

   B: No, there _____is not_____ .
   b.

   A: _____Are there_____ any reservations in Illinois?
   c.

   B: No, there _____aren't_____ .
   d.

6. **A:** Less than half of today's American Indians live on reservations.

   B: Why?

   A: _____There's_____ a lot of unemployment on many reservations. When American Indians
   a.

   need jobs, _____they_____ sometimes go to big cities.
   b.

7. **A:** Did Europeans kill Indians?

   B: Yes, _____the_____ did. Also, there _____were_____ many deaths from diseases that
   a.   b.

   Europeans brought to America.

5.9 Some, Any, A, No

Compare words used with count nouns (C) and noncount nouns (NC).

	EXAMPLES	EXPLANATION
Affirmative	(C) There is **a** big **reservation** in the Southwest.	We use *a* or *an* with singular count nouns.
	(C) I put **some apples** in the cranberry sauce. (NC) I put **some orange juice** in the cranberry sauce.	We use *some* with both plural count nouns and noncount nouns.
Negative	(C) There are**n't any** American Indian **reservations** in Illinois. (C) There are **no** American Indian **reservations** in Illinois. (NC) There is**n't any information** about Clovis Boy's family. (NC) There is **no information** about Clovis Boy's family.	We use *not any* or *no* with both plural count nouns and noncount nouns.
Question	(C) Are there **any nuts** in the cranberry sauce? (NC) Is there **any honey** in the cranberry sauce?	We use *any* with both plural count nouns and noncount nouns.

Notes:

1. You will sometimes see *any* with a singular count noun.

    *Which tribe should I write about? You can write about **any** tribe.*

    Any, in this case, means "whichever you want." It doesn't matter which tribe.

2. Don't use a double negative.

    I don't have any information. (NOT: I don't have no information.)

EXERCISE 13 Fill in the blanks with *some, any, a, an,* or *no.*

1. **A:** There were _____ *some* _____ bones near Clovis Boy.
    a.

    B: Were there _____ *any* _____ tools with him?
    b.

2. **A:** Can you name _____ *any* _____ American Indian tribes?
    a.

    B: Yes, I can name _____ *some* _____ tribes: the Navajo and the Crow.
    b.

    A: Are there _____ *any* _____ Navajos in the Southwest today?
    c.

    B: Yes, there are. There's _____ *a* _____ big Navajo reservation in the Southwest.
    d.

3. **A:** I don't use sugar, so there's _____ *no* _____ sugar in this cranberry sauce.
    a.

    B: Is there _____ *any* _____ honey?
    b.

    A: Yes, there is. There's _____ *some* _____ fruit juice in it, too. And there are _____ *some* _____
    c.   d.

    pieces of apple, too.

Navajo Code Talkers

Read the following article. Pay special attention to the words in bold. 🎧 5.7

American Indian languages are very complicated. There are many different languages, and each one has **several** dialects[1]. One of these languages is the Navajo language. **Very few** non-Navajos can speak or understand it. One exception was Philip Johnston. Johnston was not an American Indian, but he grew up on the Navajo reservation and spoke the language fluently.

In World War II, the United States was at war with Japan. The Japanese were very skillful at breaking codes[2]. They got **too much** classified[3] information. The military needed a better solution. Johnston had an idea: to use Navajo Indians to create a code in their language.

In 1942, Johnston met with **several** American military men and explained his idea. At first, they weren't interested. Then Johnston met with Major James E. Jones of the Marines and spoke **a few** Navajo words to him. He convinced the major to give his idea a try.

The Marines recruited[4] 29 speakers of Navajo to create a code based on their language. There were only **a few** military words in the Navajo language, so the Navajos had to develop **a lot of** words for these things. For example, a commanding general was a "war chief," a battleship was a "whale," and a submarine was an "iron fish."

In the first two days of code talking, more than 800 messages were sent without any errors. About 400 Navajos participated in the code program. During and after the war, they got **little** recognition for their great help in World War II. **Too many** years went by before they were finally honored for their service. It wasn't until 1992 that the U.S. government honored the Navajo code talkers for their help in winning major battles of the war.

---

1   dialect: a regional variety of language
2   code: a system of hiding the real meaning of a message
3   classified: secret; only meant to be seen by authorized people
4   to recruit: to look for and choose people to join the military

A parade in Monument Valley, Arizona, U.S.

COMPREHENSION Based on the reading, write T for *true* or F for *false*.

1. _T_ Philip Johnston learned the Navajo language as a child.

2. _F_ The Navajo language had many military words.

3. _F_ About 800 Navajos learned to use the code.

THINK ABOUT IT Discuss the questions with a partner or in a small group.

1. Why do you think that at first, the military men were not interested in Johnston's idea to create code using the Navajo language?

2. Why do you think the Navajo code would be difficult to break?

5.10 *A Few, Several, A Little*

	EXAMPLES	EXPLANATION
Count	Johnston spoke **a few words** of Navajo to Major Jones. The Navajo language has **several dialects**.	Use *a few* or *several* with count nouns.
Noncount	Johnston needed **a little time** to convince the major.	Use *a little* with noncount nouns.

EXERCISE 14 Choose the correct words to complete these sentences.

1. (*A few*/*A little*) American Indians came to help the Pilgrims in 1621.

2. They taught the Pilgrims (*a few*/*a little*) new skills for planting.

3. We read (*a little*/*several*) articles about American Indians.

4. Johnston met with (*several*/*a little*) military men.

5. He gave them (*a few*/*a little*) examples of the Navajo language.

6. (*A few*/*A little*) Navajo Indians developed a code.

7. It took (*a few*/*a little*) time to develop the code.

5.11 *A Few* vs. *Few*; *A Little* vs. *Little*

EXAMPLES	EXPLANATION
We read **a few** articles about American Indians. **Few** non-Navajos could speak the Navajo language. **Very few** young American Indians speak the language of their ancestors.	*A few* means "some" or "enough." *Few* and *very few* mean "not enough, almost none."
There's **a little** turkey left over. Let's make a sandwich. The Navajo code talkers got **little** recognition for their help in World War II. The Pilgrims had **very little** food the first winter.	*A little* means "some" or "enough." *Little* and *very little* mean "not enough, almost none."

Note:
Whether something is enough or not enough does not depend on the quantity. It depends on the perspective of the person.

EXERCISE 15 Fill in the blanks with *a little, very little, a few,* or *very few* in each conversation.

1. **A:** We read about American Indians in my English class. I'm starting to learn _____*a little*_____
   a.

   about that topic. Did you know that Eskimos are American Indians, too?

   B: Really? I know ____*very little*____ about Eskimos. In fact, I know almost nothing.
   b.

   A: They live in Alaska, Canada, and Greenland. They make their houses out of ice.

   B: What do they eat? ____*very few*____ plants grow in the cold regions.
   c.

   A: They use a lot of sea animals for food. They eat whale, seal, and fish.

   B: I like to eat ____*a little*____ fish, but I can't imagine eating it all the time. How do you
   d.

   know so much about Eskimos?

   A: I saw the movie *Eskimo.* I learned ____*a little*____ about Eskimos from the movie.
   e.

   And I read ____*a few*____ books. Do you want to borrow my books?
   f.

   B: No, thanks. I have ____*very little*____ time for reading now. I have a lot of schoolwork.
   g.

2. **A:** Let's prepare the Thanksgiving dinner together. I always like to get ____*a little*____ help.
   a.

   B: I don't think I'm going to be much help. You know I have ____*very little*____ experience
   b.

   in the kitchen.

   A: Don't worry. You can be my assistant. First, I need to put ____*a very little*____ oil on the turkey.
   c.

   B: There's ____*very little*____ oil in the house. I don't think it's going to be enough.
   d.

   A: Don't worry. I have another bottle. Next, I need you to get the spices out of the cabinet for me. We're going

   to put ____*a few*____ spices on the turkey. I also need ____*a little*____ string to tie
   e.   f.

   the legs. Then the turkey will be ready to go into the oven. Lastly, I need you to go to the store and get

   ____*a few*____ things for me. Here's a list.
   g.

   B: Shopping! That's something I can do well.

   A: Why is it that in this family, ____*very few*____ men cook the turkey? I almost never see a man
   h.

   prepare the Thanksgiving dinner. In fact, ____*very few*____ men even come into the kitchen unless
   i.

   they're hungry.

5.12 *Too Much/Too Many* vs. *A Lot Of*

EXAMPLES	EXPLANATION
My friend left the reservation because there was **too much** unemployment. If we invite **too many** people to dinner, we won't have enough food. **A lot of** Navajo Indians live in the Southwest.	*Too much* and *too many* show an excessive quantity. A problem with the quantity is presented or implied. *A lot of* shows a large quantity. No problem is presented.
I feel sick. I ate **too much**.	We can put *too much* at the end of a verb phrase. Note that the noun *food* is omitted. It is understood by the context.

Note:

Sometimes we use *a lot of* in place of *too much/too many*.

> If we invite **a lot of** people to dinner, we won't have enough food.

EXERCISE 16 Fill in the blanks with *a lot of, too much,* or *too many*. In some cases, more than one answer is possible.

1. You put _____too much_____ pepper in the potatoes, and they taste terrible.

2. On Thanksgiving Day, most people eat ___a lot too much___ and don't feel well afterwards.

3. I'm so busy before Thanksgiving. I have no time to rest. I have ___a lot of___ things to do.

4. I love garlic. This recipe calls for ___a lot of___ garlic, so it's going to be delicious.

5. She's going to bake a cherry pie for Thanksgiving. She needs ___a lot of___ cherries.

6. I think I ate ___too many___ pieces of pie. Now I feel sick.

7. We had ___too much___ food at the Thanksgiving dinner. We had to throw away a lot.

8. There are ___a lot of___ American Indian languages.

9. The Navajo code talkers gave ___a lot of___ help during World War II.

10. The code talkers sent ___a lot of___ messages successfully.

SUMMARY OF UNIT 5

Words Used before Count and Noncount Nouns

SINGULAR COUNT	PLURAL COUNT	NONCOUNT
the apple	**the** apples	**the** sugar
an apple	**some** apples	**some** sugar
no apple	**no** apples	**no** sugar
	any apples *(with questions and negatives)*	**any** sugar *(with questions and negatives)*
	a lot of apples	**a lot of** sugar
	many apples	**much** sugar *(with questions and negatives)*
	a few apples	**a little** sugar
	two apples	**two** teaspoons of sugar
	several apples	
	How many apples?	**How much** sugar?

There + a Form of *Be*

COUNT	NONCOUNT
There's one onion in the recipe. **There are** two carrots in the recipe. **Is there** a potato in the recipe? No, **there isn't.** **Are there** any nuts in the recipe? Yes, **there are.** How many nuts **are there** in the recipe?	**There is** some celery in the soup. **There isn't** any garlic in the soup. **Is there** any rice in the soup? No, **there isn't.** How much salt **is there** in the soup?

A Few/(Very) Few; A Little/(Very) Little

	COUNT	NONCOUNT
some	**A few** people brought a pie to dinner.	Do you want **a little** sugar in your tea?
not enough	It's too bad that **(very) few** Navajos speak their language today.	The Navajo code talkers got **(very) little** recognition during World War II.

A Lot Of/Too Much/Too Many

NEUTRAL (COUNT AND NONCOUNT)	PROBLEMATIC (COUNT)	PROBLEMATIC (NONCOUNT)
I cooked **a lot of** potatoes. I put **a lot of** butter on the potatoes.	You put **too many** raisins in the stuffing. It's too sweet.	You put **too much** salt in the soup. I can't eat it.

REVIEW

Read this essay by an American Indian. Circle the correct words to complete it.

My name is Joseph Falling Snow. I'm (*an/a/any*) American Indian from a Sioux[1] reservation in South Dakota.
1.

There are (*a little/little/several*) Sioux reservations; I'm from the Pine Ridge reservation. I don't live
2.

in South Dakota anymore because I couldn't find (*a/any/no*) job. There's (*a little/a few/little/few*)
3.　　　　　　　　　　　　　　　4.

work on my reservation. There's a lot of (*unemployment/unemployments*) there. (*A poverty/Poverty*) is a
5.　　　　　　　　　　　　　　　6.

big problem on my reservation. My uncle gave me (*a/an/some/any*) good (*advice/advices*). He told me
7.　　　　　　　　　　　8.

to go to (*big city/a big city*) to find (*a/an/some/any*) job. I decided to go to Minneapolis. There are
9.　　　　　　　　　10.

(*much/many/any*) job opportunities there. I had (*no/not/any*) trouble finding a job because I have
11.　　　　　　　　　　　　　　12.

(*a lot of/many/much*) (*experiences/experience*) as a carpenter.
13.　　　　　　14.

The language of my tribe is Lakota, but I know (*any/a few/very few*) words in my language. Most of the
15.

(*people/person/peoples*) on my reservation speak only English. (*A few/Any/A little*) older people still speak our
16.　　　　　　　　　　　　　　　17.

tribal language, but the language is dying out as the older people die.

(*A few/A little/Few/Little*) times a year, I go back to the reservation for a celebration called a pow wow.
18.

It gets very crowded at these times because (*much/any/a lot of*) people from our reservation and nearby
19.

reservations attend this celebration. We have (*much/too much/a lot of*) fun. We dance to our (*music/musics*) and
20.　　　　　　　　　　　　　21.

socialize with our (*friend/friends*).
22.

---

[1] Sioux *is* pronounced /su/.

FROM GRAMMAR TO WRITING

PART 1 Editing Advice

1. Some plural forms are irregular and don't take -s.

   There were a lot of childrens at the Thanksgiving dinner.

2. Use a singular noun and verb after *every*.

   Every readings teach us something new. *(es)*

3. Use the plural form of the noun after *one of*.

   One of my neighbor made a pumpkin pie. *(s)*

4. Don't use *a* or *an* before a plural noun.

   The code talkers had to create a new words. *(some)*

5. Don't put *a* or *an* before a noncount noun.

   Clovis Boy's bones give us a useful information about the past. *(some)*

6. A noncount noun is always singular.

   The American Indians gave the Pilgrims a lot of advices.

7. Use *there is* or *there are* to introduce a noun.

   There are
   Are a lot of Navajo Indians in the Southwest.

8. Don't use a specific noun after *there is/there are*.

   T   is
   There's the Grand Canyon in Arizona.

9. Include *of* with a unit of measure.

   of
   We used one cup sugar in the cranberry sauce.

10. Omit *of* after *a lot* when the noun is omitted.

    You ate a lot of turkey, but I didn't eat a lot of.

11. Use *a little/a few* to mean "some." Use *(very) little/(very) few* to mean "not enough."

    (very)
    He went to a big city to find a job because there were a few jobs on the reservation.

12. Don't use *too much* or *too many* if the quantity doesn't present a problem.

    a lot of
    She loves to go back to the reservation because she has too many friends there.

13. Don't confuse *too* and *too much/too many*.

    The potatoes are too much salty. I can't eat them.

14. Don't use a double negative.

    a
    The Navajo language doesn't have no word for "submarine."
    OR
    The Navajo language has no word for "submarine."

PART 2 Editing Practice

Some of the shaded words and phrases have mistakes. Find the mistakes and correct them. If the shaded words are correct, write C.

I love Thanksgiving. Every ~~years~~ [year], the whole family comes to our house for this holiday and a few [C] other
1.   2.

holidays. But Thanksgiving is my favorite. There are a lot of ~~childrens~~ [children] in my family, and they love to see each
3.   4.

other on Thanksgiving. They don't have ~~many~~ [much] time to see each other the rest of the year. It's so joyful to have
5.

too ~~many~~ [so many] children in the house few [a] times a year. There's a lot of noise [C] when they're here, but we don't mind.
6.   7.   8.   9.

We all bring some ~~foods~~ [food]. One of my ~~sister~~ [sister's] always makes a pumpkin pie. Her husband always makes ~~a~~ cookies
10.   11.   12.   13.

in the shape of turkeys. My other sister makes cranberry sauce. She uses a lot of ~~sugars~~ [sugar], and sometimes it's
14.

too ~~much~~ [much] sweet, but I never say anything. My brother doesn't like to cook, so he brings a lot [of] fresh fruit. My cousin
15.   16.

brings about 10 big bottles [of] soda. I prepare the sweet potatoes [C]. My mother always makes the turkey. It takes
17.   18.

much time to cook a big turkey.
19.

We have a lot [C] to prepare before Thanksgiving. My mother has very little [C] time the week before because of her
20.   21.

job. But I have a lot of [C] because I don't have ~~no~~ [any] ~~homeworks~~ [homework] that week. So I clean the house. My father likes to help,
22.   23.   24.

but he has very few [little] experience in the kitchen, so my mother asks him to do the shopping. He doesn't have much [C]
25.   26.

experience shopping either, so she always gives him ~~an~~ advice about shopping.
27.

It's always fun to spend Thanksgiving with too many [so many] people. But there's [C] one thing I don't like: ~~are~~ [there are] always a
28.   29.   30.

lot of dishes [C] to wash afterwards.
31.

WRITING TIP

There is/There are is a useful structure when you write a description. If you choose prompt 1 below, you can use *there is/are* to introduce food, clothing, and other traditions (e.g., *There is one main food everyone prepares for Thanksgiving.*). If you choose prompt 2, you can use *there are* to introduce different ethnic minorities in your country and then focus on one (e.g., *There are many ethnic minorities in Vietnam. The largest ethnic group is. . .*).

PART 3 Write

Read the prompts. Choose one and write a paragraph about it.

1. Write about a holiday celebration in your country. You may write about food, clothing, preparations, customs, etc. Use expressions of quantity.
2. Write about an ethnic minority in your native country or another country you know about. Where and how do these people live? Use expressions of quantity.

PART 4 Edit

Reread the Summary of Unit 5 and the editing advice. Edit your writing from Part 3.

Modifiers
Adverbs

Forest bathing in Jedediah Smith
Redwoods State Park, California, U.S.

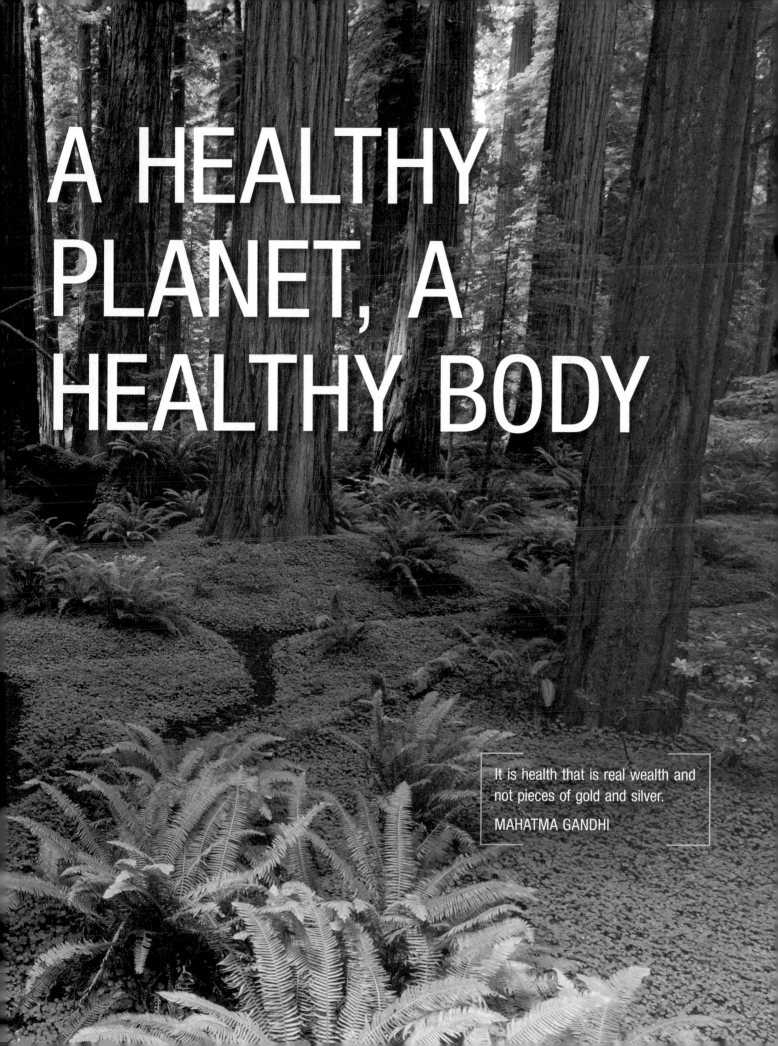

A HEALTHY PLANET, A HEALTHY BODY

It is health that is real wealth and not pieces of gold and silver.

MAHATMA GANDHI

Feeding the Planet

An increasing demand for meat and dairy puts pressure on the planet.

Read the following article. Pay special attention to the words in bold. 🎧 6.1

Can you name some things that harm our environment? If you said cars, you're **right**. If you said smoke from **large** factories, well, that's a **big** part of the problem, too. But maybe you didn't think of something in your **daily** life: your dinner. Agriculture, which produces your food, is more **harmful** to the environment than cars, trucks, trains, and airplanes combined. **Today's** farming uses our **water** supplies inefficiently[1]. Chemicals used on farms run into rivers and lakes and pollute[2] them. When **rain forests** and **grassland** are cleared for **farm** animals and crops, the result is often the extinction[3] of **wildlife**[4]. **Farming** methods release **harmful** gases into the air. These gases are an **enormous** contributor to **global** warming.

By 2050, the **world** population will be 9 billion, 2 billion more than it is today. Because of **population** growth, the problem of feeding so many people is **huge**. There will be a **growing** need for food all over the world. As countries such as China and India continue to become more **prosperous**[5], there is an **increasing** demand for meat, eggs, and dairy.

How can we increase the amount of food and maintain a **healthy** planet? Here are some solutions.

1. It is **important** to stop cutting down forests for agriculture. This is very **destructive** to the environment.

2. We don't need to eat so much meat. Producing meat wastes **valuable** resources and contributes to **global** warming.

3. We must stop wasting food. In **rich** countries, about 50 percent of food goes in the trash. In **poor** countries, a lot of food is lost between the farmer and the market because storage and transportation are not **efficient.**

It won't be **easy** to make these changes, but if we don't try, the result will be **terrible** for **future** generations. All of us have to be **thoughtful** about the connection between the food on our plates, the farmers that produce it, and the effect on the planet. As we push our **shopping** carts down the aisles of our supermarkets, our **food** choices will decide our future.

---

[1] inefficiently: in a way that is not productive or economical
[2] to pollute: to contaminate, make impure or dirty
[3] extinction: the state of no longer living or existing
[4] wildlife: animals living in their natural setting
[5] prosperous: wealthy

COMPREHENSION Based on the reading, write T for *true* or F for *false*.

1. __F__ Agriculture can cause a lot of harm to the planet.

2. __F__ Rain forests cause a lot of harm to the planet.

3. __T__ If we eat less meat, this will be better for the planet.

THINK ABOUT IT Discuss the questions with a partner or in a small group.

1. In your opinion, which is more important: feeding the population or maintaining a healthy planet? Explain.

2. Read the last line of the article again. Think about how you eat and shop for food. What choices can you make to help the environment?

6.1 Modifying a Noun

EXAMPLES	EXPLANATION
Food is part of our **daily** life. We shouldn't waste **valuable** resources.	An adjective can modify or describe a noun. (*Daily* and *valuable* are adjectives.)
Population growth is a problem. Our **food** choices affect the environment.	A noun can modify or describe another noun. (*Population* and *food* are nouns.)

EXERCISE 1 Listen to the paragraphs. Then write T for *true* or F for *false*. 🎧 6.2

1. __F__ One in ten American children is overweight.

2. __F__ Today's lifestyle includes a lot of physical activity.

3. __T__ More kids biked to school in the late 1960s than they do now.

EXERCISE 2 Listen again and fill in the blanks with the words you hear. 🎧 6.2

We know that it's ___important___ to eat well and get ___enough___ exercise.
1.   2.

Health clubs are ___full___ of people trying to get in shape. Sales of ___low___-
3.   4.

calorie foods show that Americans want to be ___thin___. However, two-thirds of
5.

___American___ adults are ___overweight___. One in three American children is
6.   7.

overweight. Weight is becoming a ___national___ problem as ___health___ costs go
8.   9.

up because of diseases related to obesity: ___heart___ disease, stroke, diabetes, and
10.

___high___ blood pressure.
11.

What is the reason for this ___growing___ problem? First, today's lifestyle does not include
12.

enough ___physical___ activity. When the United States was an ___agricultural___
13.   14.

society, farmers ate a ___big___ meal, but they also worked hard in the fields.
15.

continued

Modern technology removes _hard physical_ activity from our _daily_ lives. Most trips are _short_, within _walking_ distance of home, but most Americans drive. Only 13 percent of schoolchildren walk or bike to a school. Compare this to 48 percent in 1969. The _average_ American child spends about 35 hours a week watching TV. Kids are not _active_ enough. _today's_ kids may be the first generation to have a shorter _life_ expectancy than their parents.

6.2 Adjectives

EXAMPLES	EXPLANATION
Rich countries waste food. **Large** factories cause pollution.	An adjective can come before a noun.
We all want to have **healthy, active** kids. We all want to have **active, healthy** kids.	Two adjectives can come before a noun. We separate the adjectives with a comma when we can change the order of the adjectives without changing the meaning.
We don't do **hard physical** labor anymore. NOT: We don't do **physical hard** labor anymore.	We don't use a comma if we can't reverse the order of the adjectives.
The problem is **huge.** Feeding 9 billion people seems almost **impossible.**	An adjective can come after _be, seem,_ and the sense-perception verbs: _look, sound, smell, taste,_ and _feel._
It is important to protect the planet. **It won't be easy** to solve the problem.	An adjective can come after impersonal expressions beginning with _it._
Are you **concerned** about the future? Scientists are **interested** in finding a solution.	Some _-ed_ words are adjectives: _tired, worried, located, crowded, married, divorced, excited, disappointed, finished,_ and _frightened._
We read an **interesting** article about farming. I learned **surprising** information about our food.	Some _-ing_ words are adjectives: _amazing, exciting, boring, increasing, disappointing, frightening,_ and _growing._
It is **extremely** important to find a solution. This is a **very** difficult problem.	_Very, so, quite,_ and _extremely_ can come before adjectives.
Is farming a problem? Yes, it is a huge **one.** Do you have any ideas about how to protect the planet? There are some good **ones** in the article.	After an adjective, we can substitute a singular noun with _one_ and a plural noun with _ones._

Note:
We don't make an adjective plural.
    a **big** farm   **big** farms

GRAMMAR IN USE

In conversation, we often use informal modifiers before adjectives to express degree. Some of these words and phrases are: _pretty, sort of, kind of, really,_ and _real._ It's better not to use these in academic writing.

    I was **kind of** surprised by the article.

    The food situation sounds **really** bad.

EXERCISE 3 Fill in blanks with one of the words from the box.

growing	tired	healthy	greasy	worried	sweet	high✓
important	ones	sick	one	rich	busy	valuable

1. Burgers and fries are _____high_____ in calories.

2. It is _____important_____ to have a good diet.

3. Fries are cooked in oil. They are very _____greasy_____.

4. If you don't eat a healthy diet, you can get _____sick_____.

5. Some people eat a big breakfast. Others eat a small _____one_____.

6. Are you _____worried_____ about the future of the planet?

7. Children need to get enough sleep. It's not good to be _____tired_____ in school.

8. Cookies are very _____sweet_____.

9. Most Americans have _____busy_____ lives and don't make the time to eat well.

10. Obesity is a _____growing_____ problem. It is a bigger problem today than it was years ago.

11. We need to have a _____healthy_____ body.

12. In _____rich_____ countries, many people waste food. In poor _____ones_____, there is not enough food.

13. We shouldn't waste _____valuable_____ resources.

Students at the 24th Street School in Los Angeles, California, U.S., learn the importance of fresh food.

EXERCISE 4 Circle the correct words to complete this conversation between a husband and wife.

A: We're gaining weight. When we were younger, we used to be (*thin*/*thins*), but now that we're

1.

(*marry*/*married*), we're getting fat.

2.

B: Let's go jogging after work. There's a (*beautiful park*/*park beautiful*) where we can go.

3.

It's (*locate*/*located*) just a few blocks from our apartment.

4.

A: But after work I'm always too (*tire*/*tired*). I just want to eat dinner and watch TV.

5.

B: It's not good to eat a big meal so late at night. In many countries, people eat a big meal during the day and

(*a small one*/*a small*) at night. If we do that, we have the rest of the day to burn off the calories.

6.

A: I'm sure that's (*an idea very good*/*a very good idea*), but I don't have time to eat a big meal in the middle

7.

of the day.

B: We're always eating out in (*expensive*/*expensives*) restaurants. We should cook more at home. And we

8.

should go for a walk after dinner.

A: Good idea. Let's cook steaks tonight.

B: We need to eat less meat. Meat production is (*harm*/*harmful*) to the planet. It contributes to

9.

(*globe*/*global*) warming. I read (*an article very interesting*/*a very interesting article*) about it today.

10.   11.

A: You're right. Let's eat fish tonight.

Preparing food yourself
gives you more control
over your health.

6.3 Noun Modifiers

EXAMPLES	EXPLANATION
The **world** population is increasing. **Population** growth is a problem.	A noun can modify (describe) another noun. When two nouns come together, the first one modifies the second.
We use a **shopping** cart in a supermarket. **Farming** methods produce gas.	Sometimes a gerund (-*ing* word) describes a noun.
Potato chips have a lot of grease. My **five-year-old** son prefers candy to fruit.	The first noun is always singular. When we use a number before the noun, we usually attach it to the noun with a hyphen.
Very few **schoolchildren** walk to school. Do you have a healthy **lifestyle**?	Sometimes we write the two nouns as one word. The noun modifier and the noun become a compound word.
Today's lifestyle doesn't include much physical activity. Everyone needs a good **night's** sleep.	Sometimes a possessive noun describes a noun, especially with time words.

Pronunciation Note:

When a noun describes another noun, the first noun usually receives the greater emphasis in speaking.

I wear my __running__ shoes when I go to the __health__ club and use the __exercise__ machines.

EXERCISE 5 Fill in the blanks with one of the words from the box.

rain	world	population✓	health	shopping
farm	walking	heart	food	cow

1. ___Population___ growth is a big problem.

2. The ___World___ population will be 9 billion in 2050.

3. When we shop at the supermarket, we need to make healthy ___food___ choices.

4. When we shop, we usually use a ___shopping___ cart.

5. Some people go to ___health___ clubs to exercise.

6. One result of a poor diet is ___heart___ disease.

7. Many children live within ___walking___ distance from their schools, but they go by bus or car.

8. Cows and pigs are ___farm___ animals.

9. Cutting down ___rain___ forests is harmful to the environment.

10. Some people are allergic to ___cow___ milk.

EXERCISE 6 Fill in the blanks to complete this conversation between a mother and her son. Put the words given in the correct order. Remember to use the singular form for the first noun. Some answers are compound words.

A: We need a lot of things today. Let's take a _____ shopping cart _____.
1. cart/shopping

B: Can I sit in the _____ child seat _____?
2. child/seat

A: You're much too big. You're a six- _____ years-old _____ boy.
3. years/old

B: Mom, please buy me that cereal. It looks good. I saw it on a _____ TV commercial _____.
4. commercial/TV

A: Let's read the ingredients on the _____ cereal box _____ first. I want to see the
5. cereal/box

_____ sugar content _____ before we buy it. Let me put on my _____ eyeglasses _____.
6. content/sugar   7. glasses/eyes

Oh, dear. This cereal has 20 grams of sugar.

B: But I like sugar, Mom.

A: You know sugar is bad for your teeth. Remember what the dentist told you?

B: But I brush my teeth once a day.

A: I want you to use your _____ toothbrush _____ after every meal, not just once a day.
8. teeth/brush

B: Mom, can we buy those _____ potato chips _____?
9. chips/potatoes

A: They have too much fat.

B: How about some soda?

A: You should drink more juice. How about some _____ orange juice _____?
10. juice/oranges

B: I don't like juice.

A: Let's get in the _____ check-out line _____ and pay now. Maybe we should shop at the
11. line/check-out

_____ health food _____ store next time.
12. food/health

ABOUT YOU Make a list of things you usually have in your refrigerator. Compare your list to a partner's.

orange juice, low-fat milk
_____
_____

FUN WITH GRAMMAR

Describe your world. Write these words on a sheet of paper, numbered 1–10: *bag, building, daily, food, hard, health, room, school, shopping, world.* Then write sentences using the words as modifiers, e.g., *health* → *My brother has health problems.* You will have 10 minutes for this task. It is not a race to see who is fastest. The goal is to get the most correct answers.

The Happiest City in the U.S.

Read the following article. Pay special attention to the words in bold. 🎧 6.3

A recent study identified Boulder, Colorado, as the happiest city in the United States. Why are people in Boulder **mostly** happy with their lives? Here are three reasons.

❶ They are healthy.

When people eat **well** and exercise **regularly**, their health improves and their happiness increases, studies show.

In Boulder, there are many ways to eat **healthily**. The city has weekly farmers' markets which sell fresh fruit and vegetables. There are lots of healthy restaurants and food stores to choose from, too.

People in Boulder are also **physically** active. There are walking and bike paths throughout the city, so people can get around **easily** on foot or by bike. The city is also surrounded by a lot of natural beauty, including the Rocky Mountains, which are great for hiking, biking, and skiing. And the weather is **rarely** bad in Boulder, so people can spend a lot of time outside. Access to fresh air and sunshine can **greatly** improve people's health and happiness.

❷ They live in a small, friendly community.

The city of Boulder has about 107,000 people. Many residents know each other, and they socialize **regularly**. People in shops and cafes often greet you **in a friendly way**, too. Also, there is **hardly** any crime in Boulder, so people can walk the streets **safely** day and night.

❸ They can live **comfortably**.

In Boulder, many jobs pay **well**. People work **hard**, but **occasionally** they can take vacations and relax. This is good for their health and happiness.

Things are changing **fast**, though. Until **recently**, people could live **very cheaply** in Boulder. But today, more big companies are moving into the area, and the cost of living (housing, food, and education) has increased **dramatically**[1]. As a result, almost half of Boulder's residents feel stressed more **frequently** now.

---

[1] dramatically: a lot, greatly

Boulder, Colorado

Many of Boulder's residents are happy because they are able to spend a lot of time outdoors.

COMPREHENSION Based on the reading, write T for *true* or F for *false*.

1. __T__ The weather in Boulder is good, so people can be outside often.

2. __T__ Because Boulder isn't very big, many people know each other, and crime is low.

3. __F__ You can live very cheaply in Boulder.

THINK ABOUT IT Discuss the questions with a partner or in a small group.

1. People are happy in Boulder for three reasons. What are they? Explain each reason. Are these things true about your city?

2. What do you think of Boulder? Complete the sentence with your opinion. Then explain it.

   I would/wouldn't like to live in Boulder because…

6.4 Adverbs

EXAMPLES			EXPLANATION
subject	**verb phrase**	**adverb of manner**	An adverb of manner tells *how* or *in what way* the subject does something. We form most adverbs of manner by putting *-ly* at the end of an adjective. An adverb of manner usually follows the verb phrase.
You	can walk at night	**safely**.	
People	can live	**comfortably**.	
Costs	have increased	**dramatically**.	
Fresh air and sunshine **greatly** improve your health. Boulder residents socialize **regularly**. Many people feel stressed **frequently** now.			Other common *-ly* adverbs are: *eventually, annually, (in)frequently, certainly, greatly, suddenly, recently, directly, completely, generally, repeatedly, naturally, finally, probably, (un)fortunately, extremely, constantly.*
In Boulder, many jobs pay **well**.			The adverb for *good* is *well*.
People in Boulder are **physically** active. The weather is **rarely** bad in Boulder.			An adverb can come before an adjective.
adjective		**adverb**	Some adjectives and adverbs have the same form: *hard, fast, early, and late.* (The *-ly* in *early* is not an adverb ending.)
Residents are **hard** workers.		They work **hard**.	
He has a **fast** car.		His car goes **fast**.	
We had a **late** lunch.		We at lunch **late**.	
We went for an **early** hike.		We went for a hike **early**.	
She worked **hard** so she could live in Boulder. I **hardly** know my neighbors. There is **hardly** any crime in Boulder.			*Hard* and *hardly* are both adverbs, but they have completely different meanings. *She worked* **hard** means she put a lot of effort into the work. *Hard* comes after the verb phrase. *Hardly* means "very little" or "almost no." *Hardly* comes before many verbs, but it comes after a *be* verb.
He came home **late** from school. **Lately**, people are feeling more stress in Boulder. People are feeling more stress in Boulder **lately**.			*Late* and *lately* are both adverbs, but they have completely different meanings. *Late* means "not on time." It comes after the verb phrase. *Lately* means "recently." It comes at the beginning or end of the sentence.

She is a **friendly** person. She behaves **in a friendly manner**. He is a **lively** person. He dances **in a lively way**.	Some adjectives end in *-ly*: *lovely, lonely, friendly, lively,* and *ugly*. They have no adverb form. With these adjectives, we use an adverbial phrase (*in a _____-ly way/ manner*) to describe the action.
We gain weight **very** easily. She cooks **extremely** well. He eats **so** fast. She exercises **really** hard. You eat **quite** slowly.	*Very, extremely, so, really,* and *quite* can come before an adverb.

Note:

Though not grammatically correct, in conversation people often shorten *really* to *real*.

   *She exercises **real** hard.*

EXERCISE 7 Complete the sentences with an adverb from the box. Use each word only once.

hard	hardly ✓	honestly	neatly
quickly	regularly	very	well

A Tidy* and Happy Home

Our homes are filled with things we ____hardly____ ever use: old clothes, books,
                                      1.

papers, electronics. We try ___hard___ to throw away these items, but it's difficult. As a
                            2.

result, our homes become messy ___very___ ___quickly___ .
                                3.   **4.**

   What can we do? Marie Kondo, the author of the book *The Life-Changing Magic of Tidying*

Up, has a suggestion. Begin with your clothes. Look at each item in your closet and drawers.

First, ask yourself: Do I use this item ___regularly___? (For example, do I wear this sweater
                                        5.

often?) Also ask: Does this item make me happy? Then answer ___honestly___. If you say
                                                             6.

yes, keep the item. If you say *no,* donate it or throw it away. For the clothes you keep, fold or hang

them ___neatly___. When you are done, you will only have clothes that look good and fit
       7.

___well___ — and you will be happier.
  8.

*tidy: clean and organized

ABOUT YOU Write the adverb form of the word given. Then check (✓) the activities that you do in this way. Make statements telling how you do these activities, and explain them to a partner.

Ten Ways to Be Happy

1. __✓__ exercise __regularly__
   regular

   I exercise regularly. I go to the gym three times a week. OR

   I don't exercise regularly. I sit a lot. I hardly ever go to the gym.

2. __✓__ eat __well__
   good

3. __✓__ socialize with others __frequently__
   frequent

4. __✓__ spend time in nature __occasionally__
   occasional

5. __✓__ sleep seven or eight hours a night; don't stay up __late__ often
   late

6. __✓__ think __positively__ about most things
   positive

7. _____ treat others __nicely__
   nice

8. _____ work __hard__ but take breaks, too
   hard

9. _____ smile __happily__ at least once a day
   happy

10. _____ disconnect __completely__ from digital devices for an hour a day
   complete

6.5 Adjectives vs. Adverbs

An adjective describes a noun. An adverb describes a verb (phrase), an adjective, or another adverb.

EXAMPLES	EXPLANATION
Boulder is **easy** to get around on foot. You can get around **easily** on foot.	*Easy* is an adjective. It describes a noun—in this case, *Boulder*. *Easily* is an adverb of manner. It tells how you can go from place to place.
People in Boulder **seem happy**. I **felt great** after the hike. People always smile **happily**. The hike **greatly** improved my mood.	We use an adjective, not an adverb, after the following verbs if we are describing the subject: *smell, sound, taste, look, seem, appear,* and *feel*. We use an adverb of manner if we are describing *how* the action (the verb phrase) is done.
If you don't eat well, you can **get sick**. They **got hungry** during the hike.	We use an adjective, not an adverb, in expressions with *get*. Some expressions with *get* are *get hungry, get tired, get sick,* and *get rich*.
He's sick. He doesn't feel **well** today.	For health, we use *well*.
Boulder residents are **really** healthy. They exercise and eat **very** well.	We use an adverb before an adjective or another adverb.
As usual, they went to the farmers' market on Saturday.	We use the adjective, not the adverb, in the expression *as usual*.

EXERCISE 8 Fill in the blanks with the correct adjective or adverb form of the word given.

Here are three tips for living a ___happy___ and _____ life.
1. happy   2. healthy

Tip 1: Exercise _____. Being _____ active can _____ improve
3. regular   4. physical   5. great

how you look and feel. _____ exercise also helps you sleep better.
6. Regular

Tip 2: When you get _____ between meals, skip the junk food (like potato chips and
7. hungry

cookies). Instead, eat fruit or some nuts. Junk food tastes _____, and it's OK to eat
8. good

_____. But in large amounts, it is _____ for your health.
9. occasional   10. bad

Tip 3: Learn to cook. At one university, nutritionists _____ interviewed students about their
11. recent

diets. Many students said they _____ ate any vegetables each week because they work
12. hard

_____ all day, and they are too _____ to shop or cook. These students
13. hard   14. tired

_____ ate fast foods (such as instant noodles or pizza). Because they didn't eat
15. frequent

_____, they got _____ often. But then the students started cooking
16. good   17. sick

their own meals, and their health improved _____.
18. dramatic

ABOUT YOU Answer the questions. Discuss your answers with a partner.

1. How often do you exercise (hardly ever, occasionally, regularly)?

_____

2. When you get hungry and want a snack, what do you eat? Is it healthy? How do you feel after eating it?

_____

3. In your country, do people generally eat well or poorly? How about in the United States?

_____

A GOOD NIGHT'S SLEEP

Mike Wallace takes part in a sleep study at Johns Hopkins University in Baltimore, Maryland, U.S.

Read the following article. Pay special attention to the words in bold. 🎧 6.4

Most people need seven to nine hours of sleep. But most Americans sleep less than seven hours a night. When people aren't **rested enough**, there may be a bad result. For example, if people drive when they're **too tired**, they can cause serious accidents on the road. According to the National Transportation Administration, sleepy drivers cause 100,000 accidents each year. Airplane safety also depends on well-rested pilots. An airplane crash in 2009 killed all the passengers. The National Transportation Safety Board concluded that the pilots were **too sleepy** to make good decisions.

Sleep is **very** important to our health. In experiments with rats, where the rats were not allowed to sleep, all of them were dead in about two weeks. More studies on sleep are needed, but scientists complain that they don't receive **enough money** for sleep research.

If sleep is so important, why don't we try to go to bed earlier and get at least eight hours of sleep? About 20 percent of Americans say that they don't get **enough sleep**. Are we **too busy**? Not always.

Besides job and family responsibilities, Americans have a lot of other things that keep them out of bed. Twenty-four-hour-a-day Internet and TV and all-night supermarkets can take away from our sleep time.

What can we do to improve our sleep? Sleep experts have some recommendations:

- Don't nap during the day.
- Sleep in a dark room. **Too much light** in a room can harm sleep.
- Try not to have **too much stress** in your life.
- Don't get **too stimulated** before going to bed. Avoid activities such as watching TV or eating before bed.
- Go to bed at the same time every night.
- Avoid caffeine after lunchtime. If you drink **too much coffee** during the day, don't expect to get a good night's sleep.
- Exercise. Physical activity is **very good** for sleep. But if you exercise **too late** in the day, it will interfere with your sleep.

A good night's sleep is **very important**, so turn off the TV, shut down the computer, put away your devices, and sleep well.

COMPREHENSION Based on the reading, write T for *true* or F for *false*.

1. _F_ Most people get seven to nine hours of sleep.
2. _T_ Scientists did sleep experiments with rats.
3. _T_ A lot of money goes into research for sleep experiments.

THINK ABOUT IT Discuss the questions with a partner or in a small group.

1. What do you think scientists measure in a sleep study?

2. Do you do any of the things that sleep experts recommend that you don't do? How could improve your sleep habits?

6.6 *Too, Too Much, Too Many*, and *Enough*

EXAMPLES	EXPLANATION
The pilot was **too sleepy** to fly the airplane. You work **too hard** and don't relax.	We put *too* before adjectives and adverbs. *Too* indicates a problem.
You spend **too much time** on the computer.	We put *too much* before a noncount noun.
You spend **too many hours** watching TV.	We put *too many* before a count noun.
He doesn't sleep well because he worries **too much**.	We put *too much* at the end of the verb phrase.
Five hours of sleep is not **good enough**. You worked **hard enough**. Get some rest now.	We put *enough* after adjectives and adverbs.
Some people don't get **enough exercise**. Do you get **enough hours** of sleep?	We put *enough* before noncount and count nouns.

Note:
An infinitive can follow a phrase with *too* and *enough*.

> I'm too tired **to drive**.
> I don't have enough time **to exercise**.

GRAMMAR IN USE

Too + adjective indicates that there is too much of something and usually has a negative connotation (e.g., *That watch is too expensive.*). Sometimes we use *too* with certain positive adjectives to emphasize the feeling (e.g., *You're too kind. She's too generous.*). Such statements don't suggest a problem. They just bring attention to a large amount of something.

EXERCISE 9 Fill in the blanks with *too, too much, too many,* or *enough.*

1. Are Americans _____ too _____ busy to get a good night's sleep?

2. Some people don't get _____ enough _____ exercise because of their busy lives.

3. It's hard to sleep if you exercise _____ too _____ late in the evening.

4. If you're _____ too _____ tired when you drive, you can cause an accident.

5. Some people spend _____ too much time on the Internet. They should put away

   their electronic devices and go to bed.

6. If you drink _____ too much coffee, it can affect your sleep.

7. People drive everywhere. They don't walk _____ enough _____.

8. Try not to eat _____ too much before you go to bed.

9. Children shouldn't drink so much soda because it contains _____ too much _____ sugar.

10. We need to think about the future. We need to make sure there is _____ enough _____ food for the

    nine billion people on the planet in 2050.

11. Don't eat _____ too much meat. Try eating fish or chicken a few times a week.

ABOUT YOU Find a partner and discuss your answers to these questions.

1. How many hours do you sleep a night?

2. How many hours is enough for you?

6.7 *Too* and *Very*

EXAMPLES	EXPLANATION
We ate dinner **very** late last night. We arrived at the theater **too late**. We missed the beginning of the movie. My grandmother is 85. She's **very** old, but she's in great health. The child is six years old. He's **too** old to sit in a shopping cart.	Don't confuse *very* and *too*. *Too* indicates a problem. The problem can be stated or implied. *Very* is a neutral word. It does not indicate a problem.

Note:

We can use *a little* before *too*.

  *You woke up **a little too** late. You missed a great breakfast.*

EXERCISE 10 Fill in the blanks with *too* or *very* in this conversation between a husband and his wife.

A: I enjoyed the dinner _____ very _____ much.
1.

B: I'm glad you liked it. I worked _____ very _____ hard to prepare your favorite dishes.
2.

A: Thanks! Everything was great. But the soup was a little _____ too _____ salty.
3.

B: Oh. I thought you liked everything.

A: I did. Other than the salt, it was _____ very _____ good. And I especially liked the potatoes.
4.

B: I'm glad.

A: They were a little _____ too _____ greasy, but I ate them anyway.
5.

B: I'm afraid the meat was overcooked. I left it in the oven _____ too _____ long.
6.

A: Well, no one's perfect. I gave some to the dog.

B: What about the cake I made? Did you like that?

A: Yes. It was _____ very _____ good. The only problem was it was _____ too _____ small. I was
7. 8.

hoping to have another piece, but there was nothing left.

B: I thought you wanted to lose weight. You always say you're _____ too _____ fat and need to lose
9.

weight.

A: Fat? I'm not fat. I'm just right. But my clothes are _____ too _____ small. When I washed them, the
10.

water I used was _____ very _____ hot, and they shrank.
11.

B: They didn't shrink. You gained weight.

ABOUT YOU Write about some habits you wish to change to improve your health.
Discuss your sentences with a partner.

1. I don't get enough exercise. _____

2. I spend too much time online. _____

3. _____

4. _____

5. _____

SUMMARY OF UNIT 6

Adjectives and Adverbs

ADJECTIVES	ADVERBS
We had a **quick** lunch.	We ate **quickly**.
We had a **late** dinner.	We ate **late**.
She is a **good** cook.	She cooks **well**.
She looks **serious**.	She is looking at the label **seriously**.
As **usual**, he drank a cup of coffee.	He **usually** drinks coffee in the morning.

Adjective Modifiers and Noun Modifiers

ADJECTIVE MODIFIER	NOUN MODIFIER
a **new** machine	an **exercise** machine
old shoes	**running** shoes
a **short** vacation	a **two-week** vacation
big problems	**today's** problems

Very/Too/Enough/Too Much/Too Many

EXAMPLES	EXPLANATION
He's **very** healthy.	*very* + adjective
I slept **very** well.	*very* + adverb
I'm **too** sleepy.	*too* + adjective
It's **too** late to drive.	*too* + adverb
I'm rested **enough** to do my work.	verb + *enough*
Did you get **enough** sleep last night?	*enough* + noun
She doesn't eat ice cream because it has **too much** fat.	*too much* + noncount noun
She doesn't eat ice cream because it has **too many** calories.	*too many* + count noun
He loves coffee, but when he drinks **too much**, he can't sleep.	verb + *too much*

REVIEW

Choose the correct words to complete these sentences.

1. It's (*too*/*very*) important to get a good (*night*/*night's*) sleep.

2. Parents want their kids to eat (*good*/*well*).

3. We use a lot of resources to raise (*farm*/*farms*) animals.

4. Some farmers use chemicals to make cows grow (*fast*/*fastly*).

5. Farmers work very (*hard*/*hardly*).

6. If we use too (*much*/*many*) chemicals, we can harm the environment.

7. The (*world population*/*population world*) is increasing.

8. You seem (*sleepy*/*sleepily*). You shouldn't drive.

9. Did you get (*sleep enough*/*enough sleep*) last night?

10. I slept (*good*/*well*) last night.

11. I feel (*great*/*greatly*) today.

12. I took a two-(*hour*/*hours*) nap this afternoon.

13. Do you exercise (*regular*/*regularly*)?

14. Are you (*alert enough*/*enough alert*) to drive?

15. We ate dinner (*late*/*lately*) last night.

16. My grandfather's health is (*too*/*very*) good.

17. He's 75, but he looks like a 50-(*year*/*years*)-old man.

18. I'm always (*very*/*too*) tired to exercise after work.

19. Yesterday was an (*extreme*/*extremely*) hard day for me.

20. We like to go for a walk in the park near my house. It's (*very*/*too*) beautiful there.

21. Are you (*too*/*too much*) busy to exercise?

FROM GRAMMAR TO WRITING

PART 1 Editing Advice

1. Adjectives are always singular.

   People in poors countries don't eat a lot of meat.

2. Certain adjectives end with *-ed*.

   We're interest in taking care of the planet.
          ed

3. Put an adjective before the noun or after a linking verb, like *be*.

   She is a ~~woman very healthy~~. *OR* The woman is very healthy.
       very healthy woman

4. Use *one(s)* after an adjective to take the place of a noun.

   Do you prefer to sleep on a hard bed or a soft?
                             one

5. Put a specific noun before a general noun.

   We have to be careful about our ~~supply water~~.
                       water supply

6. A noun modifier is always singular.

   Don't eat so many potatoes chips.

7. An adverb of manner describes the action of a verb. An adjective describes a noun.

   I choose my food careful.
                   ly

   You seem seriously about exercise.

8. Don't put an *-ly* adverb of manner between the verb and the object.

   He read ~~carefully~~ the ingredients.
                  carefully

9. Adverbs of manner that don't end in *-ly* follow the verb phrase.

   He ~~late~~ came home.
              late

10. *Too* indicates a problem. If there is no problem, use *very*.

    Your father is ~~too~~ healthy.
            very

11. Don't use *too much* and *too many* before an adjective or adverb. Use *too*.

    She's too ~~much~~ tired to drive.

12. Put *enough* after the adjective.

    I'm ~~enough rested~~ to drive.
       rested enough

13. Don't confuse *hard* and *hardly*.

    I'm tired. I worked hardly all day.

    He's lazy. He hard worked at all.
                 ly

PART 2 Editing Practice

Some of the shaded words and phrases have mistakes. Find the mistakes and correct them. If the shaded words are correct, write C.

~~C~~   well   very

  I exercise regularly, and I eat very ~~good~~ most of the time. Luckily, I'm too healthy. I try to
      1.   **2.**   **3.**

eat a lot of fresh fruits and vegetables every day. I also eat a lot of wholes grains. I rarely eat
                         4.

C   fried chicken

red meat. I eat fish or chicken. But I rarely eat chicken fried because it's too much greasy. Most
5.   orange juice   **6.**   C   **7.**

mornings, I have a glass of juice orange and cereal. For lunch, I have a small meal, usually a
           8.   **9.**

C   C

tuna sandwich. For dinner, I like to eat a nice meal slowly. Most of the time, I cook dinner. But
10.   **11.**   tired

on Fridays, I have a three-hours biology course, and I late get home, so I'm too much tire to
       12.   **13.**   **14.** **15.**
                get home late

cook. Then I'm not very carefully about what I eat. My roommate offers me food, but he eats
          16.

C   C

very poorly. He often eats hamburgers and greasy fries from a fast-food place, or he brings home
17.   his food quickly **18.**

a sausage pizza. He eats quickly his food, and he drinks a lot of sweets drinks. He thinks it's
      19.   **20.**   **21.**

good enough

enough good, but I don't agree. When I eat with him, I don't eat very careful, and then I don't feel
22.   **23.** carefully

well the next day. I think it's important to have a diet very healthy. I'm going to try hardly to have
24. C   **25.**   **26.**
         a very healthy diet   hard

a better meal on Friday nights.

WRITING TIP

When comparing or contrasting, it is useful to use transition words to help connect ideas.

To show similarity, you can use transitions such as: *similarly, also, in comparison, as well, likewise,* and *like.*

 There is a lot of diverse food in the United States. **Likewise,** *in Canada people enjoy many different cuisines.*

To show difference, you can use transitions such as: *but, however, on the other hand, on the contrary, nevertheless,* and *unlike.*

 In the U.S., I eat bread every day. In Taiwan, **however,** *I ate rice instead.*

PART 3 Write

Read the prompts. Choose one and write a paragraph about it.

1. Compare food in your native culture to food in the United States.
2. Describe your eating habits today with your eating habits in your native country.

PART 4 Edit

Reread the Summary of Unit 6 and the editing advice. Edit your writing from Part 3.

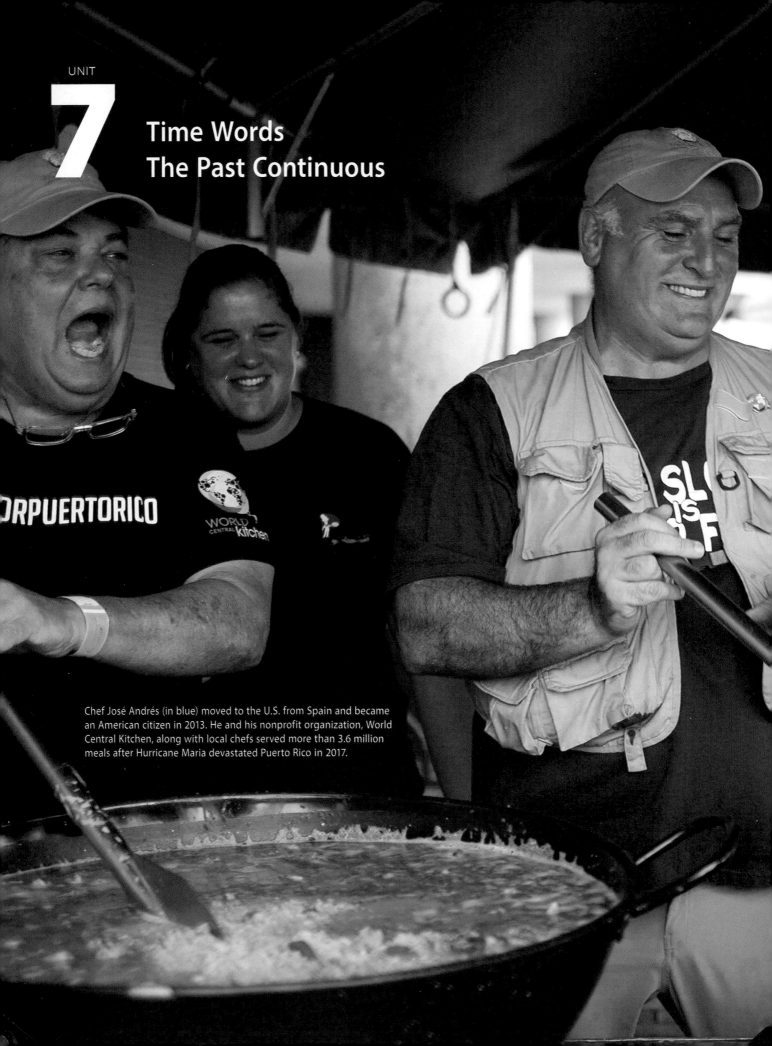

Chef José Andrés (in blue) moved to the U.S. from Spain and became an American citizen in 2013. He and his nonprofit organization, World Central Kitchen, along with local chefs served more than 3.6 million meals after Hurricane Maria devastated Puerto Rico in 2017.

A NEW START

Ellis Island

Immigrants arrive from Europe to Ellis Island around 1880.

Read the following article. Pay special attention to the words in bold. 🎧 7.1

In the 1800s, the United States experienced the largest human migration in the history of the world. As more and more immigrants came to the United States, it soon became clear that the original processing center was too small to handle such a large number. Ellis Island, in New York Harbor, was opened **on** January 1, 1892, as the new processing center. **When** the first passengers approached Ellis Island, they saw the new Statue of Liberty, which was only six years old.

The first person to enter Ellis Island was Annie Moore, a teenager from Ireland. **When** she got off the ship **after** traveling for 12 days with her two younger brothers, reporters were waiting to interview her. **After** she went through the registration process, an official gave her a 10-dollar gold coin. That day, 700 immigrants passed through Ellis Island.

During the early 1900s, immigration continued to grow. The largest number of immigrants came **in** 1907. Approximately 1.25 million immigrants came through that year.

For 62 years, Ellis Island was the main door through which millions of immigrants entered the United States. **From** the time it opened **in** 1892 **until** the time it closed

in 1954, Ellis Island processed 12 million immigrants. Sometimes more than 10,000 people passed through the registry room **in** one 24-hour period. New arrivals often waited **for** many hours **while** inspectors checked to see if they met legal and medical standards. Most did not speak English, and they were tired, hungry, and confused. Two percent (250,000 people) did not meet the requirements to enter the United States and had to return to their countries.

After it closed down, Ellis Island remained abandoned[1] **until** 1965, **when** President Lyndon Johnson decided to restore[2] it as a monument. Restoration of Ellis Island was finished **by** 1990. Visitors to this monument could see the building as it looked **from** 1918 **to** 1920. Almost two million people visited the Ellis Island monument each year **until** a storm damaged the building **in** 2012. Luckily, the exhibits did not suffer damage.

Almost half of Americans are descendants of immigrants who passed through Ellis Island many years **ago**.

---

1 abandoned: empty
2 to restore: to make something look like it did when it was new

COMPREHENSION Based on the reading, write T for *true* or F for *false*.

1. ___F___ Ellis Island was the first immigrant processing center in the United States.

2. ___T___ On the day Annie Moore arrived from Ireland, 700 immigrants passed through Ellis Island.

3. ___F___ Ellis Island processed 12 million immigrants in 1954.

THINK ABOUT IT Discuss the questions with a partner or in a small group.

1. What challenges did workers at Ellis Island face when ships arrived with large numbers of potential immigrants?

2. Imagine being a passenger on a ship approaching Ellis Island. You see the Statue of Liberty growing larger as you approach shore. Share how you feel. Include details of how old you are and why you are making this journey to America.

7.1 Time Words

TIME WORD	EXAMPLES	EXPLANATION
on	Ellis Island opened its doors **on** January 1, 1892.	We use *on* with a specific date or day.
in	Ellis Island opened **in** January. Ellis Island opened **in** 1892. **In** the early 1900s, many immigrants came to the U.S. My brother will come to the U.S. **in** two months.	We use *in*: • with a month. • with a year. • with a group of years. • to mean after a period of time.
during	**During** the early 1900s, many immigrants came to the U.S. The building at Ellis Island suffered damage **during** a storm in 2012.	We use *during* with a period of time (*the 1900s, the month of May*, etc.). We use *during* with an event (*the storm, the trip, the movie*, etc.).
for	**For** 62 years, Ellis Island was the main entrance for immigrants to the U.S.	We use *for* with a quantity of years, months, weeks, days, etc.
by	**By** 1990, restoration of Ellis Island was complete.	We use *by* to mean *up to and including a specific time*.
from . . . . . . to . . . till . . . until	Ellis Island was open **from** 1892 **to** 1954. Ellis Island was open **from** 1892 **till** 1954. Ellis Island was open **from** 1892 **until** 1954.	We use *from* with the starting time. We use *to, till*, or *until* with the ending time.
while	**While** they were restoring Ellis Island, it was closed.	We use *while* to mean *during that time*.
when	**When** Ellis Island opened on January 1, 1892, 700 people passed through.	We use *when* to mean *at that time* or *starting at that time*.
while *versus* during	New arrivals waited **while** inspectors checked their documents. New arrivals waited **during** the inspection.	We use *while* with a clause. (Clause = subject + verb) We use *during* with a noun (phrase).
until	Ellis Island remained closed **until** 1990.	We use *until* to mean *before that time and ending at that time*.
in *versus* after	I will become a citizen **in** two months. The plane will arrive **after** 9 p.m. My brother will come to the U.S. **after** he gets his visa.	We use *in* to mean *after a period of time*. We use *after* with a date, time, or action.
ago *versus* before	She got married three years **ago**. She got married **before** she came to the U.S. **Before** 1892, there was a different processing center.	We use *ago* to mean *before now*. We use *before* with an event, a date, or a time.

EXERCISE 1 Listen to this article about the Immigration Act of 1965. Fill in the blanks with the words you hear. 🎧 7.2

_____Until_____ 1892, the United States did not restrict any group of foreigners from
1.

coming as immigrants. But _____in_____ 1924, Congress passed a law to limit
2.

immigration. _____from_____ 1924 _____to_____ 1965, the United States had a quota
3.   4.

system. That means only a limited number of people could come from each country.

_____For_____ all those years, this system discriminated against certain foreigners.
5.

Northern and Western Europeans received preference over other nationalities. Asians, in

particular, were not welcome.

_____In_____ the 1960s, Americans started to see the quota system as a form of
6.

discrimination. _____While_____ President Kennedy was in office, he gave a speech about
7.

immigration restrictions. He called this system "intolerable." Members of Congress invited

experts to give their opinions. _____During_____ their discussions, they said that very little
8.

would change as a result of changing the law. Congress passed a bill to eliminate the quota

system. When President Johnson signed the bill into law _____On_____ October 3, 1965,
9.

he said, "It does not affect the lives of millions." But he was completely wrong.

_____In_____ the first five years _____after_____ the bill passed, immigration
10.   11.

from Asian countries increased by 400 percent _____In_____ the 1950s, six percent of
12.

immigrants were Asian. _____By_____ the 1990s, 31 percent of immigrants were from
13.

Asian countries. Other immigrants and political refugees started coming from Africa and Latin

America. _____By_____ the end of the twentieth century, there was a great change in the
14.

American population.

When we see the diversity in the United States today, it is hard to imagine that many years

_____ago_____, certain groups of people were not allowed into the United States.
15.

EXERCISE 2 Circle the correct time word to fill in the blanks.

1. I stayed in my country (until/by) I got a visa.

2. I applied for my visa (in/on) January.

3. I waited (for/from) January (till/at) June to get my visa.

4. I was very excited (*when*/*while*) I got my visa.

5. I got my visa five years (*before*/*ago*).

6. (*While*/*During*) my trip to the U.S., I couldn't sleep.

7. (*While*/*During*) I was on the airplane, I couldn't sleep.

8. I never thought about learning English (*by*/*until*) I applied for my visa.

9. I arrived in New York (*on*/*in*) July 4, 2014.

10. I was at the airport (*during*/*for*) three hours.

11. (*Until*/*By*) 3:30 p.m., I passed through immigration and customs and was ready to start my life in the U.S.

12. I hope my parents will come here (*in*/*after*) a few years.

13. I hope my parents will come here (*during*/*after*) they get their visas.

EXERCISE 3 Fill in the blanks with one of the time words from chart 7.1.

1. My grandfather came to the U.S. _____when_____ he was 36 years old.

2. My grandfather came to the U.S. many years ____ago____.

3. He lived in Poland ____until____ 1911.

4. He arrived at Ellis Island ____in____ May of 1911.

5. He was alone and scared. He was nervous ____While____ he was in line.

6. In Poland, he didn't study English. He didn't speak a word of English ____Until____ he started to work in the U.S. Then he learned a little.

7. My grandmother was without her husband ____from____ 1911 ____to____ 1921.

8. My grandfather worked ____for____ ten years to save money to bring his wife and children to the U.S. Finally, ____In____ 1921, he sent money to bring his family.

9. ____During____ the long trip, my aunt became sick.

10. My grandmother arrived with my mother and her siblings ____On____ August 13, 1921.

11. ____When____ the inspectors examined them, they decided to put my aunt in the hospital. My grandmother was afraid the officials would send them back.

12. ____By____ the end of the week, my aunt was better.

13. ____When____ my aunt felt better, she passed the health inspection. They all took a train to Chicago and started their new life there.

ABOUT YOU Complete each statement about leaving your country. Share your answers with a partner.

1. I stayed in my country until _I won the diversity lottery._

2. During my trip to the U.S., _we styed in Dubia for night_

3. I traveled for _18 hours._

4. While I was on the airplane/boat/road, _It was too cold and boring._

5. I arrived on _29/Dec/2016._

6. When I arrived, _we stayed in very small home._

7. I never knew _about US hard life._ until I came to the U.S.

7.2 *When* and *Whenever*

EXAMPLES	EXPLANATION
When I went to New York a few years ago, I visited Ellis Island.	*When* means *at that time* or *after that time*.
Whenever I go to New York, I enjoy myself.	*Whenever* means *any time* or *every time*.

Note:

In the present, *when* and *whenever* are often interchangeable.

> *When/Whenever my grandfather tells me about his life, I find it very interesting.*

EXERCISE 4 Add a main clause to complete each statement. Share your answers with a partner.

1. Whenever people travel by airplane, _they have to pass through security._

2. Whenever passengers pass through security, _they have to find their gate._

3. Whenever passengers are on an airplane, _they fly from country_

4. Whenever people fly to another country, _they will land new country_

5. Whenever immigrants come to the U.S., _they will have hard time at first._

6. Whenever I'm on an airplane, _I got sleep immediatly_

7. When I got my visa, _I will be happy_

8. When I arrived in the U.S., _I need to struggle to set my new life_

FUN WITH GRAMMAR

Create a story. Form groups of three. Your teacher will write five time words on the board. Each team will write a brief story correctly using those time words (e.g., *for*: Martin worked at the company for ten years.). Be creative! The group with the most interesting story and the most correct sentences wins. Be careful: some of these words can have an additional use other than a time word (e.g., This gift is *for* Mike.).

IMMIGRANTS:
Building Businesses and Communities

Read the following article. Pay special attention to the words in bold. 🎧 7.3

The United States is home to many immigrants and refugees who have come for different reasons. In 1994, Hamdi Ulukaya immigrated to the United States. **When** he **arrived** from Turkey with $3,000, he **was hoping** to learn English and find work. Today his Greek yogurt company, Chobani, has annual sales of about $1.5 billion and employs more than 2,000 people.

Mr. Ulukaya grew up in a small village in eastern Turkey. Many of the villagers were shepherds[1] who took their sheep, goats, and cows into the mountains when the weather was warm. They made yogurt and cheese from the milk. **When** he **was studying** business and English in New York state, he **had** the idea to start a feta cheese[2] company, making cheese from his family's recipe. Then he saw an ad for a yogurt factory for sale. He bought the factory and started a new company, Chobani, which means *shepherd* in Turkish.

In 2010, the company **was growing** and Ulukaya needed more employees. It was important to him to support the community around his factory. Many immigrants and refugees from Africa, Asia, and Eastern Europe **were living** in the area. They needed work and he needed workers. He gave them help with language, training, and transportation, and in return they worked hard. Years later, he opened the world's largest yogurt factory in Twin Falls, Idaho. He hired refugees from the community to work at the new factory. Today approximately 30 percent of his employees are immigrants or refugees. Ulukaya said, "The minute that they got the job, that's the minute they stopped being refugees." There are people from 19 different countries working at Chobani.

Ulukaya knew his employees **were working** hard, but they **were** still **struggling** to support their families. In 2016 he announced a profit-sharing program for employees, which is very rare in manufacturing. Mr. Ulukaya said, "I've built something I never thought would be such a success, but I cannot think of Chobani being built without all these people. Now they'll be working to build the company even more and building their future at the same time." **When** he **immigrated**, Ulukaya **was looking** for work. He created it not only for himself, but for many other immigrants, too.

---

[1] shepherd: a person who takes care of sheep
[2] feta cheese: cheese made from the milk of a goat or sheep

Hamdi Ulukaya, left, with employees in Twin Falls, Idaho, U.S.

COMPREHENSION Based on the reading, write T for *true* or F for *false*.

1. ___F___ Ulukaya came to the U.S. to start a business.
2. ___T___ Chobani employs many immigrants and refugees.
3. ___T___ Ulukaya shares his success with his employees.

THINK ABOUT IT Discuss the questions with a partner or in a small group.

1. What do you think Ulukaya's quote about refugees means?

2. Would you like to work at a company like Chobani? Complete the sentence with your opinion. Then explain it.

   I would/wouldn't like to work for Chobani because. . .

7.3 The Past Continuous—Form

To form the past continuous, we use *was* or *were* + the present participle (*-ing* form of the verb).

SUBJECT	WAS/WERE (+ NOT)	PRESENT PARTICIPLE	
I	was	reading	about immigrants.
He	was	studying	business.
You	were	asking	about Turkey.
They	were not	living	in Turkey.

Notes:

1. The contraction for *was not* is *wasn't*. The contraction for *were not* is *weren't*.
2. We can put an adverb between *was/were* and the present participle.

   *He was **already** studying English at that time.*
3. The past continuous is also called the past progressive.

Compare statements, *yes/no* questions, short answers, and *wh-* questions.

STATEMENT	YES/NO QUESTION & SHORT ANSWER	WH- QUESTION
They **were living** in Turkey in 2003.	**Were** they **living** in a home? No, they **weren't**.	Where **were** they **living**?
They **weren't living** in their country.	**Were** they **living** in a refugee camp? Yes, they **were**.	Why **were** they **living** in a refugee camp? Why **weren't** they **living** in their country?
A volunteer **was helping** them in the U.S.	**Was** the volunteer **helping** them with English? Yes, she **was**.	Who else **was helping** them?

EXERCISE 5 Listen to the conversation. Then write T for *true* or F for *false*. 🎧 7.4

1. __F__ The man was studying medicine when the war broke out.

2. __F__ He needed permission from the refugee agency to go to America.

3. __F__ The man was in the same refugee camp as his parents.

EXERCISE 6 Listen to the conversation again. Fill in the blanks with the words you hear. 🎧 7.4

A: Before you came to the U.S., _were you living_ with your parents?
   _{1.}

B: No, I __wasn't__ . I __was studying__ at a university in another city.
   _{2.}   _{3.}

A: What __were__ you __studying__ ?
   _{4.}   _{5.}

B: I __was planing__ to become a doctor, but a war broke out. I ran to a refugee camp in
   _{6.}

Kenya. While I __was living__ in the refugee camp, I tried to get information about my
   _{7.}

family back home, but I couldn't.

A: That's terrible. While you __were living__ in the refugee camp,
   _{8.}

__were__ you __planning__ to come to the U.S.?
   _{9.}   _{10.}

B: Of course, I __was thinking__ about it. I __was studying__ English with the hope
   _{11.}   _{12.}

of coming to the U.S. I didn't know if I would get permission. But finally the United Nations gave me permission.

A: Who __was waiting__ for you at the airport when you arrived?
   _{13.}

B: A man from a refugee agency. When I arrived, he __was holding__ a sign with my name on
   _{14.}

it. He could easily identify me because I __was wearing__ a name tag.
   _{15.}

A: Did you ever find your family?

B: Yes, I did. They __were living__ in a refugee camp in Zambia.
   _{16.}

EXERCISE 7 Fill in the blanks with the past continuous form of the verb given. In some cases, you just need to complete the short answer.

1.

A: I read an article about Annie Moore, the first immigrant to come to Ellis Island. Did you read it, too?

B: Yes. She __was traveling__ to the U.S. with her younger brothers.
   _{a. travel}

A: __were they traveling__ with their parents, too?
   _{b. they/travel}

B: No, they __weren't__ .
   _{c.}

A: Why __weren't they traveling__ with their parents?
   _{d. they/not/travel}

B: Their parents came to the U.S. first. They __were waiting__ for their children at Ellis Island.
   _{e. wait}

continued

Time Words, The Past Continuous 181

2.

A: What ___*were you doing*___ at about nine o'clock last night?

                  a. you/do

___*Were you sleeping*___? I called you and texted you, but you didn't answer.

          b. you/sleep

B: I ___*was watching*___ a program on TV about immigration.

              c. watch

I ___*was taking*___ notes because I want to write an essay about it.

           d. take

3.

A: My great-grandmother came through Ellis Island.

B: ___*She was traveling*___ alone?

             a. she/travel

A: No, she ___*wasn't*___. She was just a little girl. She

                 b.

___*was immigrating*___ to the U.S. with her parents and her brother. Her aunt

          c. immigrate

___*was already living*___ in the U.S.

        d. already/live

4.

A: Where ___*were you living*___ when you heard about the assassination of the

               a. you/live

president?

B: We ___*were living*___ in Rwanda.

            b. live

A: ___*Were you working*___?

      c. you/work

B: Yes, I ___*was*___.

              d.

A: Where ___*were you working*___?

          e. you/work

B: At a hospital. My wife was at home. She ___*was taking*___ care of the children.

                                          f. take

7.4 The Past Continuous with a Specific Time

EXAMPLES	EXPLANATION
In 1993, he **was working** in a hospital.	We use the past continuous to show what was in progress at a specific time in the past.

ABOUT YOU Find a partner. Tell your partner if the following things were happening in your life in January, 2019.

1. go to school

   I was (not) going to school in January 2019. I

2. work

   I was working in 2019

3. exercise

   I was exercing in 2019.

4. study English

   I was studying English 2019.

5. live in the U.S.

   I was living in the US 2019

6. live with my parents

   I was not living with

7. look for a new apartment

   I was not

8. go out every night with friends

   _____

9. travel

   _____

10. celebrate the New Year with friends

    _____

ABOUT YOU Find a partner. Ask each other questions with *What were you doing . . . ?* at these times.

1. at six o'clock this morning

   A: *What were you doing at six o'clock this morning?*

   B: *I was sleeping.*

2. at ten o'clock last night

3. at nine o'clock this morning

4. at five o'clock yesterday afternoon

5. at this time yesterday

6. at this time last year

7.5 The Past Continuous with a *When* Clause

EXAMPLE	EXPLANATION
He **was working** in a hospital **when** he **heard** the news.	We use the past continuous with the simple past in the same sentence to show the relationship of a longer past action to a shorter past action.
When Annie Moore **arrived** at Ellis Island in 1892, her parents **were waiting** for her.	We use *when* + the simple past in the clause with the shorter action. We use the past continuous in the clause with the longer action.

Note:

If the main clause precedes the time clause, do not separate the two clauses with a comma.

> He was working in a hospital when he heard the news.

If the time clause precedes the main clause, separate the two clauses with a comma.

> When he heard the news**,** he was working in a hospital.

GRAMMAR IN USE

The past continuous is used to recount events or tell stories. It helps set the scene and portray the mood. The past continuous can also build suspense, which then may be interrupted by an action in the story in the simple past.

> The wind **was howling,** and a fresh layer of snow **was** quickly **covering** everything in sight. One lonely car **was inching** along on the slippery road. Suddenly the car stopped . . .

EXERCISE 8 Use the past continuous for the longer action and the simple past for the shorter action.

1. She ___was traveling___ to the U.S. when she ___met___ her future husband.
   (travel)   (meet)

2. When I ___was arriving___ at the airport, my uncle ___was waiting___ for me.
   (arrive)   (wait)

3. They ___were living___ in a refugee camp when they ___got___ permission
   (live)   (get)
   to come to the U.S.

4. I ___was watching___ a program on TV about immigration when I ___fell___
   (watch)   (fall)
   asleep.

5. We ___were living___ in the U.S. when a war ___broke___ out in our country.
   (live)   (break)

6. My wife ___was taking___ care of the kids at home when we ___heard___ the
   (take)   (hear)
   news about the president.

7. When the first ship ___arrived___ at Ellis Island in 1892, reporters
   (arrive)
   ___were waiting___ to write about the arrival of the first immigrants there.
   (wait)

8. I ___was driving___ to the airport to pick up my aunt and uncle when I
   (drive)
   ___got___ a flat tire.
   (get)

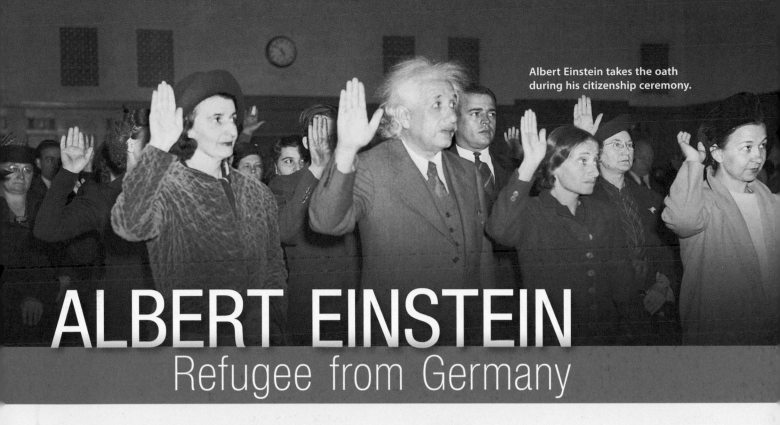

Albert Einstein takes the oath during his citizenship ceremony.

ALBERT EINSTEIN
Refugee from Germany

Read the following article. Pay special attention to the words in bold. 🎧 7.5

Of the many refugees who came to the United States, one will always be remembered throughout the world: Albert Einstein. Einstein changed our understanding of the universe.

Einstein was born in Germany in 1879 to Jewish parents. When he graduated from college in Switzerland in 1900, he was planning to become a teacher of physics and math, but he couldn't find a job in those fields. Instead, he went to work in a patent[1] office as a technical expert from 1902 to 1909. **While** he **was working** at this job, he **studied** and **wrote** in his spare[2] time. In 1905, when he was only 26 years old, he published three papers about the basic structure of the universe. His theory of relativity explained the relationship of space and time. He returned to Germany to accept a research position at the University of Berlin. However, in 1920, **while** he **was lecturing** at the university,

anti-Jewish groups often **interrupted** his lectures, saying they were "un-German."

In 1921, Einstein visited the United States for the first time. During his visit, he talked not only about his scientific theories, but also about world peace. **While** he **was traveling** outside the country in 1933, the Nazis **came** to power in Germany. They took his property, burned his books, and removed him from his university job.

The United States offered Einstein refugee status, and, in 1940, he became a U.S. citizen. He received many job offers from all over the world, but he decided to accept a position at Princeton University in New Jersey. He lived and worked there until he died in 1955.

_____

[1] patent: a document that identifies the owner of a new invention. Only the person or company who has the patent can sell the invention.

[2] spare: free

COMPREHENSION Based on the reading, write T for *true* or F for *false*.

1. _____ Einstein taught math and physics while he was living in Switzerland.

2. _____ In 1933, Einstein returned to his university job in Germany.

3. _____ Einstein developed his theory of relativity while he was living in the United States.

1. Do you think Einstein faced the same difficulties as other refugees who came to the United States? Why or why not?

2. Look at the photo of the citizenship ceremony. What does it make you think about?

7.6 The Past Continuous with a *While* Clause

EXAMPLES	EXPLANATION
While Einstein **was living** in Switzerland, he **developed** his theory of relativity. **While** Einstein **was traveling** outside of Germany, the Nazis **came** to power.	We use the past continuous with the simple past in the same sentence to show the relationship of a longer past action to a shorter past action. We use *while* + the past continuous in the clause with the longer action. We use the simple past in the clause with the shorter action.
Einstein was living in the U.S. **when** he **died.** **While** he **was living** in the U.S., he wrote many papers.	We use *when* + the simple past with the shorter action. We use *while* + the past continuous with the longer action.

Notes:

1. We can use *when* in place of *while* with a continuous action.

> *While* Einstein was living in Switzerland, he developed his theory.

> *When* Einstein was living in Switzerland, he developed his theory.

2. We cannot use *while* with an action that is not continuous.

> NOT: Einstein was living in the U.S. while he died.

3. The simple past form of *be* often has a continuous meaning.

> While Einstein **was** outside the country, the Nazis took his property.

4. We use the past continuous in both clauses if the two actions occurred at the same time.

> While Einstein **was working** at the patent office, he **was thinking** about his theory.

EXERCISE 9 Use the past continuous for the longer action and the simple past for the shorter action.

1. While I ___was traveling___ to the U.S., I _____met_____ a nice man on the airplane.

(travel)   (meet)

2. Einstein _____ about his theory of relativity while he _____

(write)   (work)

   in a patent office.

3. While he _____, some people _____ his lectures.

(teach)   (interrupt)

4. While I _____ the story about Einstein, I _____ to use my

(read)   (have)

   dictionary to look up the word "patent."

5. While I _____ for permission to come to the U.S., I _____ to
        wait   start

study English.

6. While the teacher _____ about immigration, one of the students
                      talk

_____ an interesting question.
        ask

7. I _____ a movie on the airplane while I _____ to the U.S.
      watch   travel

EXERCISE 10 Fill in the blanks with the simple past or the past continuous of the verb given to complete this conversation.

A: I __was looking__ through some old boxes when I _____ this picture of you and
        1. look   2. find

Grandpa when you were young. How did you meet Grandpa?

B: One day I _____ in the park in my hometown in Poland when he
                3. walk

_____ me to ask what time it was. We started to talk, and then he asked
        4. stop

me to go for a cup of coffee with him. We dated, but a few months later his family applied for the

green card lottery in the U.S. While we _____, they _____
                                          5. date   6. receive

a letter that gave them permission to immigrate to the U.S.

A: What happened next?

B: At first, I was worried that I'd never see your grandfather again. But he _____
                                                                              7. write

to me often and _____ me whenever he could. About a year later, he went back
                  8. call

to Poland to visit me. While we _____ in a restaurant, he
                                  9. eat

_____ me to marry him.
        10. ask

A: Did you get married right away?

B: Yes. We got married a few weeks later, but then he had to return to the U.S. I couldn't go to the U.S. with

him. I had to wait several years.

A: That's awful. What did you do while you _____?
                                            11. wait

B: I took English classes. Finally, I got permission to come. When I _____ at the
                                                                      12. arrive

airport, he _____ with roses and balloons.
              13. wait

7.7 The Simple Past vs. The Past Continuous with *When*

Both the simple past and the past continuous can be used in a sentence that has a *when* clause. However, the time sequence is completely different.

EXAMPLES	EXPLANATION
When Einstein **graduated** from college, he **tried** to get a job as a teacher. Einstein **came** to live in the U.S. **when** he **lost** his German citizenship.	If we use the simple past in both clauses, *when* means *after*.
When Einstein **entered** college, he **was living** in Switzerland. Einstein **was living** in the U.S. **when** he **died**.	If we use the simple past after *when* and the past continuous in the main clause, *when* means *at the same time*.

EXERCISE 11 Fill in the blanks with the simple past or the past continuous of the verb given.

1. Henri _____was living_____ in a refugee camp when he got his visa.

        live

   When he got to the U.S., he _____needed_____ to find a job.

        need

2. He _____ in a hospital when he heard the news about the president.

      work

   When he _____ permission, he came to the United States.

      get

3. When they arrived in the U.S., volunteers _____ them.

      help

   When they arrived in the U.S., a volunteer _____ for them at the airport.

      wait

4. They _____ in the U.S. when their fourth child was born.

      live

   When their fourth child was born, they _____ to a bigger apartment.

      move

5. When Henri learned enough English, he _____ to work in a hotel.

      start

   He _____ in a hotel when his daughter was born.

      work

6. Henri _____ morning English classes when he found a job.

      take

   Henri _____ to night classes when he found a job.

      change

7. When Einstein entered college, he _____ to become a teacher.

      study

   When Einstein entered college, he _____ in Switzerland.

      live

8. Einstein _____ a resident of the U.S. when he lost his German citizenship.

      become

   Einstein _____ in the U.S. when he died.

      live

7.8 Using the *-ing* Form after Time Words

When the main clause and the time clause have the same subject, we can delete the subject of the time clause and use a present participle (verb + *-ing*) after the time word.

EXAMPLES

1. Einstein left high school **before he finished** his studies.

   Einstein left high school **before finishing** his studies.

2. **After Einstein left** high school, he studied mathematics and physics.

   After leaving high school, Einstein studied mathematics and physics.

Note:

In the second set of examples above, notice that the subject (Einstein) becomes part of the main clause.

EXERCISE 12 Change these sentences. Use a present participle after the time word. Make any other necessary changes.

1. After ~~Einstein entered~~ *entering* the university, ~~he~~ *Einstein* developed his theory.

2. Einstein passed an exam before he entered the university.

3. He left high school before he received his diploma.

4. After Einstein developed his theory of relativity, he became famous.

5. He became interested in physics after he received books on science.

6. After Einstein came to the U.S., he got a job at Princeton.

7. Before he came to the U.S., Hamdi Ulukaya lived in Turkey.

8. While the children were living in the refugee camp, they didn't go to school.

9. The parents were working while they were raising a family.

SUMMARY OF UNIT 7

Time with Dates, Days, Time Periods, etc.

TIME WORD	EXAMPLES

from . . .
  to
  till
  until
	From 1892 **to** 1954, Ellis Island was an immigrant processing center.
	From 1892 **till** 1954, Ellis Island was an immigrant processing center.
	From 1892 **until** 1954, Ellis Island was an immigrant processing center.

during	**During** that time, 12 million immigrants passed through Ellis Island.
for	New arrivals had to wait **for** many hours.
in	**In** 1905, Einstein wrote about relativity. I became a resident **in** March. He'll take his citizenship test **in** six months.
by	Restoration of Ellis Island was finished **by** 1990.
ago	One hundred years **ago**, new arrivals passed through Ellis Island.
on	We came to the U.S. **on** Wednesday.
until	Ellis Island remained closed **until** 1990.
after	**After** class, I saw a movie about immigration.
before	He became a citizen **before** his twentieth birthday.

Time Words with Clauses

TIME WORD	EXAMPLES
when	**When** my grandfather came to the U.S., he passed through Ellis Island. Henri was working in a hospital **when** he heard the news about the president.
while	**While** Einstein was traveling, the Nazis took his property in Germany.
whenever	**Whenever** you enter the U.S., you have to make a declaration of things you're bringing in.
until	Ellis Island remained closed **until** the restoration was complete.

Uses of the Past Continuous

USE	EXAMPLES
To describe a past action that was in progress at a specific moment	At 9:45 a.m., I **was driving** to the airport to pick up my brother. Where **were** you **living** in December, 2013?
With the simple past, to show the relationship of a longer past action to a shorter past action	Einstein **was living** in New Jersey when he died. While Einstein **was living** in Switzerland, he developed his theory of relativity.

REVIEW

Circle the correct words to complete each statement.

1. (*While*/*When*) Ellis Island opened (*on*/*in*) January 1, 1892, 700 immigrants passed through.

2. (*During*/*For*) the early 1900s, immigration was high.

3. Ellis Island closed as an immigrant processing center (*in*/*at*) 1954.

4. (*When*/*While*) Annie Moore arrived with her two brothers, her parents (*waited*/*were waiting*) for them.

5. (*While*/*For*) many years, immigrants from Asian countries weren't welcome.

6. The immigration law didn't change (*until*/*by*) 1965 (*when*/*while*) President Johnson (*signed*/*was signing*) a new law.

7. President Johnson started restoration of Ellis Island. It was finished (*until*/*by*) 1990.

8. (*While*/*Whenever*) people enter another country, they have to pass through customs.

9. (*During*/*While*) we were visiting New York last year, we (*decided*/*were deciding*) to see the Statue of Liberty.

10. You can visit the Statue of Liberty (*of*/*from*) 8:30 a.m. (*till*/*at*) 5 p.m.

11. Einstein died while he (*was living*/*lived*) in Princeton, New Jersey.

12. He lived in the U.S. (*for*/*during*) 22 years.

13. I came to the U.S. five years (*before*/*ago*).

14. When I (*arrived*/*was arriving*) in the U.S., I was so happy.

15. Before (*to come*/*coming*) to the U.S., I studied English.

16. I will become a citizen (*after*/*in*) five years.

FROM GRAMMAR TO WRITING

PART 1 Editing Advice

1. Put the subject before the verb in all clauses.

    my mother came
    When ~~came my mother~~ to the U.S., our family was so happy.

2. Use *when,* not *while,* if the action has no duration.

    When
    ~~While~~ she arrived, we were waiting for her.

3. Be careful to choose the correct time word.

    for
    She traveled ~~during~~ 10 hours.

    on
    She arrived ~~in~~ May 2.

4. Don't confuse *before* and *ago.*

    ago
    I came to the U.S. three years ~~before~~.

5. After a time word, use an *-ing* form, not a base form.

    learning
    After ~~learn~~ English, she found a job.

6. Don't forget *be* and *-ing* with the past continuous.

    ing
    At 9:30 last night, I was watch a program about immigration.
    ^

    were
    They ‸ talking about famous immigrants on this program.
    ^

7. Don't forget to use a comma if the time clause precedes the main clause.

    When he heard the news ‚ he was studying at the university.
    ^

PART 2 Editing Practice

Some of the shaded words and phrases have mistakes. Find the mistakes and correct them. If the shaded words are correct, write C.

C
I left my country three years ago. But my husband didn't come with me.

1. for
He wanted to stay in our country ~~during~~ two more years until he
2.   3.

finished college. While I got here, I started to study English right away.
4.

While I going to school, I worked in the school library.
5.   6.

My husband was plan to get a degree in engineering when a war broke
7.   8.   9.

out in our country. When started the war, he left the country quickly
10.

and went to a neighboring country. He was in a refugee camp during one
11.

year. While he was living in the camp, he started to study English. He applied
12.

for permission to come to the United States. After wait for one year, he finally got
13.

permission. When he was getting here, we were so excited to see each other again.
14.   15.

He's learning English quickly. After he learns English well enough, he's

going to enter an engineering program. I know he'll be happy until he gets
16.

his engineering degree. Until then, he will continue to work and study. While he
17.   18.

finishes his program, we will celebrate.

WRITING TIP

Use time words (*before, after, while*) to combine short simple sentences into more sophisticated sentences.

I graduated from college in 2001. I wasn't sure what to do with my life.

***When** I graduated from college in 2001, I wasn't sure what to do with my life.*

Make your writing smoother by using present participles after time words when each clause has the same subject.

After Jack moved to Boston, he decided to pursue a career in politics.

***After moving** to Boston, Jack decided to pursue a career in politics.*

PART 3 Write

Read the prompts. Choose one and write a paragraph about it.

1. Write about a major historical event that took place in your country or in another part of the world. What was happening when this event took place? What happened afterwards? If you research your paragraph, provide your sources.
2. Write about an important event that took place in your life or in the life of a famous person.

PART 4 Edit

Reread the Summary of Unit 7 and the editing advice. Edit your writing from Part 3.

APPENDIX A

SUMMARY OF VERB TENSES

VERB TENSE	FORM	MEANING AND USE
SIMPLE PRESENT	I **have** class Mondays. He **doesn't have** class today. **Do** you **have** class today? **What do** you **do** every day?	• facts, general truths, habits, and customs • used with frequency adverbs, e.g., *always, usually, sometimes, never* • regular activities and repeated actions
PRESENT CONTINUOUS	I **am studying** biology this semester. He **isn't studying** now. **Are** you **studying** this weekend? **What is** she **studying** at college?	• actions that are currently in progress • future actions if a future time expression is used or understood
PRESENT PERFECT	I **have seen** the movie *Titanic*. He **has seen** *Titanic* five times. **Have** you **seen** *Titanic*? **Why have** you never **seen** *Titanic*?	• action that started in the past and continues to the present • action that repeats during a period of time from the past to the present • action that occurred at an indefinite time in the past
PRESENT PERFECT CONTINUOUS	She **has been working** there for years. I **haven't been working** regularly in a while. **Have** you **been working** here long? **Where have** you **been working** lately?	• an action that started in the past and continues to the present
SIMPLE PAST	The students **liked** the class discussion. They **didn't like** the homework. **Did** you **like** the discussion? **What did** you **like** about the discussion?	• a single, short, past action • a longer past action • a repeated past action
PAST CONTINUOUS	She **was watching** TV when I called. I **wasn't watching** TV when you called. **Were** you **watching** TV around 10? **What were** you **watching**?	• an action in progress at a specific past time • often with the simple past in another clause to show the relationship of a longer past action to a shorter past action
PAST PERFECT	I **had** just **left** when she arrived. We **hadn't left** yet when she arrived. **Had** you already **left** the party when she arrived? **How long had** you **known** each other before you got married?	• used to indicate the first of two past events
PAST PERFECT CONTINUOUS	The movie **had been playing** for 10 minutes when they arrived. The movie **hadn't been playing** for too long when they arrived. **How long had** the movie **been playing**?	• a continuous past action that was completed before another past action • used with action verbs, e.g., *arrive, ask, eat, enter*
FUTURE WITH *WILL*	I **will go** to the store He **won't go** to the store. **Will** you **go** to the store? **When will** you **go** to the store?	• future plans/decisions made in the moment • strong predictions • promises and offers to help

FUTURE WITH *BE GOING TO*	He**'s going to study** all weekend. He **isn't going to study** Saturday. **Are** you **going to study** Saturday? **What are** you **going to study** Saturday?	• future plans that are already made • predictions
FUTURE CONTINUOUS	I **will be sleeping** at midnight. They**'re going to be attending** a concert at that time.	• actions that will occur in the future and continue for an expected period of time
FUTURE PERFECT	She **will have finished** by 10 o'clock.	• actions that will be completed before another point in the future
FUTURE PERFECT CONTINUOUS	I **will have been standing** here for an hour when the train finally arrives.	• actions that will continue up until a point in the future

APPENDIX B

NONACTION VERBS

DESCRIPTION	FEELINGS	DESIRES	MEASUREMENTS	MENTAL STATES	SENSES
appear* be* consist of look* look like resemble seem	appreciate care dislike forgive hate like love mind miss	hope need prefer want wish	cost measure* weigh*	agree believe concern disagree doubt forget guess know imagine mean recognize remember* suppose surprise think* understand	belong contain feel* have* hear* hurt notice own possess see* smell* sound*

*Words that also have an active meaning

APPENDIX C

IRREGULAR VERB FORMS

BASE FORM	PAST FORM	PAST PARTICIPLE	BASE FORM	PAST FORM	PAST PARTICIPLE
be	was/were	been	fight	fought	fought
bear	bore	born/borne	find	found	found
beat	beat	beaten	fit	fit	fit
become	became	become	flee	fled	fled
begin	began	begun	fly	flew	flown
bend	bent	bent	forbid	forbade	forbidden
bet	bet	bet	forget	forgot	forgotten
bid	bid	bid	forgive	forgave	forgiven
bind	bound	bound	freeze	froze	frozen
bite	bit	bitten	get	got	gotten
bleed	bled	bled	give	gave	given
blow	blew	blown	go	went	gone
break	broke	broken	grind	ground	ground
breed	bred	bred	grow	grew	grown
bring	brought	brought	hang	hung	hung
broadcast	broadcast	broadcast	have	had	had
build	built	built	hear	heard	heard
burst	burst	burst	hide	hid	hidden
buy	bought	bought	hit	hit	hit
cast	cast	cast	hold	held	held
catch	caught	caught	hurt	hurt	hurt
choose	chose	chosen	keep	kept	kept
cling	clung	clung	know	knew	known
come	came	come	lay	laid	laid
cost	cost	cost	lead	led	led
creep	crept	crept	leave	left	left
cut	cut	cut	lend	lent	lent
deal	dealt	dealt	let	let	let
dig	dug	dug	lie	lay	lain
dive	dove/dived	dove/dived	light	lit/lighted	lit/lighted
do	did	done	lose	lost	lost
draw	drew	drawn	make	made	made
drink	drank	drunk	mean	meant	meant
drive	drove	driven	meet	met	met
eat	ate	eaten	mistake	mistook	mistaken
fall	fell	fallen	overcome	overcame	overcome
feed	fed	fed	overdo	overdid	overdone
feel	felt	felt	overtake	overtook	overtaken

BASE FORM	PAST FORM	PAST PARTICIPLE	BASE FORM	PAST FORM	PAST PARTICIPLE
overthrow	overthrew	overthrown	stick	stuck	stuck
pay	paid	paid	sting	stung	stung
plead	pled/pleaded	pled/pleaded	stink	stank	stunk
prove	proved	proven/proved	strike	struck	struck/stricken
put	put	put	strive	strove	striven
quit	quit	quit	swear	swore	sworn
read	read	read	sweep	swept	swept
ride	rode	ridden	swell	swelled	swelled/swollen
ring	rang	rung	swim	swam	swum
rise	rose	risen	swing	swung	swung
run	ran	run	take	took	taken
say	said	said	teach	taught	taught
see	saw	seen	tear	tore	torn
seek	sought	sought	tell	told	told
sell	sold	sold	think	thought	thought
send	sent	sent	throw	threw	thrown
set	set	set	understand	understood	understood
sew	sewed	sewn/sewed	uphold	upheld	upheld
shake	shook	shaken	upset	upset	upset
shed	shed	shed	wake	woke	woken
shine	shone/shined	shone/shined	wear	wore	worn
shoot	shot	shot	weave	wove	woven
show	showed	shown/showed	wed	wedded/wed	wedded/wed
shrink	shrank/shrunk	shrunk/shrunken	weep	wept	wept
shut	shut	shut	win	won	won
sing	sang	sung	wind	wound	wound
sink	sank	sunk	withdraw	withdrew	withdrawn
sit	sat	sat	withhold	withheld	withheld
sleep	slept	slept	withstand	withstood	withstood
slide	slid	slid	wring	wrung	wrung
slit	slit	slit	write	wrote	written
speak	spoke	spoken			
speed	sped	sped			
spend	spent	spent			
spin	spun	spun			
spit	spit/spat	spit/spat			
split	split	split			
spread	spread	spread			
spring	sprang	sprung			
stand	stood	stood			
steal	stole	stolen			

Note:

The past and past participle of some verbs can end in -ed or -t.

burn	burned or burnt
dream	dreamed or dreamt
kneel	kneeled or knelt
learn	learned or learnt
leap	leaped or leapt
spill	spilled or spilt
spoil	spoiled or spoilt

APPENDIX D

GERUNDS AND INFINITIVES

Verbs Followed by Gerunds

admit	detest	miss	resent
advise	discuss	permit	resist
anticipate	dislike	postpone	risk
appreciate	enjoy	practice	stop
avoid	finish	put off	suggest
can't help	forbid	quit	tolerate
complete	imagine	recall	understand
consider	keep	recommend	
delay	mention	regret	
deny	mind	remember	

Verbs Followed by Infinitives

agree	claim	know how	seem
appear	consent	learn	swear
ask	decide	manage	tend
attempt	demand	need	threaten
arrange	deserve	offer	try
be able	expect	plan	volunteer
beg	fail	prepare	want
can afford	forget	pretend	wish
care	hope	promise	would like
choose	intend	refuse	

Verbs Followed by Either Gerunds or Infinitives

begin	love	start
continue	prefer	stop*
hate	remember*	try (in past form *tried*)*
like	can (not) stand	

*Difference in meaning between use of gerund and infinitive

Adjectives Followed by Infinitives

afraid	easy	lucky	sad
ashamed	embarrassed	necessary	shocked
careful	excited	pleased	sorry
certain	glad	prepared	stupid
challenging	good	proud	surprised
delighted	happy	ready	upset
determined	hard	relieved	useful
difficult	important	reluctant	willing
disappointed	impossible	rewarding	wrong
eager	likely	right	

APPENDIX E

VERBS AND ADJECTIVES FOLLOWED BY A PREPOSITION

MANY VERBS AND ADJECTIVES ARE FOLLOWED BY A PREPOSITION.

accuse someone of
(be) accustomed to
adjust to
(be) afraid of
agree with
(be) amazed at/by
(be) angry about
(be) angry at/with
apologize for
approve of
argue about
argue with
(be) ashamed of
(be) aware of
believe in
blame someone for
(be) bored with/by
(be) capable of
care about
care for
compare to/with
complain about
concentrate on
(be) concerned about
consist of
count on
deal with
decide on
depend on/upon
(be) different from
disapprove of
(be) divorced from
dream about/of
(be) engaged to
(be) excited about

(be) familiar with
(be) famous for
(be) fond of
forget about
forgive (someone) for
(be) glad about
(be) good at
(be) grateful (to someone) for
(be) guilty of
(be) happy about
hear about
hear of
hope for
(be) incapable of
insist on/upon
(be) interested in
(be) involved in
(be) jealous of
(be) known for
(be) lazy about
listen to
look at
look for
look forward to
(be) mad about
(be) mad at
(be) made from/of
(be) married to
object to
(be) opposed to
participate in
plan on
pray to
pray for

(be) prepared for/to
prevent (someone/something) from
prohibit (someone/something) from
protect (someone/something) from
(be) proud of
recover from
(be) related to
rely on/upon
(be) responsible for
(be) sad about
(be) satisfied with
(be) scared of
(be) sick of
(be) sorry about
(be) sorry for
speak about
speak to/with
succeed in
(be) sure of/about
(be) surprised at
take care of
talk about
talk to/with
thank (someone) for
(be) thankful (to someone) for
think about
think of
(be) tired of
(be) upset about
(be) upset with
(be) used to
wait for
warn (someone) about
(be) worried about
worry about

APPENDIX F

NONCOUNT NOUNS

GROUP A	**Nouns that have no distinct, separate parts**			
	milk	juice	paper	cholesterol
	oil	yogurt	rain	blood
	water	poultry	air	electricity
	coffee	bread	soup	lightning
	tea	meat	butter	thunder

GROUP B	**Nouns with parts too small or insignificant to count**		
	rice	hair	sand
	sugar	popcorn	corn
	salt	snow	grass

GROUP C	**Nouns that are classes or categories**	
	money or cash (nickels, dimes, dollars)	mail (letters, packages, postcards, flyers)
	furniture (chairs, tables, beds)	homework (compositions, exercises, readings)
	clothing (sweaters, pants, dresses)	jewelry (necklaces, bracelets, rings)

GROUP D	**Abstract nouns**					
	love	happiness	nutrition	patience	work	nature
	truth	education	intelligence	poverty	health	help
	beauty	advice	unemployment	music	fun	energy
	luck/fortune	knowledge	pollution	art	information	friendship

GROUP E	**Subjects of study**		
	history	grammar	biology
	chemistry	geometry	math (mathematics*)

*Note: Even though *mathematics* ends with *s*, it is not plural.

Quantity Words with Count and Noncount Nouns

SINGULAR COUNT	PLURAL COUNT	NONCOUNT
a tomato	tomatoes	coffee
one tomato	**two** tomatoes	**two cups of** coffee
	some tomatoes	**some** coffee
no tomato	**no** tomatoes	**no** coffee
	any tomatoes (with questions and negatives)	**any** coffee (with questions and negatives)
	a lot of tomatoes	**a lot of** coffee
	many tomatoes	**much** coffee (with questions and negatives)
	a few tomatoes	**a little** coffee
	several tomatoes	**several cups of** coffee
	How many tomatoes?	**How much** coffee?

Count or Noncount Nouns with Changes in Meaning

COUNT	NONCOUNT
Avocados and nuts are **foods** with healthy fats.	We have a lot of **food** at home.
He wrote a **paper** about hypnosis.	I need some **paper** to write my composition.
He committed three **crimes** last year.	There is a lot of **crime** in a big city.
I have 200 **chickens** on my farm.	We ate some **chicken** for dinner.
I don't want to bore you with my **troubles**.	I have some **trouble** with my car.
She went to Puerto Rico three **times**.	She spent a lot of **time** on her project.
She drank three **glasses** of water.	The window is made of bulletproof **glass**.
I had a bad **experience** on my trip to Paris.	She has **experience** with computers.
I've learned about the **lives** of my grandparents.	**Life** is sometimes happy, sometimes sad.
I heard a **noise** outside my window.	Those children are making a lot of **noise**.
Some **fruits** have a lot of sugar.	I bought some **fruit** at the fruit store.

APPENDIX G

USES OF ARTICLES

The Indefinite Article

A. To classify a subject

EXAMPLES	EXPLANATION
Chicago is **a** city. Illinois is **a** state. Abraham Lincoln was **an** American president.	• We use *a* before a consonant sound. • We use *an* before a vowel sound. • We can put an adjective before the noun.
Chicago and Los Angeles are cities. Lincoln and Washington were American presidents.	We do not use an article before a plural noun.

B. To make a generalization about a noun

EXAMPLES	EXPLANATION
A dog has sharp teeth. **Dogs** have sharp teeth.	We use an indefinite article *(a/an)* + a singular count noun or no article with a plural noun.
An elephant has big ears. **Elephants** have big ears.	Both the singular and plural forms have the same meaning.
Coffee contains caffeine. **Love** makes people happy.	We do not use an article to make a generalization about a noncount noun.

C. To introduce a new noun into the conversation

EXAMPLES	EXPLANATION
I have **a cell phone**. I have **an umbrella**.	We use the indefinite article *a/an* with singular count nouns.
I have **(some) dishes**. Do you have **(any) cups**? I don't have **(any) forks**. I have **(some) money** with me. Do you have **(any) cash** with you? I don't have **(any) time**.	We use *some* or *any* with plural nouns and noncount nouns. We use *any* in questions and negatives. *Some* and *any* can be omitted.
There's **an elevator** in the building. There isn't **any money** in my wallet.	*There* + a form of *be* can introduce an indefinite noun into a conversation.

The Definite Article

A. To refer to a previously mentioned noun

EXAMPLES	EXPLANATION
There's **a dog** in the next apartment. **The dog** barks all the time.	We start by saying *a dog*. We continue by saying *the dog*.
We bought **some grapes**. We ate **the grapes** this morning.	We start by saying *some grapes*. We continue by saying *the grapes*.
I need **some sugar**. I'm going to use **the sugar** to bake a cake.	We start by saying *some sugar*. We continue by saying *the sugar*.
Did you buy **any coffee**? Yes. **The coffee** is in the cabinet.	We start by saying *any coffee*. We continue by saying *the coffee*.

B. When the speaker and the listener have the same reference

EXAMPLES	EXPLANATION
The number on this page is 203.	The object is present, so the speaker and listener have the same object in mind.
The president is talking about **the** economy.	People who live in the same country have things in common.
Please turn off **the lights** and shut **the door** before you leave **the house**.	People who live in the same house have things in common.
The house on the corner is beautiful. I spent **the money you gave me**.	The listener knows exactly which one because the speaker defines or specifies which one.

C. When there is only one in our experience

EXAMPLES	EXPLANATION
The sun is bigger than **the moon**. There are many problems in **the world**.	The *sun*, the *moon*, and the *world* are unique objects.
Write your name on **the top** of the page.	The page has only one top.
Alaska is **the biggest** state in the U.S.	A superlative indicates that there is only one.

D. With familiar places

EXAMPLES	EXPLANATION
I'm going to **the store** after work. Do you need anything? **The bank** is closed now. I'll go tomorrow.	We use *the* with certain familiar places and people— *the bank, the zoo, the park, the store, the movies, the beach, the post office, the bus, the train, the doctor, the dentist*—when we refer to the one that we habitually visit or use.

Notes:

1. Omit *the* after a preposition with the words *church, school, work,* and *bed.*
   He's **in church**.   They're **at work**.
   I'm going **to school**.   I'm going **to bed**.

2. Omit *to* and *the* with *home* and *downtown.*
   I'm going **home**.   Are you going **downtown** after class?

continued

E. To make a formal generalization

EXAMPLES	EXPLANATION
The shark is the oldest and most primitive fish.	To say that something is true of all members of a group, use *the* with singular count nouns.
The computer has changed the way people deal with information.	To talk about a class of inventions, use *the*.
The ear has three parts: outer, middle, and inner.	To talk about an organ of the body in a general sense, use *the*.

Note:

For informal generalizations, use *a* + a singular noun or no article with a plural noun.

> **The computer** *has changed the way we deal with information.* (Formal)
> **A computer** *is expensive.* (Informal)
> **Computers** *are expensive.* (Informal)

Special Uses of Articles

NO ARTICLE	ARTICLE

Personal names:
  John Kennedy
	The whole family:
	  the Kennedys

Title and name:
  Queen Elizabeth
	Title without name:
	  the Queen

Cities, states, countries, continents:
  Cleveland
  Ohio
  Mexico
  South America
	Places that are considered a union:
	  the United States
	Place names: the _____ of _____
	  the District of Columbia

Mountains:
  Mount Everest
	Mountain ranges:
	  the Rocky Mountains

Islands:
  Staten Island
	Collectives of islands:
	  the Hawaiian Islands

Lakes:
  Lake Superior
	Collectives of lakes:
	  the Great Lakes

Beaches:
  Palm Beach
  Pebble Beach
	Rivers, oceans, seas:
	  the Mississippi River
	  the Atlantic Ocean
	  the Dead Sea

Streets and avenues:
  Madison Avenue
  Wall Street
	Well-known buildings:
	  the Willis Tower
	  the Empire State Building

Parks:
  Central Park
	Zoos:
	  the San Diego Zoo

NO ARTICLE	ARTICLE

Seasons:
    summer   fall   spring   winter
    Summer is my favorite season.
 	
Note: After a preposition, *the* may be used.
    In (the) winter, my car runs badly.
	Deserts:
	    the Mojave Desert
	    the Sahara Desert

Directions:
    north   south   east   west
	Sections of a piece of land:
	    the West Side (of New York)

School subjects:
    history   math
	Unique geographical points:
	    the North Pole the Vatican

Name + *College* or *University*:
    Northwestern University
	The University/College of _____
	    the University of Michigan

Magazines:
    Time   *Sports Illustrated*
	Newspapers:
	    the *Tribune* the *Los Angeles Times*

Months and days:
    September   Monday
	Ships:
	    the *Titanic* the *Queen Elizabeth II*

Holidays and dates:
    Mother's Day
    July 4 (month + day)
	The day of month:
	    the fifth of May
	    the Fourth of July

Diseases:
    cancer   AIDS
    polio   malaria
	Ailments:
	    a cold a toothache
	    a headache the flu

Games and sports:
    poker
    soccer
	Musical instruments, after *play*:
	    the drums the piano
	Note: Sometimes *the* is omitted.
	    She plays (the) drums.

Languages:
    English
	The _____ language:
	    the English language

Last month, year, week, etc. = the one
before this one:
    I forgot to pay my rent last month.
    The teacher gave us a test last week.
	The last month, the last year, the last
	week, etc. = the last in a series:
	    December is the last month of the year.
	    Vacation begins the last week in May.

In office = in an elected position:
    The president is in office for four years.
	In the office = in a specific room:
	    The teacher is in the office.

CONNECTORS

Sentences Types

There are three basic sentences types: simple, compound, and complex.
Simple sentences usually have one subject and one verb.

> S   V
> Students love textbooks.

Simple sentences can have more than one subject and/or verb.

> S   S   V
> Children and adults like pizza.

Compound sentences are usually made up of two simple sentences (independent clauses) with a **connector** (a coordination conjunction such as *and, but, or, yet, so,* and *for*):

>   coord
> S V   conj S   V
> They worked hard all semester, **but** they did not finish the project.

Complex sentences have one independent clause and at least one dependent clause. The dependent clause is often an adverb clause, which begins with a **connector** (a subordinating conjunction such as *while, although, because,* and *if*):

> sub
> conj dependent clause   independent clause
> **Although** the test was very difficult, all the students received a passing grade.

Coordinating Conjunctions

Coordinating conjunctions join two independent clauses to form a compound sentence. Use a comma before a coordinating conjunction in a compound sentence.

>   coord
> independent clause   conj   independent clause
> The test was very difficult, **but** all the students received a passing grade.

Subordinating Conjunctions

Subordinating conjunctions introduce a dependent clause in a complex sentence. When a dependent clause begins a sentence, use a comma to separate it from the independent clause.

>   dependent clause   independent clause
> **Although** the test was very difficult, all the students received a passing grade.

When a dependent clause comes after an independent clause, no comma is used.

>   independent clause   dependent clause
> All the students received a passing grade **although** the test was very difficult.

Transition Words

Transition words **show the relationship between ideas in sentences**. A transition followed by a comma can begin a sentence.

independent clause   transition   independent clause

The test was very difficult. **However**, all the students received a passing grade.

Connector Summary Chart

PURPOSE	COORDINATING CONJUNCTIONS	SUBORDINATING CONJUNCTIONS	TRANSITION WORDS
To give an example			For example, To illustrate, Specifically, In particular,
To add information	and		In addition, Moreover, Furthermore,
To signal a comparison			Similarly, Likewise, In the same way,
To signal a contrast	but yet	while, although	In contrast, However, On the other hand, Conversely, Instead,
To signal a concession	yet	although, though, even though	Nevertheless, Even so, Admittedly, Despite this,
To emphasize			In fact, Actually,
To clarify			In other words, In simpler words, More simply,
To give a reason/cause	for	because, since	
To show a result	so	so	As a result, As a consequence, Consequently, Therefore, Thus,
To show time relationships		after, as soon as, before, when, while, until, since, whenever, as	Afterward, First, Second, Next, Then, Finally, Subsequently, Meanwhile, In the meantime,
To signal a condition		if, even if, unless, provided that, when	
To signal a purpose		so that, in order that	
To signal a choice	or		
To signal a conclusion			In conclusion, To summarize, As we have seen, In brief, In closing, To sum up, Finally,

CAPITALIZATION AND PUNCTUATION

Capitalization Rules

RULE	EXAMPLES
The first word in a sentence	**M**y friends are helpful.
The word *I*	My sister and **I** took a trip together.
Names of people	**A**braham **L**incoln; **G**eorge **W**ashington
Titles preceding names of people	**D**octor (**D**r.) **S**mith; **P**resident **L**incoln; **Q**ueen **E**lizabeth; **M**r. **R**ogers; **M**rs. **C**arter
Geographic names	the **U**nited **S**tates; **L**ake **S**uperior; **C**alifornia; the **R**ocky **M**ountains; the **M**ississippi **R**iver **Note:** The word *the* in a geographic name is not capitalized.
Street names	**P**ennsylvania **A**venue (**A**ve.); **W**all **S**treet (**St**.); **A**bbey **R**oad (**R**d.)
Names of organizations, companies, colleges, buildings, stores, hotels	the **R**epublican **P**arty; **C**engage **L**earning; **D**artmouth **C**ollege; the **U**niversity of **W**isconsin; the **W**hite **H**ouse; **B**loomingdale's; the **H**ilton **H**otel
Nationalities and ethnic groups	**M**exicans; **C**anadians; **S**paniards; **A**mericans; **J**ews; **K**urds; **I**nuit
Languages	**E**nglish; **S**panish; **P**olish; **V**ietnamese; **R**ussian
Months	**J**anuary; **F**ebruary
Days	**S**unday; **M**onday
Holidays	**I**ndependence **D**ay; **T**hanksgiving
Important words in a title	*Grammar in Context; The Old Man and the Sea; Romeo and Juliet; The Sound of Music* **Note:** Capitalize *the* as the first word of a title.

Punctuation Rules

PUNCTUATION	EXAMPLES
A period (.) is used at the end of a declarative sentence.	This is a complete sentence**.**
A question mark (?) is used at the end of a question.	When does the movie start**?**
An exclamation mark (!) is used at the end of an exclamation. It expresses a strong emotion. It can also be called an exclamation point.	This book is so interesting**!**
A comma (,) is used:	
• before the connectors *and*, *but*, *so*, and *or* in a compound sentence.	• She gave Tomas a pen, but he wanted a pencil.
• between three or more items in a list.	• He needs a notebook, a pen, and a calculator.
• after a dependent clause at the beginning of a complex sentence. Dependent clauses include time clauses, *if* clauses, and reason clauses.	• If it's cold outside, you should wear a coat.
• between the day and the date and between the date and the year.	• The test will be on Friday, May 20. The school opened on September 3, 2010.
• between and after (if in the middle of a sentence) city, state, and country names that appear together.	• She lived and taught in Shanghai, China, for five years.
• after time words and phrases, prepositional phrases of time, and sequence words (except *then*) at the start of a sentence.	• Finally, the test was over, and the student could leave. After the movie, they decided to go out for coffee.
An apostrophe (') is used to indicate either a contraction or a possession:	
• Use an apostrophe in a contraction in place of the letter or letters that have been deleted.	• I'm happy to see you. You've read a lot of books this year.
• Add an apostrophe and the letter -*s* after the word. If a plural word already ends in -*s*, just add an apostrophe.	• That is Yusef's book. The teachers' books include the answers.
Quotation marks (") are used to indicate:	
• the exact words that were spoken by someone. Notice that the punctuation at the end of a quote is inside the quotation marks.	• Albert Einstein said, "I have no special talent. I am only passionately curious."
• language that a writer has borrowed from another source.	• The dictionary defines punctuation as "the use of specific marks to make ideas within writing clear."
• when a word or phrase is being used in a special way.	• The paper was written by a "professional" writer.

GLOSSARY

- **Adjective** An adjective gives a description of a noun.

  It's a *tall* tree.   He's an *old* man.   My neighbors are *nice*.

- **Adverb** An adverb describes the action of a sentence or an adjective or another adverb.

  She speaks English *fluently*.   I drive *carefully*.

  She speaks English *extremely* well.   She is *very* intelligent.

- **Adverb of Frequency** An adverb of frequency tells how often an action happens.

  I *never* drink coffee.   They *usually* take the bus.

- **Affirmative** *Affirmative* means "yes."

  They *live* in Miami.

- **Apostrophe** ' We use the apostrophe for possession and contractions.

  My *sister's* friend is beautiful. (possession)

  Today *isn't* Sunday. (contraction)

- **Article** An article comes before a noun. It tells if the noun is definite or indefinite. The indefinite articles are *a* and *an*. The definite article is *the*.

  I have *a* cat.   I ate *an* apple.   *The* teacher came late.

- **Auxiliary Verb** An auxiliary verb is used in forming tense, mood, or aspect of the verb that follows it. Some verbs have two parts: an auxiliary verb and a main verb.

  You *didn't* eat lunch.   He *can't* study.   We *will* return.

- **Base Form** The base form of the verb has no tense. It has no ending (*-s, -ed, or -ing*): *be, go, eat, take, write*.

  I didn't *go*.   We don't *know* you.   He can't *drive*.

- **Capital Letter** A B C D E F G . . .

- **Clause** A clause is a group of words that has a subject and a verb. Some sentences have only one clause.

  She speaks Spanish.

Some sentences have a **main clause** and a **dependent clause**.

MAIN CLAUSE	DEPENDENT CLAUSE (reason clause)
She found a good job	*because she has computer skills.*

MAIN CLAUSE	DEPENDENT CLAUSE (time clause)
She'll turn off the light	*before she goes to bed.*

MAIN CLAUSE	DEPENDENT CLAUSE (*if* clause)
I'll take you to the doctor	*if you don't have your car on Saturday.*

- **Colon** :

- **Comma** ,

- **Comparative** The comparative form of an adjective or adverb is used to compare two things.

  My house is *bigger* than your house.

  Her husband drives *faster* than she does.

  My children speak English *more fluently* than I do.

- **Consonant** The following letters are consonants: *b, c, d, f, g, h, j, k, l, m, n, p, q, r, s, t, v, w, x, y, z.*

    NOTE: *Y* is sometimes considered a vowel, as in the world *syllable.*

- **Contraction** A contraction is two words joined with an apostrophe.

    He's my brother.   *You're* late.   They *won't* talk to me.

    (*He's = He is*)   (*You're = You are*)   (*won't = will not*)

- **Count Noun** Count nouns are nouns that we can count. They have a singular and a plural form.

    1 *pen*–3 *pens*   1 *table*–4 *tables*

- **Dependent Clause** See **Clause**.

- **Exclamation Mark** !

- **Frequency Word** Frequency words (*always, usually, generally, often, sometimes, rarely, seldom, hardly ever, never*) tell how often an action happens.

    I *never* drink coffee.   We *always* do our homework.

- **Hyphen** -

- **Imperative** An imperative sentence gives a command or instruction. An imperative sentence omits the subject pronoun *you.*

    Come here.   *Don't be* late.   Please *help* me.

- **Infinitive** An infinitive is *to* + the base form.

    I want *to leave.*   You need *to be* here on time.

- **Linking Verb** A linking verb is a verb that links the subject to the noun, adjective, or adverb after it. Linking verbs include *be, seem, feel, smell, sound, look, appear,* and *taste.*

    She *is* a doctor.   She *looks* tired.   You *are* late.

- **Main Clause** See **Clause**.

- **Modal** The modal verbs are *can, could, shall, should, will, would, may, might,* and *must.*

    They *should* leave.   I *must* go.

- **Negative** *Negative* means "no."

    She *doesn't speak* Spanish.

- **Nonaction Verb** A nonaction verb has no action. We do not use a continuous tense (*be* + verb *-ing*) with a nonaction verb. Nonaction verbs include: *believe, cost, care, have, hear, know, like, love, matter, mean, need, own, prefer, remember, see, seem, think, understand, want,* and sense-perception verbs.

    She *has* a laptop.   We *love* our mother.   You *look* great.

- **Noncount Noun** A noncount noun is a noun that we don't count. It has no plural form.

    She drank some *water.*   He prepared some *rice.*

    Do you need any *money?*   We had a lot of *homework.*

- **Noun** A noun is a person, a place, or a thing. Nouns can be either count or noncount.

    My *brother* lives in California.   My *sisters* live in New York.

    I get *advice* from them.   I drink *coffee* every day.

- **Noun Modifier** A noun modifier makes a noun more specific.

    fire department   *Independence* Day   *can* opener

- **Noun Phrase** A noun phrase is a group of words that form the subject or object of a sentence.

  A very nice woman helped me.   I bought *a big box of cereal*.

- **Object** The object of a sentence follows the verb. It receives the action of the verb.

  He bought *a car*.   I saw *a movie*.   I met *your brother*.

- **Object Pronoun** We use object pronouns (*me, you, him, her, it, us, them*) after a verb or preposition.

  He likes *her*.   I saw the movie. Let's talk about *it*.

- **Paragraph** A paragraph is a group of sentences about one topic.

- **Parentheses** ( )

- **Period** .

- **Phrasal Modal** Phrasal modals, such as *have to* and *be able to*, are made up of two or more words.

  You *have got to* see the movie.   We *have to* take a test.

- **Phrase** A group of words that go together.

  Last month my sister came to visit.   There is a strange car *in front of my house*.

- **Plural** *Plural* means "more than one." A plural noun usually ends with *-s*.

  She has beautiful *eyes*.   My *feet* are big.

- **Possessive Form** Possessive forms show ownership or relationship.

  Mary's coat is in the closet.   *My* brother lives in Miami.

- **Preposition** A preposition is a short connecting word. Some common prepositions are: *about, above, across, after, around, as, at, away, back, before, behind, below, by, down, for, from, in, into, like, of, off, on, out, over, to, under, up,* and *with*.

  The book is *on* the table.   She studies *with* her friends.

- **Present Participle** The present participle of a verb is the base form + *-ing*.

  She is *sleeping*.   They were *laughing*.

- **Pronoun** A pronoun takes the place of a noun.

  John likes Mary, but *she* doesn't like *him*.

- **Punctuation** The use of specific marks, such as commas and periods, to make ideas within writing clear.

- **Question Mark** ?

- **Quotation Marks** " "

- **Regular Verb** A regular verb forms the simple past with *-ed*.

  He *worked* yesterday.   I *laughed* at the joke.

- **-s Form** A simple present verb that ends in -s or -es.

    He *lives* in New York.   She *watches* TV a lot.

- **Sense-Perception Verb** A sense-perception verb has no action. It describes a sense. Some common sense-perception verbs are: *look, feel, taste, sound,* and *smell.*

    She *feels* fine.   The coffee *smells* fresh.   The milk *tastes* sour.

- **Sentence** A sentence is a group of words that contains a subject and a verb and gives a complete thought.

    SENTENCE: She came home.

    NOT A SENTENCE: When she came home

- **Singular** *Singular* means "one."

    She ate a *sandwich.*   I have one *television.*

- **Subject** The subject of the sentence tells who or what the sentence is about.

    My sister got married last April. *The wedding* was beautiful.

- **Subject Pronoun** We use a subject pronoun (*I, you, he, she, it, we, you, they*) before a verb.

    They speak Japanese.   *We* speak Spanish.

- **Superlative** The superlative form of an adjective or adverb shows the number one item in a group of three or more.

    January is the *coldest* month of the year.

    My brother speaks English the *best* in my family.

- **Syllable** A syllable is a part of a word. Each syllable has only one vowel sound. (Some words have only one syllable.)

    change (one syllable)   after (af·ter = two syllables)

    look (one syllable)   responsible (re·spon·si·ble = four syllables)

- **Tag Question** A tag question is a short question at the end of a sentence. It is used in conversation.

    You speak Spanish, *don't you?*   He's not happy, *is he?*

- **Tense** Tense shows when the action of the sentence happened. Verbs have different tenses.

    SIMPLE PRESENT: She usually *works* hard.

    PRESENT CONTINUOUS: She *is working* now.

    SIMPLE PAST: She *worked* yesterday.

    FUTURE: She *will work* tomorrow.

- **Verb** A verb is the action of the sentence.

    He *runs* fast.   I *speak* English.

Some verbs have no action. They are linking verbs. They connect the subject to the rest of the sentence.

    He *is* tall.   She *looks* beautiful.   You *seem* tired.

- **Vowel** The following letters are vowels: *a, e, i, o, u.*

    NOTE: *Y* is sometimes considered a vowel, as in the world *syllable.*

INDEX

Note: All page references in blue are in Split Edition A

A

A few, several, a little, 143–144, 146
Ability/permission, modals, 202–203
Action verbs, present continuous, 53–54
Active voice, 341–342, 354
    summary, 354
Adjectives, 168
    adverbs versus, 162–163
    clauses, 284–307
    comparatives, 317–319
    gerunds, with, 267
    infinitives after, 273–274
    modifiers, 154–156
    possessive, 98–99
    superlatives, 311–313
    too, too much, too many, enough, 165–166, 168
    too, very, 166–168
Adjective clauses, 284–307
    relative pronouns, objects, 291–294, 304
    relative pronouns, objects of prepositions, 295–297, 304
    relative pronouns, place, 301–304
    relative pronouns, possessive, 298–299, 304
    relative pronouns, subjects, 288–290, 304
    relative pronouns, time, 301–304
    summary, 304
    where and *when*, 301–304
    who/that, 290
    whose + noun, 298–299, 304
Adverbs, modifiers, 153–154, 160–162, 168
    adjectives versus, 162–163
    comparatives, 317–319
    nouns, modifying, 153–154
    present perfect, 233
    summary, 168
    superlatives, 311–313
Advice, modals, 205–207
Affirmative statements
    simple present, 16–17
Another and *other*, 373–375, 378
Articles, 361–381
    another and *other*, 373–375, 378
    definite pronouns, 376–378
    generalizations, 362–363
    indefinite pronouns, 376–378
    nonspecific nouns, 366–367, 370–371
    quantity words, 370–371
    specific nouns, 367–371

    subjects, classifying, 363–364
    subjects, defining, 363–364
    summary, 378
As . . . as, comparatives, 324–325, 334
As many/much . . . as, comparatives, 326–327

B

Be
    contractions, 5, 10–11
    forms, simple present, 5–10, 36
    going to, 60–64
    negative statements, 8
    present continuous, 43–44
    simple past, 76–77, 88
    there + be, 138–140
    uses, 7
    wh- questions, 12–14
Be + not, 8
Be going to, 60–64
Be supposed to, 201–202

C

Can, could, modals, 202–203
Clauses, adjectives, 284–307
Comparatives, 316–337
    adjectives, 317–319
    adverbs, 317–319
    as . . . as, 324–325, 334
    as many/much . . . as, 326–327
    like and *alike*, 331–334
    long words, 334
    same . . . as, 327–329, 334
    short words, 334
    similarity, 331–333
    summary, 334
    use, 319–322
Comparison nouns, 141
Complements, questions about, 114–116, 118
Comprehension exercises
    a few, several, a little, 142–143
    adjective clauses, 286–287, 300–301
    adverbs, modifiers, 152–153
    articles, 360–361, 365–366, 372–373
    as . . . as, 323–324
    be forms, 4–5
    comparatives, 316–317
    count and noncount nouns, 130–131
    frequency words, 28–29
    future, 57–58

CREDITS

NOTES